R VENKATARAMAN

R VENKATARAMAN
A Centenary Tribute

Foreword by
President Pratibha Devisingh Patil

RUPA

This Anthology Copyright © Lakshmi Venkataraman Venkatesan 2012
Preface Copyright © KP Singh Deo

The copyright for the individual pieces vests with
the individual contributors

First published in 2012 by
Rupa Publications India Pvt. Ltd.
7/16, Ansari Road, Daryaganj,
New Delhi 110 002

Sales Centres:

Allahabad Bengaluru Chennai
Hyderabad Jaipur Kathmandu
Kolkata Mumbai

All rights reserved.
No part of this publication may be reproduced, stored in a
retrieval system, or transmitted, in any form or by any means,
electronic, mechanical, photocopying, recording or otherwise,
without the prior permission of the publishers.

R Venkataraman Birth Centenary Editorial Board
Chairman: KP Singh Deo
Members: Gopalkrishna Gandhi, Inder Malhotra,
Lakshmi Venkataraman Venkatesan (convenor),
Late PC Alexander, Shovana Narayan, Soli Sorabjee and Tarun Das

The individual contributors assert the moral right
to be identified as the authors of this work.

Printed in India by
Replika Press Pvt. Ltd.

Contents

Preface ix
Convenor's Note xiii
Foreword xv

AN EXEMPLARY STATESMAN

The People's President 3
    AP Venkateswaran

An Inspiration for Future Generations 10
    DN Patodia

A Multifaceted Personality 16
    Era Sezhiyan

India's Presidents – in Good Times and in Times of Crisis 25
    Fali S Nariman

R Venkataraman As State And Central Minister 43
    G Ramachandran

A Personal Tribute 53
    Lord Geoffrey Howe

The Value of Decency 58
    Gopalkrishna Gandhi

RV's Shining Services to India 70
    Inder Malhotra

The Gentleman Politician *K Natwar Singh*	77
A True Statesman *K Parasaran*	80
A Statesman and Manager *K Subrahmanyam*	84
The Harbinger of Industrial Growth in Tamil Nadu *KS Narayanan*	89
Satyamurti – A Forgotten Patriot *KV Ramanathan*	98
The True Spirit of Democracy *M Hamid Ansari*	110
The Copybook President *MK Narayanan*	114
An Able Achiever *MK Venkatachalam*	119
Helping India Scale New Heights *MM Pallam Raju*	131
R Venkataraman's Role in the SSI Success Story *MS Parthasarathy*	135
The Karmayogi of Raisina Hill *Meira Kumar*	139
A Stickler for Propriety *Najma Heptulla*	143
Entrepreneurship Development Through Small-Scale Industries in India *PC Alexander*	148
My Recollections *P Murari*	154
The Father of Industrialisation of Tamil Nadu *PR Ramasubrahmaneya Rajha*	164

In Service of the Services *Admiral (Retd) RH Tahiliani*	169
India's Youth and the Challenge of Sustainable Development *RK Pachauri*	172
The Trade Union Movement as a Political Force *TS Sankaran*	179
The Minister and the Mandarin *VS Arunachalam*	187

A PATRON OF THE ARTS

A Constant Source of Support *Amjad Ali Khan*	199
The Epitome of Graciousness *Kapila Vatsyayan*	201
A Music Aficionado *L Subramaniam*	205
A Saint among Politicians *Padma Subrahmanyam*	210
RV's Contribution to the Arts *Shovana Narayan*	216
The Essence of a Truly Humanising Culture *Yamini Krishnamurthi*	221

PERSONAL VIGNETTES

RV The Person *K Venkataraman*	227
A Nation Finding its Feet *Lloyd and Susanne Rudolph*	233

My Grandfather: An Inspiration *Siddharth Ramachandran*	242
Growing Up with Grandpa *Tara Venkatesan*	246
Tribute to Mama *Vyjayantimala Bali*	250
Messages	255
Contributors	272
Ramaswamy Venkataraman: A Profile	292

Preface

December 2010–2011 marks the birth centenary year of Ramaswamy Venkataraman: the eighth president of India, a grass roots politician, a personable parliamentarian, a sagacious statesman, a globalist, a humanist – a person extraordinaire.

This volume of forty-eight articles is a distinctive tribute to this great leader, an initiative that I think he would have appreciated. It includes homage to 'RV', as he was affectionately called by many. Going beyond, it also incorporates reflections by contributors on the various issues that concerned, energised and fulfilled his engagements with his times. It is visualised as a document showcasing the problems and prospects of the India of this generation and, in keeping with his optimistic gaze into the future, of the India when today's young will be its guardians.

The book, divided into four main sections – An Exemplary Statesman, A Patron of the Arts, Personal Vignettes and Messages – has many sub-themes woven into the rich tapestry of RV's life.

Eminent lawyer Fali S Nariman analyses where R Venkataraman stands in the long and illustrious line-up of India's presidents. Variously characterised as the 'Karmayogi of Raisina Hill' by Lok Sabha Speaker Meira Kumar and 'a true friend of the working class' by Sheila Dikshit, the chief minister of Delhi, Vice-

President of India M Hamid Ansari sums up his contribution, saying, 'R Venkataraman embodied the correct spirit of "political virtue", and his conduct, both personal and public, is worthy of emulation by today's leaders'. Governor of West Bengal MK Narayanan echoes these sentiments, drawing a parallel between the early 1990s and the present, and feels that the need of the hour is to handle the political situation adroitly. Former Prime Minister AB Vajpayee, expressing his personal warmth for RV and his ability to make friends across the political spectrum, comments, 'I had special regard and respect for him. He did not allow party considerations to come in the way of our personal relations.'

Admiral (Retd) Tahiliani encapsulates the admiration for RV among India's defence establishment: 'R Venkataraman's close connection with the defence services extended well beyond his tenure as defence minister of India. He embodied the qualities instilled in the forces'. General (Retd) KV Krishna Rao talks of RV's great interest in the progress of the armed forces, particularly their professional efficiency and welfare.

As RV's deputy, I can personally testify to the enormous concern, compassion and care that he exhibited towards the war-wounded, widows, ex-servicemen and their families.

'R Venkataraman made immensely significant contributions to India's missile programme, during his tenure as defence minister, propagating self-reliance,' asserts MM Pallam Raju, minister of state for defence. The late defence expert and analyst K Subrahmanyam speaks of RV's sharp memory and fully cooperative spirit, guiding the Kargil Review Panel even at the ripe old age of eighty-nine.

RV's passion and keen interest in science and technology is underscored when Nobel Laureate Dr Pachauri discusses the pressing environmental issues of the day as he highlights the importance of taking cues from R Venkataraman's approach to conflict resolution and the balancing of competing interests. In a lively article titled 'The Minister and the Mandarin', Dr VS Arunachalam, who was his scientific advisor, says appreciatively, 'R Venkataraman's contribution towards defence and technological innovations was immense. He is responsible to a great extent for India's technological superiority in defence today.'

RV's pioneering role on the international stage, beginning with his successful vindication of Indian soldiers in Malaysia in 1946 and spanning over six decades thereafter, is brought to life by a letter written by two American professors watching him campaign, sitting atop a bale of hay in the villages of Tanjore in 1957. The deep personal impression he made on Lord Howe, former deputy prime minister of Britain, is reflected in his article. He also did not confine his energies to India alone. Former Federal President of Germany Richard von Weizsäcker's message reveals how RV was able to forge strong, mutually beneficial connections across very different cultures and ideologies.

Known as the father of industrialisation in the state of Tamil Nadu, RV indeed laid the foundation for India's future economic growth by playing a pioneering role in development of entrepreneurship through small-scale industries, as Late PC Alexander, former governor of Tamil Nadu and Maharashtra, claims. Eminent industrialist KS Narayanan seconds these thoughts, 'RV gave a major boost to the Tamil Nadu industry, with innovative reforms and policies.'

'A true patron of the arts, he was the essence of a truly humanising culture with the ability to understand classical forms of art, and appreciate the spiritual, lofty and subtle thought that infuse them,' writes renowned danseuse Dr Yamini Krishnamurthi. Noted scholar Dr Kapila Vatsyayan points out in a humorous aside how RV occasionally even supported 'crazy' plans to ensure that cultural events took off successfully. The famous sarod player Ustad Amjad Ali Khan says confidently,

'I am sure most of the musicians and dancers of India can speak volumes about the love and encouragement they received from President R Venkataramanji. We will always miss his presence, but I am sure we can feel his presence while we are performing even now.'

RV's public persona is well known, but what was he like in private? asks his son-in-law Dr K Venkataraman. Siddharth and Tara give rare glimpses of the inspiration RV was to his grandchildren.

While prominent dancer Dr Padma Subrahmanyam describes him as 'A Saint among Politicians', Swami Dayananda Saraswati adds, 'RV was highly committed, with an insight into the spiritual oneness as unfolded by the Gita. And this helped him relate to all forms of religious prayers without any tinge of patronising attitude.'

Known above all for his decency and his indomitable human spirit, would Ramaswamy Venkataraman, who would have turned a hundred years old this year, be an anachronism today? wonders Gopalkrishna Gandhi, former governor, West Bengal, who had served RV over half a dozen years. 'Perhaps he would. And yet, "his" era was not some bygone age, it was yesterday. So near and yet so far.'

KP Singh Deo
(Chairman, R Venkataraman
Birth Centenary Editorial Board)

Convenor's Note

Scores of R Venkataraman's friends, admirers and family were inspired to commemorate his birth centenary with a festschrift. The challenging task was to capture the essence of this multifaceted personality, who endeared himself to one and all by the sheer force of his personality.

When you embark on such a demanding journey, just where do you start to acknowledge those that joined, guided and rallied around this formidable undertaking? The wholehearted enthusiasm of Gopalkrishna Gandhi, who had served R Venkataraman steadfastly for over half a dozen years, set the ball rolling a little over a year ago. The eight members of the editorial board, Late PC Alexander, Tarun Das, Gopalkrishna Gandhi, Inder Malhotra, Shovana Narayan, Soli Sorabjee and I, under the able leadership of KP Singh Deo, reached out to an impressive array of luminaries who have had the privilege of knowing RV through his remarkable journey, from Rajamadam village to Rashtrapati Bhavan, in the service of India. This serious endeavour was backed by the unstinted support of RK Mehra of Rupa Publications, also the publishers of RV's autobiography *My Presidential Years*.

What followed was an outpouring of response from national and international political leaders, chiefs of armed forces, captains of industry, bureaucrats, spiritual leaders, musicians and dancers. Articles, anecdotes, photographs and messages – the editorial board amassed a veritable treasure chest in its quest for paying homage to RV.

For me personally, it has been an unprecedented honour to be associated with bringing out this book, as member-convenor of the editorial board. I have the impossible task of thanking all those who have made this volume a fitting tribute to my father. I have no pretensions of being able to do justice in my personal capacity. So, with the utmost humility, on behalf of RV's three daughters, Padma, Vijaya, myself, and our families, I would like to place on record:

Our deep admiration and appreciation to HE Pratibha Devisingh Patil, the president of India, for her inspiring foreword, underscoring the warmth and high esteem President Patilji and R Venkataraman had for each other.

Our heartfelt gratitude to the forty-six eminent personalities and experts for their invaluable contributions to the festschrift. It is only the lack of space that prevents us from naming each individual, who took time out to highlight what he or she shared with RV – a mutual regard and respect beyond measure.

Our indebtedness to the determined and diligent efforts of the members of the editorial board and to Rupa Publications for bringing out this book, within an extremely short period, in time for R Venkataraman's year-end centenary celebrations.

Finally, my father's spirit would be gladdened, for sure, to witness such an august articulation from his favourite colleagues and friends, many of whom paid their respects to RV in person, and to those who unfailingly attended the ongoing events throughout this centenary year.

31 October 2011   Lakshmi Venkataraman Venkatesan
(Member-Convenor, social entrepreneur
and daughter of R Venkataraman)

Foreword

It was during the mid-nineteen eighties when Shri R. Venkataraman was the Vice-President of the country and Chairman of the Rajya Sabha that I could closely interact with him in my capacity as the Deputy Chairperson of the Rajya Sabha. Above all, I was deeply impressed by his simplicity, humanitarian approach, sharpness of mind and courage of conviction. A great national figure with a reformist approach, he always supported women's empowerment and their socio-economic development. I had the occasion to reflect on his thoughts and philosophy when I read with great interest his autobiography, "My Presidential Years".

Shri R. Venkataraman who was the 8th President of India, was indeed a versatile personality known for his statesmanship, administrative acumen and intellectual depth. His contributions to national life for over a period of eight decades, were far reaching. His understanding of people's aspirations equipped him with the knowledge required to give expression to issues that concerned them, and to find responses which were acknowledged to be pragmatic and realistic.

Shri R. Venkataraman began his career as a lawyer but was soon drawn into the country's freedom movement. He was deeply influenced by the surge for freedom that swept the nation under the leadership of Mahatma Gandhi. He rejected the option of joining an attractive Civil Service under the colonial administration and chose to be a lawyer. While practicing law independently, he took up several public issues of far reaching consequences. His active participation in the "Quit India Movement of 1942" led to his imprisonment for two years. After independence, he served in various capacities in public life – as a Legislator, a Minister, the Vice-President and then as the President of the country. He was a distinguished Parliamentarian, who began his parliamentary career in 1950 with his election to the first Parliament of India. Known for his constructive approach, his wit and humour often helped him on many an occasion to defuse tensions in the Parliament. As a Minister, in the erstwhile Madras State and at the Centre, he rapidly acquired a reputation of one who handled his numerous portfolios with dexterity and keenness to achieve time bound objectives.

Shri R. Venkataraman had a deep understanding of constitutional matters and upheld the Constitution on all occasions, especially during the days of political instability when the country witnessed the dawn of coalition governments at the Centre. His integrity and fair play, his wisdom and humaneness enhanced the dignity of the office of President upholding the essence of a strong Parliamentary democracy.

Shri R. Venkataraman was one of India's noblest sons who served the nation selflessly and with dedication. Throughout his life, he was interested in the welfare of the public and interacted with a large number of people from various fields and from all sections of society. He was a grassroots political leader who had healthy and strong association with trade unions. It is important that the work and the lives of persons such as Shri R. Venkataraman are brought out to inspire the younger generations to serve the nation with sincerity and commitment.

I pay my tributes to late Shri R. Venkataraman and wish the Birth Centenary Celebrations every success.

New Delhi

Pratibha Devisingh Patil
October 25, 2011

AN EXEMPLARY STATESMAN

The People's President

AP Venkateswaran

> R Venkataraman served the people in many diverse capacities before assuming the post of president of India. The experience he brought to the presidency was tempered with humility, even as he utilised the office to promote the development of fields ranging from missile development to the performing arts.

Even when I was a student in the 1950s in Presidency College, Madras (as Chennai was known at that time), R Venkataraman was a very well-known public figure in the country – as a senior member of the Congress party, a freedom fighter and also a member of the Constituent Assembly of free India. He served in the Madras state cabinet where he was a prominent figure, and also in the union cabinet as minister of finance and minister of defence. He had the experience and the qualifications necessary to become the president of India, which he was destined to become in 1987, after serving for a term as vice-president of the country.

My father, Justice ASP Ayyar, who was in the Madras High Court, knew him well and had high regard for his sterling abilities, both as a lawyer and later on as the minister for industries in K Kamaraj's state cabinet. As mentioned earlier, he was an important member of the state cabinet for many years, holding various important portfolios such as industries, power, labour, transport and cooperation, before his election to the Lok Sabha in 1977 from the Madras constituency. He was re-elected to the Lok Sabha in 1980 and was appointed union minister of finance in Indira Gandhi's cabinet.

In the early years of India's independence, all of us in the country, from the smallest children in schools to the students in the universities, were highly inspired by and enthused with intense patriotic fervour, and followed attentively all the unfolding developments in the country. How one wishes that the same zeal and energy was evident in our people today, when India is increasingly beset with so many difficulties, which are often created within the country, as well as those which are being caused from outside by those who are inimical to us. The earlier cohesion that existed seems to have given way to unnecessary mutual recrimination and increasing conflict. What is worse, corruption is eating into the very vitals of the nation. We seem to have forgotten and forsaken the struggle waged by our forefathers to win independence for India. It is high time that all of us, as Indians, regained and revitalised ourselves, drawing inspiration from the exhilarating early years of our rebirth as an independent nation, after having suffered from centuries of foreign rule.

R Venkataraman had joined the Quit India Movement along with K Kamaraj Nadar, and had been detained under the British colonial government's Defence of India Rules. He had been keenly interested in the labour movement ever since he became a lawyer practising in the High Court of Madras. He had helped to organise the labour movement in the state, founding the *Labour Law Journal* in 1949 and was actively connected with the trade unions, including those of plantation workers, railway and dock workers, and working journalists. When the transfer of power to India became imminent, he was a member of the legal team sent to Singapore to defend Indians charged with having collaborated with the Japanese occupation forces. It was a natural progression into politics from then onwards, leading to his election as a member of the provisional government in 1950 and to the Lok Sabha in 1952. Even though he was re-elected in 1957, he gave up his seat in the Lok Sabha to serve as a minister in the Madras state cabinet, holding various portfolios with distinction.

R Venkataraman, as the minister of industries in Madras, can claim credit for single-handedly transforming Tamil Nadu from being a largely agrarian state to an industrialised centre of the country. He was responsible for bringing the automobile industry into the state, in the early years after Independence. Today, Tamil Nadu accounts for over 40 per cent of the production of automobiles and ancillaries. The production today includes such well-known international brands as Hyundai, General Motors, Volkswagen, Mitsubishi, and Honda. With the opening up of the Indian economy, BMW and Nissan have also set up their assembly lines.

As a delegate of India to the United Nations in New York during the General Assembly sessions for many years, from 1953 to 1961, R Venkataraman was a familiar and highly respected figure in that world organisation, representing the country. He also served in the UN Administrative Tribunal from 1955 to 1979 and was also its president from 1968 to 1979. He visited a large number of countries of the world during this period as well.

It was during his visits to the UN that I had the pleasure and privilege of personally getting to know him. I was then India's vice-consul and later consul in New York for two years (1957–1959). Like a truly great man, R Venkataraman never had any airs about him. He mixed freely with the high and the low, and was ever gentle and kind to everyone he met, especially towards young people he encountered. Ever since those days I have had a high regard and respect bordering on affection towards him. I cherish that memory.

Later on, when I was political counsellor in the Embassy of India, Moscow, R Venkataraman had accompanied K Kamaraj on his visit to the USSR in the mid-1960s. The Soviet government had extended to Kamaraj full honours as to a head of state and had even placed a special aircraft at his personal disposal, for the entire duration of the visit. My ambassador, TN Kaul, had deputed me to travel with the delegation throughout the visit, since I was the only Tamil-speaking officer at that time in the mission. It was a valuable opportunity for me to renew my acquaintance with R Venkataraman and also to observe Kamaraj from very close quarters. Kamaraj was being called 'kingmaker' at the time, since his support was crucial for anyone who aspired to become prime minister in the Congress party. Of course, this situation changed soon thereafter.

When I met R Venkataraman again, it was during my posting in New Delhi as secretary (east) in the Ministry of External Affairs, many years later, in the 1980s. R Venkataraman was occupying the esteemed post of vice-president of India. He invited my wife and me to the musical evenings he regularly hosted at his residence on Maulana Abdul Kalam Azad Road, where, apart from the music concerts, we got to know him and his family for their rare human warmth and hospitality.

My personal association with R Venkataraman continued when I became foreign secretary, and I had the pleasant task of briefing him about various state visitors from abroad. This relationship continued, at a personal level, even after my resignation, following the contretemps resulting from the off-the-cuff remarks by Prime Minister Rajiv Gandhi at his press conference at Vigyan Bhavan on 21 January 2007. That was a period of considerable personal turbulence in the relationship between President Giani Zail Singh and Prime Minister Rajiv Gandhi. The growing confrontation between them could have easily taken an ugly turn, leading to a constitutional crisis within the country, with unpredictable negative consequences, but for the wise counsel tendered to the prime minister by then Vice-President R Venkataraman.

My close personal relationship with R Venkataraman continued even after I left the government and he succeeded as the president of India, after the five-year term of Giani Zail Singh had come to an end. Every time we met, since then, has been an occasion to remember and to cherish, due to the unfailing warmth and friendliness that he and Mrs Venkataraman showed to me and my family.

A little-known fact is the vital contribution made by R Venkataraman to India's missiles development, when he held the portfolio of the minister of defence, under Prime Minister Indira Gandhi. He allotted ₹388 crore and shifted APJ Abdul Kalam, who was then with the space programme, to the Ballistic Missile Development Programme. This had led to the development by the Integrated Guided Missile Development Programme of the Agni, Prithvi, Akash, Trishul, Nag and Brahmo missiles, capable of carrying nuclear warheads, which are today an important component of the country's overall defence capacity. He had also set up a committee of the three chiefs of staff of the army, navy and air force to oversee developments.

APJ Abdul Kalam, who himself became the president of India later, recalls this event in his book *Wings of Fire* and says about R Venkataraman: 'He advised us to list all the resources we needed to achieve our goals, overlooking nothing, and then include in the list our own positive imagination and faith. "What you imagine, is what will transpire. What you believe is what you will achieve," he said.'

After finally leaving the Rashtrapati Bhavan in 1992, R Venkataraman continued to take a keen interest in the developments of India in myriad fields. After the promulgation by the Indian Parliament of the Kalakshetra Foundation Act in 1994 which was preceded by a presidential ordinance, R Venkataraman became the chairman of the Kalakshetra Foundation in Chennai. He successfully restored Kalakshetra to its former glory as during the time of Rukmini Devi. He had played a pivotal role in revitalising the foundation after an Act of Parliament had declared it an institution of national importance. His keen interest in the country's welfare and progress was always evident, and this was reflected in the speeches he made at the functions he was invited to address, all over the country.

In my discussions with him I found, to my pleasant surprise, that R Venkataraman was very aware that among all the oldest civilisations in the world, only the civilisations of China and India still remain, with an unbroken link to their past. Even the Chinese civilisation had lost many of its earlier links due to internal turmoil, and it was only India where the culture of the people remained intact. At birth, marriage and death, the same rituals are practised in India and the same prayers are chanted as they were six thousand years ago. What can give a greater sense of belonging to one than this unique sense of one's own identity! Alas, over the centuries, decadence had slowly set in and the strength of the people was slowly sapped. Meanwhile, the very prosperity of India attracted the jealousy of others from across the oceans, and internal rivalries exposed the country to invaders.

It took all of a thousand years for India to rise again as an independent nation. To ensure that history does not repeat itself, we must learn from the example of our true leaders. It is here that the example set by R Venkataraman throughout his life should serve as a beacon light for those who follow him. It is truly said that courage is the first amongst virtues. Without courage, it is impossible to practise any virtue. All the ills which beset our nation today can be traced to the lack of courage of our people to stand up to the challenges which confront them. Merely to lament over our inability to stand up to the challenges that face us will not help in resolving them. Whether it is corruption that pervades our society as never before, or sycophancy, or the temptation to speak pleasant falsehood over unpleasant truth to gain advantage to oneself, the wholesale erosion of societal values constitutes a greater danger to us from within than any danger that may come from outside. Let us heed the ancient call to arise, awake and to stop not till the goal is reached, of recapturing our values as a nation.

R Venkataraman was a true leader in every sense of the word and displayed courage of conviction in everything that he did in his life. Mahatma Gandhi also taught us that if Right does not fight Might, Might will rule alone. I would venture here to recall an old Indian proverb which states: A thousand lions, led by a donkey, will be defeated by a thousand donkeys led by a lion! Merely to affirm, as has become fashionable today, that negotiations have been successful after giving in to pressure from the other side, reflects no credit on oneself.

In conclusion, I for one feel deeply that the passing away, a year ago of a truly multifaceted leader amongst us, like R Venkataraman, has left a deep void in the political, economic and social life of this country which it would be very difficult to fill.

An Inspiration for Future Generations

DN Patodia

> *As president, R Venkataraman brought to the office all the skills acquired not only as a lawyer, but also as a politician of long standing, expertly handling political crises even as he guided the development of India's economic and geo-political interests.*

Born in a highly respected and dignified family and brought up in the sylvan surroundings of village Rajamadam in Madras state (now Tamil Nadu), the lifespan of R Venkataraman, popularly known as RV, is an illuminating and inspiring story of a true patriot and a hero who immensely contributed to the making and shaping of post-Independence India and its democratic and secular character.

A law graduate, he joined mainstream politics soon after starting his career as a trade union lawyer, participated in the Quit India Movement and courted arrest. Throughout his political career, by the virtue of his sheer dedication, sharp intellect and disciplined behaviour, he was constantly entrusted with greater responsibilities, was elected to the provisional Parliament in 1950 and thereafter, to the first Lok Sabha in 1952.

In 1957, although re-elected to the Lok Sabha, RV was invited by the charismatic K Kamaraj to join the government of the then Madras state as a minister of industries, labour, power and transport. With a progressive outlook and foresight, he introduced several far-reaching measures to promote industrial growth on a wide scale, thus sowing the seeds of all-round industrial and economic development in the state as we can see today.

Coming back to the centre as a member of the Planning Commission between 1967 and 1971, he brought a new culture of economic resurgence with a greater vision of inclusive growth and emphasis on rural upliftment.

In 1980, Indira Gandhi entrusted him with the significant portfolio of finance, and as a true democrat dedicated to greater economic freedom, he introduced several far-reaching measures for comprehensive growth of the economy, permitting larger participation of the private sector. A champion for rural development, he held a definite view that adoption of Western patterns was not particularly suitable for Indian conditions, and designed his economic package with remarkable precision to give shape to his cherished vision and promote growth with wider participation and greater transparency within a well-calibrated monetary frame and taxation structure.

In his scheme of building a modern, strong and progressive India, RV always placed security and defence amongst the nation's top priorities, and invariably supported building our own strong defence structure along with the needed nuclear capacity, rather than looking for outside help all the time. As the country's defence minister, he forcefully outlined his vision for building a strong defence.

RV was elected to the high office of vice-president of India in August 1984. He was a gentleman to the core, dignified and helpful in all situations and highly disciplined in his manners. While presiding over the Rajya Sabha, using sweet and persuasive behaviour blended with experience, he succeeded brilliantly in bringing a new order of sobriety and discipline befitting the upper house, and received wide appreciation from all sections across party lines.

At the pinnacle of his political career, between 1987 and 1992, as president of India, he was confronted with the most challenging and critical period of post-Independence India, a period deeply inflicted by coalition politics and frequent shuffles of governments at the centre. RV had to work with four different prime ministers. That period, between the resignation of VP Singh as prime minister and the appointment of Chandra Shekhar, fraught with internal squabbles and changing loyalties, was particularly precarious. Added were the other critical situations arising from several unforeseen events, such as the Sri Lankan crisis, the Bofors deal, and the assassination of Rajiv Gandhi. In such a testing period of great uncertainty and one crisis taking over the other, RV, a person of great wisdom, deep understanding and political foresight, handled all the sensitive issues with great skill, sagacity and wisdom. And in such difficult times, as a *rashtrapati*, he presided over the nation with great honour and dignity.

During the years of his presidency, he kept himself fully abreast of all the important events in India and abroad; instead of depending on government briefings alone, he invariably invited eminent persons from different walks of life, including politicians, economists, jurists, administrators, businessmen and journalists, for free and frank exchange of views, which, at crucial moments, helped him immensely in taking appropriate and judicious decisions on sensitive issues.

Even after completing his term as president of India in 1992, RV continued to remain equally well-informed of all the important events and very often, looking at the constant drift in ethical values, he used to express his deep concern.

Formation of governments by multi-party coalitions was, in his view, neither morally desirable nor democratically appropriate. Mad race for acquiring power, forming unduly large cabinets to accommodate partners and fighting for allocation of plump portfolios, all for the sake of staying in power, were all, according to RV, the byproduct of unholy coalitions leading invariably to ineffective leadership, and national interests getting subordinated to political survival.

Some of the events that we have lately witnessed only confirm the apprehensions expressed by RV from time to time. The manner in which the government failed miserably to deal with the Naxalites and Maoists; political leaders mudslinging each other, a prominent political leader accusing the home minister of intellectual arrogance, and the manner in which important decisions are indefinitely deferred by forming GOMs (Group of Ministers) – about 169 such GOMs have already been formed – and, on the external front, the manner in which our external affairs minister was treated with contempt in another country, and how certain nations interfere in our internal affairs, are all very clearly the symptoms of a weak and diluted leadership, lacking authority and direction.

Anticipating problems arising from such unethical alliances whenever occasions arose, RV, in his great foresight and wisdom, was always forthright in making constructive recommendations. In 1991, when the country was facing a critical situation, he was bold enough to suggest forming a national government, at least till the crisis was over.

On another occasion, to prevent multi-party coalitions, he even recommended some basic changes in the Constitution to ensure a two-party system under which splinter parties would not be able to get elected to Parliament. On yet another occasion, to bring more stability, he even suggested that at the time of moving a 'No Confidence' motion, the name of a new prime minister, to replace the incumbent one, should simultaneously be recommended.

History will judge that had some of the profound recommendations made by RV been accepted, the quality and character of India's political system could have been different, more ethical and more stable, better equipped to tackle the critical problems facing the country today.

While deeply concerned about such political developments, RV was at the same time always enthusiastic and appreciative of several other profound measures, such as the Right to Information Act, Employment Guarantee Scheme, Education for All, and other major initiatives, including growth of infrastructure, better network of roads, extensive coverage of telecommunications and generation of more electric power across the rural India.

A person of progressive outlook, RV was an ardent supporter of economic reforms. Following liberalisation measures introduced in the 1980s, subsequently intensified in 1991, RV was all praise for the successful efforts of Manmohan Singh in achieving a higher growth rate, placing India on the fast track of economic development and bringing laurels from all over the world.

However, looking at the overall pattern of economic development, it was his considered view that instead of transplanting Western concepts to India, we should develop an indigenous model, judiciously blending Western concepts with Indian traditions and values. A champion of inclusive growth, he always pleaded for simultaneous emphasis on development of rural and agricultural sectors, so as to ensure that the fruits of growth were more equitably distributed all over and the curse of rural poverty could more effectively be removed. He very often expressed his great concern that even sixty years after Independence such a large section of our population was uneducated and undernourished, denied even of the minimum needs of life like health, sanitation and housing.

A highly devoted and pious person, RV nourished deep respect for India's ancient values and rich heritage, and in keeping with such values he dedicated his remarkable publication *My Presidential Years* to the sacred memory of Mahaswamy Shri Chandrashekharendra Saraswati Jagadguru Shankaracharya.

An inspired man, a relentless fighter and a discriminating observer of current events with historical perspective, his profound contribution in the shaping of modern India will be inscribed in golden letters, and will always remain a source of great inspiration and guidance for the generations to come. I offer my most respectful salutations to this great son of India.

A Multifaceted Personality

Era Sezhiyan

> *RV proved himself as a man of excellence at every stage of his life. Despite the long list of achievements, he remained simple as always.*

President R Venkataraman – known to many of us in Tamil Nadu as 'RV' – was an inhabitant of Pattukkottai in Thanjavur district of former Madras province. His father, K Ramaswami Iyer, was the leading lawyer in the district. RV and my eldest brother Sourirajan – 'Souri' to RV – were classmates in the Board High School, Pattukkottai. They used to study together, both in our house and in RV's, a sprawling big house in Pattukkottai's Big Street. After high school, RV went to Madras to complete his graduation in economics and law. He was registered as an advocate in 1935.

As a Lawyer

We in Pattukkottai were hoping that, in the tradition of professional hereditary followed in those days, RV would come here to take over the legal vocation developed by his father. But RV had his own ideas, as he chose to appear mostly in the courts for the cause of workers and trade unions, without monetary consideration. He soon became a trade union leader and a renowned organiser of the labour wing of the Congress party.

Apart from the organised labour in factories, he took keen interest in the unorganised labour, particularly in the agricultural sector. Majority of the agricultural workers in the Cauvery delta of Thanjavur and Trichy districts and in the coastal region of Andhra belonged to the scheduled classes and other backward communities. That way, RV fulfilled twin objectives: first, that of Mahatma Gandhi, of social emancipation of Harijans, and second, of the socialistic approach of Jawaharlal Nehru in improving the welfare of the working class.

At the call of the Quit India Resolution on 8 August 1942, RV immediately took part in the agitation and was sentenced to two years' imprisonment. I was then a student in the Annamalai University. In those days, getting arrested under the British regime for political reasons was an honour for a politician.

With the imminent approach of India's independence, the Government of India formed in 1946 a panel of lawyers to safeguard the interests of the Indians in Malaysia and Singapore who were charged with collaborating with the Japanese invaders during the Second World War. There were a significant number of people from the Thanjavur district who had gone to those countries as employees in the commercial ventures and rubber plantations. There were also persons associated with Subhas Chandra Bose's Indian National Army charged with serious offences by the British government. The panel consisted of leading lawyers K Bashyam, RV, and KF Nariman (Bombay). The lawyers were successful in getting many of the accused freed from the serious charges raised against them, and in releasing the rest with some nominal punishment.

At that time, there was a serious criminal case against a group of boys accused of having conspired and killed a British officer, and the final judgment gave a death sentence to all the accused. Rajaji (C Rajagopalachari) tried his best to secure pardon for them in consideration of their tender ages. But the date of hanging was fixed. When all hope was lost, RV hit upon a legal point to get a stay order on the hanging by making an appeal through a counsel in England to the Privy Council. Later, the boys were let off by the Government of India. RV's timely move in finding a subtle point of law saved the lives of the young boys. Rajaji paid a tribute to RV as a 'very intelligent lawyer'.

From 1947 to 1950, RV stayed in Madras to practise in the Madras High Court and was soon elected Secretary of the Madras Provincial Bar Association. With his long experience and erudite scholarship in labour laws, he started in 1949 the *Labour Law Journal*, which became a valuable source of reference for trade unions and lawyers.

As a Minister of Tamil Nadu

RV was a member of the Provisional Parliament (1950-52), of the first Lok Sabha (1952-57). In 1957, he got elected to the second Lok Sabha, but K Kamaraj, chief minister of Madras state, wanted him in his cabinet. RV resigned his membership of Lok Sabha and was entrusted with heavy portfolios like industry, labour, power, transport, cooperation, communications and commercial taxes. Further, he was made the leader of the legislative council.

RV's capacity for hard work was phenomenal. The Madras province was industrially backward. With missionary zeal and administrative dexterity, he soon put the state on the industrial map of India. He was responsible for establishment of Guindy Industrial Estate and Ambattur Industrial Estate in Madras' suburbs, which gave rise to formation of such industrial estates throughout the state. These estates helped small entrepreneurs in development of small and medium industries. Large housing schemes under the State Housing Board were started around major cities in the state.

RV initiated cooperative societies, not only to assist small industrial ventures, but also in rural parts, to involve traditional cultivators and agricultural labour for additional employment and income opportunities. He established industrial cooperatives for small tea growers and cooperative textile mills. For the first time in Madras state, he encouraged the establishment of large-scale industries like paper, aluminum, cement and automobile auxiliary units. During his tenure of ten years, he made Madras the third most industrialised state in India. He is known as the 'Father of Industrialisation of Tamil Nadu'.

I was elected to Parliament in 1962. Whenever RV came to Delhi, he would invariably invite me for breakfast or dinner with him at the Tamil Nadu House. He enjoyed talking freely on political situations and personalities in the state and national level. Once when we were dining, C Subramaniam, then union minister of steel and heavy industries, dropped in and exclaimed: 'How is it that a pious Congress minister and an aggressive DMK MP are joined here in conspiring?' RV replied: 'He is my schoolmate.' CS wondered: 'He looks much younger to you!' RV cleared: 'I said "schoolmate". His brother Sourirajan was my classmate. But Sezhiyan also studied in the same high school as I did, therefore a schoolmate.'

In the Planning Commission

In the 1967 general election, the Congress party lost its continuous dominance in many states, including Tamil Nadu. Though RV lost the parliamentary election in the state, the centre willingly made him a member of the Planning Commission, in charge of industry, labour, power, transport, communications and railways, almost an extension at the national level of his work in the state, along with addition of the railways, the gargantuan undertaking crisscrossing throughout the subcontinent.

When RV joined the Planning Commission in 1967, the entire process of planning was in a state of suspension. The third Five Year Plan (1961–66) had ended, but the fourth FYP (for the period 1967–72) prepared under the stewardship of Asoka Mehta, was not taken up due to the economic crisis caused by two years of drought, devaluation and distressing recession. Instead of the Five Year Plans, the government proceeded with Annual Plans for three years, from 1966 to 1969, euphemistically called 'Plan Holiday'.

About the prime objective of planning, RV stated in a symposium on 10 September 1969: 'Soon after freedom, we adopted planning as a means to accelerate economic development. In the newly independent countries, political freedom was only the first and initial step of their large mass of people, steeped in ignorance and poverty and of uniting and welding them into progressive and prosperous nations. Economic development thus became to be the prime objective of the governments in the post-independent era in the most underdeveloped countries.'

What RV had stated four decades ago is still relevant to the planning process in India.

As a Minister in the Central Government

In the 1977 General Election to the sixth Lok Sabha, RV was successful in the South Madras constituency; at the same time, the Congress party incurred unprecedented defeat in the North. In the states of UP, Bihar, Madhya Pradesh, Rajasthan, Himachal Pradesh, Haryana, Punjab and Delhi, the Congress (I) party, led by Indira Gandhi, got only two seats in the Lok Sabha out of a total of 238 in those nine states put together. As most of the former ministers and long-standing Congress leaders, including Indira Gandhi got defeated, RV was the most experienced and important spokesman for the party with respect to financial issues in the Parliament.

On the return of Indira Gandhi to power at the centre in 1980, the natural choice of RV as the finance minister was not surprising. He introduced the scheme of bearer bonds and cash assistance, and subsidies for exports, to meet the balance of payment position of the country. Along with finance, he held temporary charge of industries till 1 August 1981. As finance minister, he also served as the governor of the International Bank of Reconstruction and Development (IBRD) and the Asian Development Bank (ADB).

From January 1982 to August 1984, RV was the defence minister. During his tenure there, he gave special attention to scientific research in order to strengthen self-sufficiency and defence-preparedness of the country.

I was a member of the Rajya Sabha from 3 April 1978 to 2 April 1984. As a leading member of the Janata Party in the opposition, I had several occasions to participate in the debates and confront RV in debates on budget proposals and financial allocations. Members of the Rajya Sabha normally were not much involved in the debates on budget proposals on the grounds that constitutionally, they come under the purview of the Lok Sabha and that as such, the Rajya Sabha had no *locus standi* in them. Though in adopting demands for grants and passing money bills the Lok Sabha has supremacy, I asserted the right of Rajya Sabha to consider the details and give its recommendations for the final consideration of Lok Sabha. RV always understood and appreciated my points raised in the Rajya Sabha and paid attention to them. If there was anything valid in my points of order, he did not hesitate to accept them.

As I retired from the Rajya Sabha in April 1984, I was not there when RV was elected vice-president in August 1984 and took over the ex-officio chairmanship of Rajya Sabha. But because of my work in the Janata Party as a member of its Working Committee and the Parliamentary Board, I was to be in Delhi for long duration and often went to the Central Hall of Parliament House and the library. Even opposition members in the Rajya Sabha were appreciative of RV's successful efforts as chairman to uphold the dignity and discipline of the House.

As President of Indian Republic

The highest honour bestowed on RV was his election to be the eighth president of the Indian Republic. In the poll on 25 July 1987, R Venkataraman, supported by the Congress party and its allies, was elected by a majority of seventy-two per cent of the total value of the votes cast by the electoral college, against the score of twenty-eight per cent obtained by the runner-up candidate VR Krishna Iyer.

During his tenure of five years, President Venkataraman had to face several critical constitutional issues that were not confronted by any of his predecessors.

When he became the head of the state, the head of the executive as prime minister was Rajiv Gandhi, who had a good relationship with and high respect for the president. But the popularity of Prime Minister Rajiv Gandhi was sullied by the Bofors scam of a Swedish arms deal. Further, the resignation of VP Singh from the cabinet and his return to Parliament in a by-election weakened Rajiv Gandhi's position. The CAG Report on the Bofors transactions added fuel to the fiery trend of the opposition. At one stage, all the opposition members resigned. The ensuing 1989 election to the tenth Lok Sabha marked a turning point in the political history of free India.

The unprecedented majority of 415 seats obtained by Rajiv Gandhi in 1984 was decimated to a doleful 197 in the 1989 poll.

Free India, for the first time, had a 'hung Parliament' which meant that there was no single party having requisite majority in the House to form the government. In England, whenever there was no majority for any one party or group of parties, the monarch had the discretion to call the leader of the party having the largest number of members to form the government. In India, after the 1989 election, the Congress party had 197 members in the Lok Sabha, but its leader Rajiv Gandhi refused to form the government; next in the number game was the Janata Dal, headed by Vishwanath Pratap Singh, with 143 seats. Normally, in selecting the leader in a 'hung assembly', the governor in his Raj Bhavan used to satisfy himself about the possibility of the person to form the government, by inspecting the parade of Assembly members. President Venkataraman had more respect for the democratic character of our parliamentary system when he called VP Singh to form the government, with the stipulation that the prime minister should prove his strength on the floor of Lok Sabha.

The National Front government of VP Singh secured the requisite majority in the confidence motion in the Lok Sabha with support of the Leftist Parties, the BJP, some Independents and other smaller parties.

In 1990, when the Bharatiya Janata Party, whose support ensured a majority in the House to VP Singh's government, communicated to the president their withdrawal of support to the ruling party, President Venkataraman did not take note of it but advised Prime Minister VP Singh to seek a vote of confidence in the House.

After laying down his office on 25 July 1992, RV became a free man and unhesitatingly gave his noble thoughts on the governance of a functioning democracy. In his address at the Indian Institute of Public Administration, New Delhi on 18 October 2000, RV said:

> I had the dubious distinction of appointing three prime ministers and working with four of them in five years. Governments, depending on the whims and fancies of small parties supporting from inside or outside, were all the time trying to survive in office and had no time to serve the country or the people. Coalition partners demand the pound of flesh and disrupt the governments, if denied. In short, the tail wags the head.

A Gentleman

Though he had committed himself politically from the very beginning as a firm Congress member, RV always remained a confirmed democrat and a most noble person.

At every stage in his life, in every position he occupied, amidst all splendour and glory, RV remained a simple man, humane and friendly, smiling and soft, towards everyone who met him.

India's Presidents – in Good Times and in Times of Crisis

Fali S Nariman

Among India's presidents in times of peace and of crisis, R Venkataraman stands tall.

A commentator on India's presidency has described it as 'a quiescent volcano[1]'. The constitutional position of the Crown in England (to which India's head of state has been compared)[2] was described, 150 years ago, in more elegant terms by Walter Bagehot, a renowned political journalist of his time:

> To state the matter shortly, the Sovereign has, under a constitutional monarchy, three rights – the right to be consulted, the right to encourage, and the right

---

[1] Pandit, HN, *The PM's President*, S. Chand Co. Ltd., 1974 (p3).
[2] KM Munshi differed. He wrote:
  The President's position essentially differs as stated above from that of the British Crown as to (i) the oath; (ii) the election; (iii) the basis of allegiance of people; (iv) impeachability, and (v) the powers specifically conferred necessarily involving personal discretion. (Munshi, KM, *The President under the Indian Constitution*, Bharatiya Vidya Bhawan, 1963).

to warn. And a king of great sense and sagacity would want no others. He would find that his having no other would enable him to use these with singular effect. He would say to his (First) Minister: 'The responsibility of these measures is upon you. Whatever you think best must be done. Whatever you think best shall have my full and effectual support. But you will observe that for this reason and that reason what you propose to do is bad; for this reason and that reason what you do not propose is better. I do not oppose, it is my duty not to oppose; but observe what I warn'. Supposing the king to be right, and to have what kings often have, the gift of effectual expression, he could not help moving his Ministers. He might not always turn his course, but he would always trouble his mind.[3]

In India's quasi-federal polity with a parliamentary system of government, there is a head of state at the centre whose job is to keep the 'Ship of State' (the union) on an even keel; and there is also a governor at the head of each state. The head of state has hardly ever 'rocked the ship' except during some periods of the first presidency. In the states, however, there have been several occasions when governors have 'played politics', sometimes on their own, more often at the behest of the central government that appointed them. R Venkataraman was a 'textbook' president. He would often confide in Gopalkrishna Gandhi, saying: 'I will not clutch at jurisdiction', implying (at the same time) that

---

[3]Bagehot, Walter, *The English Constitution*, Fontana Press, 1991 (p 113). At a late stage of the debate in India's Constituent Assembly, Dr Ambedkar had said that 'like the English king, our president will have not only Bagehot's three rights (the right to advise, to warn and to be consulted), but also the "prerogative powers", of appointing the prime minister and the dissolution of the House'. (CA Debates, Vol.VII, p 1158).

he would not hesitate to exercise his constitutional functions whenever an appropriate occasion arose.

In the life of almost every president of India these past sixty years, there have been occasions when the president has exercised his individual powers of persuasion – and his 'right to warn'. It is only in crisis situations that the true mettle and personality of the person occupying the highest office in the land is revealed.

Amongst all our presidents of the past, the role of Rajendra Prasad, India's first head of state, has been unique. He did not respond to crisis situations – he was responsible for creating them! During a full decade in office as president – India's only head of state to be elected for two successive terms – he maintained strong views about his role. Having the 'gift of effective expression', these views did frequently 'trouble the mind' of then Prime Minister Jawaharlal Nehru. In private, however, Prasad often complained to his friend Minoo Masani (both were members of India's Constituent Assembly) that Panditji did not allow him to exercise the powers which he was sure he had under the document he had helped get passed in India's Constituent Assembly. Years later, Masani was to say that Rajendra babu did not have the force of Nehru's personality, gave in too readily, and yet went on grumbling (as he gave in) saying: 'this is not the way we framed the Constitution'. Masani added: 'When people say what is wrong with this Constitution, I say nothing is wrong; what is wrong is us, we have destroyed the Constitution because people in Delhi love power too much to tolerate either a "strong president" or a "strong state".' In the past, there have been many votaries of this view.

Within two months of being elected, Rajendra Prasad wrote a three-page paper titled, 'Questions relating to the powers of the President under the Constitution of India'. One of the questions was: 'Does the Constitution contemplate any situation where the President "has to act independently" of the ministers?'

The queries were addressed to Panditji, who passed them on to India's first attorney general, Setalvad.[4]

Setalvad responded firmly and authoritatively – as only he could do – opining that the position of the king in England and India's president were analogous; whilst India's president did have a discretion in selecting the prime minister and deciding when to dissolve Parliament, either at the instance of the prime minister or when he personally felt the overarching force of public opinion, he had to always follow the 'advice' of his council of ministers.

Well into his second term in office, Rajendra babu was not convinced that he was only a constitutional head of state: in 1960, in a speech to the India Law Institute, he said that our Constitution contained no provision 'which in so many words lays down that the President is bound to act on ministerial advice'. This statement created a stir. As my good friend Granville Austin has said[5]: 'it set the presidential fox among the constitutional geese'. But the journalistic reaction to this statement tended to favour the president's position.[6]

After Sarvepalli Radhakrishnan was elected to succeed Rajendra Prasad in May 1962, the contention over presidential powers subsided. If we are to believe what HN Pandit says in his book on the years in office of Radhakrishnan, acquaintances who called on India's second president at Rashtrapati Bhavan were invariably treated to a worm's-eye view of the presidency. 'What is a president after all?' Radhakrishnan would (reportedly)

---

[4]Pandit, HN, *The PM's President – A New Concept on Trial*, S. Chand & Co (Pvt.) Ltd., 1974, (Appendix I. p 91); See also Austin, Granville, *Working a Democratic Constitution – The Indian Experience*, Oxford University Press, 1999 (p 21).

[5]Austin, Granville, *Working a Democratic Constitution – the Indian Experience* Oxford University Press, 1999 (p 24).

[6]ibid. p 25.

say. 'Anyone nearing seventy-five and who has lost his will-power is fit enough to be President of India.' Nearing seventy-five himself, India's second president, however, never lost his will-power during his period in office. For instance, presidential 'pressure' was clearly perceived after India's defeat in the war with China in 1962, with growing clamour for the resignation of Krishna Menon, minister of defence, a very close friend of Panditji. Menon had been blamed for India's defeat, but Nehru, in failing health, would not drop him. It was then that Radhakrishnan diplomatically wrote to the prime minister: *'as you have said* we have to accept Menon's resignation'. (Nehru had said nothing of the sort!) It was a tactful exhibition of presidential pressure in relation to sustained public opinion. The comment of Radhakrishnan's biographer[7] to this incident was that, 'the recognised procedure of the President, acting on the advice of the Prime Minister, was reversed'.[8] Again, when it was reported – soon after President Radhakrishnan took office – that he had told the United States ambassador, Chester Bowles, that upon Nehru's departure from office, he might take temporary charge of government, set policy and administration right, and then step aside for a democratically chosen prime minister, there was a storm of protest by the constitutionalists. Radhakrishnan's biographer has not discussed this incident – he dismisses it as having been said 'in jest'.[9]

President Zakir Hussain – the scholar-president who succeeded Radhakrishnan but who died in office just over two years after being elected, had said that the presidency was a

---

[7]Gopal on Radhakrishan, p 315.
[8]P 315
[9]Gopal on Radhakrishan p 328 and Austin, Granville, p 26. In retirement President Radhakrishan himself had described this as, 'a tissue of lies': see Datta, CL, *With Two Presidents,* Vikas Publishing House, 1971.

'unique institution'. His biographer (D Sheikh Ali) says that Zakir Hussain believed that, in theory, the Indian presidency was 'more powerful than the President of the United States where Woodrow Wilson reduced his Cabinet to office boys, but in India, he (President of India) cannot write his own speech to Parliament, like the British Monarch, he is merely to read what is written for him.'[10]

VV Giri succeeded President Zakir Hussain, after resigning his own office as vice-president and thus creating a constitutional void that necessitated Chief Justice Hidayatullah taking over for a brief period, as acting president. Giri was 'the dark horse' who got elected shortly after the split of the old Congress party when Indira Gandhi, (then head of the Congress [I]) backed him against Sanjeeva Reddy, nominee of the Congress (O). The only recorded crisis during VV Giri's presidentship was his own election to the office of president. It was challenged before the Supreme Court under the Presidential and Vice-Presidential Elections Act, 1952. After a long hearing, and after much oral evidence (the president himself appearing for the first time in court and giving his version of events), a bench of five judges of the Supreme Court upheld the election.[11]

After Giri, the gravest crisis faced by any president in India was that to which President Fakhruddin Ali Ahmed was exposed. He was elected president in August 1974, but unfortunately died in office before completing his term. The 'crisis' was when he was confronted with signing the Proclamation of the Internal Emergency of 25 June 1975; he signed, the inevitable consequence of which was the rounding up of all his erstwhile friends and compatriots, who were all preventively detained

---

[10]Ali, D Sheikh, *Zakir Hussain Life and Times,* Vikas Publishing House, 1991 (p 291).
[11]Kirpal Singh vs. VV Giri – AIR 1970 S.C. 2092 (5J)

in jails spread across the country. One of the lessons of the Internal Emergency (which lasted till March 1977) has been not to place reliance on constitutional functionaries. They failed us – the ministers of government, members of Parliament, judges of the Supreme Court and even the president of India. It was because the president of India so readily agreed to sign the Proclamation of Emergency on the night of 25 June 1975, even before the cabinet (council of ministers) knew anything about it, that three years later (after revocation of the Internal Emergency in March 1977) a constitutional amendment was deliberately enacted by Parliament – the Constitution (Forty-fourth Amendment) Act, 1978 which declared (Article 352 [3]) that in future a president could not sign a Proclamation of Emergency unless the decision of the council of ministers was communicated to him *in writing*.

But the signing of the Emergency Proclamation was not a stray incident. Constitutional functionaries have failed us not merely when the times were bad, but in other times as well. In the general elections of March 1977, the Janata government was swept into power, on a tidal wave of protest against the 'Phoney Internal Emergency' (June 1975–January 1977). Promptly, a circular was issued in May 1977 by Charan Singh, then home minister in the Morarji Desai government. Charan Singh addressed letters to the chief ministers of nine states, asking them to recommend dissolution of state assemblies, even though some of the states' allotted term of five years had not expired. It was a pressure tactic not envisaged by the Constitution. But it worked. When the circular was challenged by one state government (State of Rajasthan) the Supreme Court of India upheld it – in May 1977 by a majority of 7:2.[12] It was only in 1994 that the court had second thoughts – but then it was too

---

[12]State of Rajasthan vs. Union of India – AIR 1977 S.C. 1361

late. In Bommai's case (1994), in a nine-judge bench, the same court (though now differently composed) which had put its imprimatur on undemocratic executive action, declared that the decision of the seven-judge bench in the state of Rajasthan was no longer 'good law'.[13]

Indira Gandhi came back to power in 1980 when the Janata wave petered out. And what did she do? As the saying goes, what was 'sauce for the goose' was made 'sauce for the gander'! Relying on the Supreme Court judgment of May 1977, she instructed her Home Minister Zail Singh to draft a Proclamation under Article 356 for nine State Assemblies – dissolving them and imposing president's rule. And it was President N. Sanjeeva Reddy[14] who signed the Proclamation but (as he reportedly said) 'with hesitation'.

Granville Austin records in his book[15] that Sanjeeva Reddy said: 'given the precedent how could I say No. I told Indira that Morarji had been wrong in principle and to dissolve again was still wrong.' But right or wrong, he assented to the Proclamation – like the ill-fated Duchess of Kent in the limerick of old, 'who said she would not go but she went'! Sanjeeva Reddy had succeeded Fakhruddin sahib after the general elections of March 1977.

During the Emergency imposed in June 1975, when many members of Parliament belonging to opposition parties were placed under preventive detention, the government of the day rushed through Parliament the Constitution (Forty-Second Amendment) Bill, 1976. One of its provisions, which soon became law, substituted a new clause for Article 74(1). It read: 'There

---

[13]SR Bommai vs. Union of India – AIR 1994 S.C. 1918.
[14]Austin, Granville, *Working a Democratic Constitution*, Oxford University Press, 1999, p 536.
[15]ibid. p 536.

shall be a Council of Ministers with the Prime Minister at the head to aid and advise the President who shall, in the exercise of his functions, act in accordance with such advice.'

What was previously left to constitutional convention had now been incorporated as a constitutional mandate in the written text. After the 1976 Amendment, the role of India's head of state was intended to be confined to that of a titular functionary; he must have no 'elbow room'; he must act according to the wishes of his ministers. When the Janata government came to power in the wake of the end of the Emergency and after the March 1977 elections, it moved a Constitutional Amendment in 1978, adding a proviso to the substituted provision that had been introduced in 1976 (which was like a breath of fresh air). It read: 'Provided that the President may require the Council of Ministers to reconsider such advice, either generally or otherwise, and the President shall act in accordance with the advice tendered after such reconsideration.'

Even though the Constitutional Amendment obliges him to act in accordance with the reconsidered advice given by his council of ministers, there is no constitutional prescription as to the time when the president should so act. This omission in our written Constitution was exploited by Giani Zail Singh, India's next president (July 1982–July 1987).

When the Post Office Bill 1987 was submitted to him for assent, there was much criticism of its provisions, particularly the one which permitted an interception of all communications through the mail by the government of the day. Although the Bill was passed by both Houses of Parliament and submitted to President Giani Zail Singh for assent, Gianiji paused. He did not assent. He paid heed to the groundswell of public opinion.

The British Constitution is not written. But it recognises that the British monarch, on rare but important occasions, is entitled to intervene in public affairs in a way that may be decisive. As the constitutional historian of England, Walter Bagehot, used to say, 'the greatest wisdom of a constitutional King would show itself in well-considered inaction'. Gianiji might have been untutored about what went on in Westminster, but he had astute political horse sense: he could sense that people were behind him when he delayed (and then withheld) assent to the Post Office Bill. And in politics, nothing succeeds like success. As a consequence, the public outcry against the Bill gathered greater momentum, and the Bill lay unsigned on the desk of his successor (R Venkataraman). The latter expressed his own displeasure at the Bill, returning it to the prime minister of the day, VP Singh, in January 1990.[16]

The cruel assassination of Indira Gandhi was a great shock to the nation. But the reaction to this event proved to be Zail Singh's finest hour. He could think on his feet – and he did. The burning question was who should be asked to become prime minister. Zail Singh did not dither or vacillate. In the *Memoirs of Giani Zail Singh* (by Manohar Singh Batra[17]) it is recorded that Gianiji firmly told the two union ministers, Pranab Mukherjee and PV Narsimha Rao – possible aspirants to the prime ministership in his view – 'about my decision to place the mantle of the Prime Ministership on Rajiv Gandhi'. Both of them, (the biographer recalls), gladly agreed that the president's decision 'was correct'.

As to how presidents function in times of acute crises we have the version of President R Venkataraman[18] himself (the only president who has penned a memoir of his presidential years). He writes about the crisis occasioned by the resignation of Chandra Shekhar as prime minister – the first question was whether the

---

[16]Venkataraman, R, *My Presidential Years,* Harper Collins, 1994 (p 84)
[17]Batra, Manohar Singh, *Memoirs of Giani Zail Singh,* Har Anand Publications Pvt. Ltd., 1997 (p 205).
[18]*My Presidential Years.*

prime minister, after the acceptance of his resignation by the president, and after having been asked to continue in office until the national elections later that year, was competent to pilot any legislation in the Lok Sabha, and the second question was, what could the president do to carry on the administration of government in the event of Parliament not passing the Finance Bill; at the time it was a distinct possibility.

Slightly departing from his position as constitutional head (a 'textbook president' as he liked to describe himself) Venkataraman wrote a letter to the Speaker Rabi Ray, as well as to the prime minister, expressing his own view based on British precedents, viz., that the prime minister did have the power to function in legislative and administrative matters, even after the acceptance of the resignation of a prime minister. It worked like magic. After these letters, the tragic and menacing cloud on the political horizon lifted, with the Lok Sabha adopting all financial business, and the president endorsing the same. The following communiqué was then issued from Rashtrapati Bhavan:

> On March 6, 1991, the Prime Minister Mr. Chandra Shekhar and his Council of Ministers tendered their resignations and wanted to seek a fresh mandate from the people. The President accepted the resignations and requested the Council of Ministers to continue in office till alternative arrangements were made.
>
> Since financial provisions to defray expenditure after March 31, 1991, had to be made, the President stated that orders on the request for fresh polls would be made separately.
>
> A number of representations were made to the President in favour of and against the dissolution of the Lok Sabha. Questions whether the President could

resort to issue of an ordinance in case Parliament failed to pass budgetary measures to cover expenditure during 1991-92 also cropped up.

The President consulted eminent lawyers and jurists and also party leaders and reached the conclusion that it would be safer to have the financial provisions passed by Parliament.

As necessary budgetary and other legislative measures have since been passed by both Houses of Parliament and as the Union Council of Ministers headed by Mr. Chandra Shekhar has already resigned and recommended a fresh poll and no political party has staked a claim to form an alternative government, the President dissolves the Lok Sabha with immediate effect. A Presidential Order under sub-clause (B) of Clause 2 of Article 85 of the Constitution dissolving the Lok Sabha has been issued.

The President has also directed the constitution of the new Lok Sabha on or before the 5th of June, 1991. Official notification in this regard will be published in due course.

The President wishes to thank all jurists, political leaders and eminent men who have helped him with their advice, counsel and suggestions.

The significance of this has been mentioned in *My Presidential Years*:

It would be seen from the communiqué that I did not base the dissolution of the Lok Sabha solely on recommendation of the outgoing Prime Minister but on the other factor also, namely that no political party had come forward to form a government. I also laid down a healthy convention that budgetary and financial provisions should be handled by Parliament and not through an ordinance. I introduced the innovation of fixing a date for the constitution of the new Lok Sabha which is sustained by the British practice.

Former President Venkataraman had been compelled, by force of circumstances, to depart from the written text of the Constitution – to innovate, to improvise – but without violating either his oath of office or his position as president under India's Constitution.

In a personal letter to me (dated 18 October 1992), after he demitted office as president, R Venkataraman said that he proposed to write about his presidential years 'as they may have some relevance either as good precedent to follow, or as sad mistakes to be avoided ... .'

Shankar Dayal Sharma was elected to the highest office after the full term of President R Venkataraman. Sharma was then presented by the government of the day with the Representation of People Ordinance 1996, recommended to him by the entire cabinet. This ordinance aimed at shortening the period of the poll campaign at elections from three weeks to two weeks. The Constitutional Schedule Caste (Amendment) Ordinance was also submitted to him by the cabinet for promulgation – it was intended to extend reservations in public employment to a large number of 'Dalit Christians'. Former President Shankar Dayal Sharma returned these two ordinances, refusing to promulgate them, since they were recommended by the government of the day on the eve of elections; and according to him this would not pass the test of 'constitutional propriety'.[19]

During the presidentship of KR Narayanan (1997–2002), who succeeded President Shankar Dayal Sharma, then Prime

---

[19] See *The Times of India*, 28 March 1996: 'The President sends back Ordinances: constitutional propriety in question.'

Minister IK Gujral and his council of ministers sent to the president for promulgation a Proclamation under Article 356 of the Constitution, for the imposition of president's rule in the State of Bihar. Acting under the proviso to Article 74(1) of the Constitution, the president returned the proclamation for reconsideration by the council of ministers, giving elaborate reasons (as he invariably did) for his decision. This became widely known, and the union government and Prime Minister Gujral refrained from sending back the Proclamation to him a second time. If it had, Narayanan would have had to sign it, but the public (We the People) would have been against it. In politics, as in most things, discretion is often the better part of valour.[20]

President APJ Abdul Kalam had his share of crises. The Bihar Dissolution Bill which (to my regret) he signed in haste when he was away in Moscow, was struck down by a Constitution Bench of the Supreme Court of India in Rameshwar Prasad's case 2006 (2) SCC 1: by majority (3:2). But his role in the Office of Profit Bill was exemplary.

Kalam's biographer, his secretary PM Nair, says in his book:[21]

> The President's position is very clear in the Constitution. Article 111 gives three options to him: give assent, withhold assent or return the Bill to the Houses with a message for reconsideration – the latter two applicable only in the case of non-money bills. The Article which gives such a right to the president also vests the Parliament with a right to resubmit that Bill after reconsideration

---

[20] Austin, Granville, *Working a Democratic Constitution – The Indian Experience*, Oxford University Press, 1999 (p 582).
[21] Nair, PM, *The Kalam Effect – My Years with the President*, Harper Collins, 2008 (p 110-13).

to the President with or without amendments. When that happens, he 'shall not withhold assent therefrom'. The phrasing of the article takes into account the need to do so without delay.

Exercising this right, the president decided to send a message to Parliament. This was the first time a president was exercising such a constitutional right, and correctly so. In my view, he would have been at fault if he did not do so. He showed that he was not a rubber-stamp president. The message ran thus:

> I received on 25 May, 2006, the Parliament (Prevention of Disqualification) Amendment Bill, 2006, duly passed by both Houses of Parliament for my assent under Article 111 of the Constitution of India.
>
> 2. While having the highest regard for the sagacity and mature wisdom of my fellow Parliamentarians and with due deference to the Parliament, I would like the Parliament to re-consider the proposed Bill:
> (a) in the context of the settled interpretation of the expression 'Office of Profit' in Article 102 of the Constitution, and
> (b) the underlying Constitutional principles therein.
> 3. While re-considering, among other things, the following may be specifically addressed:
> (i) evolution of generic and comprehensive criteria which are just, fair and reasonable and can be applied across all States and Union Territories in a clear and transparent manner,
> (ii) the implication of including for exemption the names of offices the holding of which is alleged to disqualify a member and in relation to which petitions for disqualification are already under process by the competent authority, and

(iii) soundness and propriety of law in making the applicability of the amendment retrospectively.
4. As provided under Article 111 of the Constitution, I, therefore, hereby return the Bill to the Houses for reconsideration with this message.

(signed) A.P.J. Abdul Kalam
30 May 2006

Parliament reconsidered the Bill and as thought fit by that body, passed it again without any amendment. Of course, the government, out of regard to the president, also resolved to refer the entire matter to a Parliamentary Committee to evolve norms. The Bill was reconsidered and passed again in the meanwhile. Thus re-passed, it came back to the president for assent on 1 August 2006. Having exercised his right under Article 111 of the Constitution, he was duty-bound to discharge his constitutional responsibility under the same Article by assenting to it – which he did on 18 August 2006.

Being an erudite scientist, Kalam was also innovative. In February 2005 I was witness, in Parliament, to a bit of astute constitutional statesmanship by the country's then president, Kalam, when he delivered his customary address to both Houses of Parliament to herald in the new session. As is well-known, India's Constitution provides that the president is to address the Houses of Parliament at the beginning of each session. It does not say who is to prepare this address – this is determined by convention. Since the president acts only on the advice of his council of ministers, the address is prepared by the government of the day. But on the morning of 25 February 2005, President Kalam made a departure – he had with him the full text of the written speech prepared by his government. But he chose to begin with a poem in Tamil, a poem composed not by the government of the day but by himself the previous night. He called it 'Where are We?'

> Where are we?
> Where are we now, dear friends,
> In the Maha Sabha that shapes as history,
> The call of heartbeats of Indian people,
> People ask us, people ask us;
> Oh! Parliamentarians, the sculptors of Mother India,
> Lead us unto light, enrich our lives.
> Your righteous toil is our guiding light,
> If you work hard, we all can prosper.
> Like King, so the people,
> Nurture great thoughts, rise up in actions, May righteous methods be your guide;
> May you all prosper ever with Almighty's grace.

It was a criticism of parliamentarians and their erstwhile manner of functioning, firmly expressed, but with a light touch. It was meant as a gentle exhortation from the people's president to the country's representatives not to walk out of legislative chambers, but to work hard and do their job. Since the president could not alter the text of his address to the Houses of Parliament, he devised the expedient of saying what he had to say in verse – and fortunately, it was well received.

The president of India, as its first citizen, has the constitutional right, and correspondingly, the duty to interpose in public affairs of great moment, giving of his wisdom – privately, never publicly; quietly, never with fanfare. An elected president notionally represents the collective will of the people – he can use it (and must use it) to temper the occasional excesses of its elected representatives.

I believe that on those very rare occasions when Parliament (or the government) chooses to do something which the president of India believes to be unconstitutional – or even morally wrong or improper, it is his function, right and duty to intervene and to make known his views: an illustrative instance in point would be an excessive prolongation (by a proposed constitutional amendment) of the life of an existing Parliament: which would keep in office a government whose normal term has run out, and which is anxious to avoid elections.

But then, how must a president, as a constitutional head of state, express his disapproval? It was a former chief justice of Pakistan who provided the answer many years ago. CJ Munir was asked by his country's president (during that country's initial experiment with parliamentary democracy) whether he could constitutionally refuse to give his assent to a Bill passed by the National Assembly (Pakistan's first Constitution after independence was like ours – fashioned on the Westminster model). Chief Justice Munir's answer went something like this:

> If you think it is a matter of the gravest importance, and you cannot in all conscience accept the measure presented to you, you can, and you must (if you are true to your oath) refuse assent – but having refused assent you must then resign; the system must go on; people will know why you resigned, and will sort things out with their governments.

Pearls of wisdom: they show how important, and how potentially effective, is the great office of the president in a parliamentary democracy: but they also show that the words of the Constitution, though important, are never decisive: because the silences in our constitutional law speak louder than words.

R Venkataraman As State And Central Minister
A Nostalgic Civil Servant Reminisces

G Ramachandran

Before he moved to New Delhi to become, successively, a member of the Union Planning Commission, union minister, vice-president of India and then president, R Venkataraman made a name for himself as a minister in the cabinet of Madras state. A civil servant recounts his work ethic – RV's all-out push for development blending seamlessly with an understanding of the realities of the political scene.

It was said of Oliver Goldsmith, that there was nothing which he did not touch, and that there was nothing that he touched in which he did not shine. Venkataraman's scintillating record as trade union leader, labour law specialist, parliamentarian, state and central minister and holder of the two highest constitutional offices of our land evokes the kind of praise, which was bestowed on Goldsmith by his friends in Samuel Johnson's literary circle.

As one among the few surviving civil servants who had the privilege of serving under him, both at the commencement of his ministerial career in the State of Madras (as Tamil Nadu was then called) and towards its climax at the centre in the 1980s, I propose to focus exclusively on his work and achievements as minister, and on his relationship with civil servants. In thus limiting the scope of my article, I could be confident that I am writing about matters within my official knowledge as one of his aides who had assisted him in dealing with them.

When Venkataraman joined the Kamaraj cabinet in 1957, I was director of handlooms – one of the departments assigned to him. The handloom industry occupied then, as it still does, an important place in the economy of the state, being second only to agriculture in terms of the employment it provided. It was not, therefore, surprising when Madras became the first state to set up a separate department to deal with handloom industry. I, then only in the seventh year of my service, was named the director. The policy of both state and central governments then was to bring weavers into the cooperative fold and channelise all assistance for production and marketing of handloom cloth through weavers' cooperatives. In pursuance of this policy, the director of handlooms was also designated an ex-officio joint registrar of cooperative societies, technically under the control of the registrar of cooperative societies. This anomalous arrangement, fraught with possibilities of inter-personal conflict, worked smoothly in practice due to the support extended to me by Venkataraman, who also held charge of the cooperation portfolio. Venkataraman was fair and objective in dealing with those working under him, and was a great consensus builder.

At the same time, he was a taskmaster. He kept up continuous and relentless pressure on me to form new cooperative societies, to enroll more weavers and to formulate new schemes for improving quality of production and for opening new outlets for marketing. He accorded prompt approvals for the schemes proposed by the department. Wherever the Government of

India's sanctions were needed, they were obtained quickly by effective follow-up action and, if need be, through personal intervention at the ministerial level. The result was that we could absorb forty per cent of the total allocations from the handloom fund, whereas normally we could have obtained only about twenty per cent or so.

Though in his distinguished career as a minister in his state, Venkataraman held a number of portfolios – industries, labour, power, cooperation, housing, commercial taxes and law – it is for his stellar performance as minister of industries that he will be forever remembered in the annals of the state. The pace and pattern of industrialisation in any state in that era – the era of licence and 'quota raj' as it was derisively called – were set by the policies and procedures of the central government. As a member of Parliament, Venkataraman had acquired a keen insight into the working of central ministries and had earned the respect and confidence of those who mattered in Delhi. His 'strike rate' in securing approvals for industrial projects in both the public and private sector in the state was therefore high. He also ensured that the state fulfilled promptly its commitments, which he had undertaken with regard to provision of infrastructure, and thus earned the respect and goodwill of the centre, which in those days called all the shots in the industrial sector. In short, in that era of controls and licensing by the centre, he 'managed' the environment in the proper sense of that term, and not in the pejorative sense, which the term has acquired in recent years.

Two major projects on which Venkataraman's heart was set were the Integrated Neyveli Project and the Salem Steel Plant – both involving massive central investment. Of the two projects, the Neyveli project had secured necessary approvals a little before he became a minister. But through the two representatives of state government – industries secretary and finance secretary – on the Board of Neyveli Lignite Corporation, he kept a close watch over the progress of the project, sorting out problems promptly and sometimes proactively. He easily solved problems connected with land acquisition, industrial relations, and deputation of experienced technical personnel from state government as needed to man senior positions in the corporation. When the power segment of the project was completed, he agreed to a reasonable rate for the power supplied to the state electricity board – the monopsony – and thus ensured the viability of the lignite power project, despite some protest from the electricity board. Venkataraman could thus take a long-term view of what was good for the state.

As regards the Salem Steel Plant, taking note of the centre's lukewarm response to repeated pleas of the state, Venkataraman sought to 'up the ante' by commissioning a pre-feasibility study by MN Dastur & Co. There were then many influential bureaucrats in the Planning Commission and central ministries, who opposed the project tooth and nail because they wanted to confine the steel industry to the Bengal–Bihar belt. But Indira Gandhi, who saw the justice of the demand of the state, made a statement in Parliament in April 1970, announcing the decision of the Government of India to set up steel plants in Visakhapatnam, Bellary–Hospet area, and Salem. As joint secretary to prime minister at that time, I drew some satisfaction in taking the draft statement, as desired by the prime minister, to Venkataraman, then a member of the Planning Commission in charge of industries, for his comments before it was finalised. Venkataraman should have experienced a great sense of fulfilment when he incorporated, with the concurrence of Gadgil, deputy chairman, a reference to the southern steel plants in the Fourth Plan Document at the very last minute before the document was presented to the Parliament in May 1970. To complete the long-drawn tale of this project, which in emotional terms meant so much to the people of Tamil Nadu, the government eventually decided to set up only a special steel plant at Salem. It so happened that I was the expenditure secretary in the ministry of finance at that time. I cleared the project in my capacity as chairman of the Project Investment Board (PIB). Based on the recommendation of PIB, the central cabinet accorded its approval to the project in February 1977, just three weeks before the general election. There was then no code of conduct proscribing sanction of projects on the eve of elections. The Janata government, which came to power in March 1977 and undertook a review of projects already sanctioned and on which action had not commenced, confirmed the decision of the previous government on the Salem Plant. Venkataraman's long-cherished dream became a reality – albeit in a truncated form.

No account of Venkataraman's record as minister in his state can be considered complete if note is not taken of his contribution to the growth of the state's economy in his capacity as minister in charge of power. As a planning secretary and part-time member of the state electricity board, I can bear testimony to the vigour with which he pushed through programmes for generation and distribution of power. The installed capacity was doubled and a massive programme of rural electrification was undertaken, with the accent on energisation of pump sets. Madras led all other states then in percentage of villages electrified and number of pump sets connected to power. At that time, the state depended primarily on hydel (hydro-electric) power. During his tenure, for the first time, a big switch to thermal power took place, with commencement of action on the first stage of Ennore Thermal Project. It has also to be stressed that all this expansion of the grid was accomplished without impairing the financial health of the state electricity board. Tariffs for different categories of consumers, including agriculturists, were periodically adjusted, enabling the state electricity board to cover operational costs, depreciation and also pay in full the interest due on loans advanced to it by the state government.

It was this record of the power sector in the state, which led the Planning Commission to appoint Venkataraman as chairman of a committee at national level to review the working of state electricity boards. The committee recommended that SEBs should over a period of time aim at covering operational costs, interest reserve, electricity duty and return on capital – aggregating to eleven per cent on capital. For a long time, this recommendation remained the benchmark against which the performance of electricity boards was judged.

When Venkataraman took over the Ministry of Finance in January 1980, the outlook for the budget of 1980–81 was extremely bleak, in view of the severe and widespread drought of 1979 and massive expenditure on assistance to states for drought relief. The prices of imported petroleum crude had tripled in 1979 in the wake of the overthrow of the Shah's regime in Iran, and the attempts of the finance ministry under HM Patel to pass on these increases to the consumer had been successfully thwarted by the petroleum minister. The cost of production of fertilisers being based largely on Naphtha, LSHS, and fuel oil had also risen sharply and remained to be passed on to the consumers. Venkataraman was quick to recognise that unless the administered prices of these products were suitably enhanced, the country would face an economic disaster. Under his direction, proposals for substantial upward revision of the prices of these were worked out and with the preliminary approval of the prime minister, these proposals were placed before the cabinet. Incidentally, these proposals, instead of being referred to the concerned ministries for concurrence, which it would have been difficult if not possible to obtain, were straightaway taken to the cabinet, under a business rule which empowered the finance ministry to take any proposal which it considered essential for the management of the economy direct to the cabinet. After a heated discussion, the cabinet approved – one could say acquiesced in the proposals of the finance minister. With the increases in administered prices a few days ahead of the budget, the finance minister could present a mild budget, with both tax increases and deficit financing being kept at moderate levels. Venkataraman enhanced the appeal of his budget further by annulling in one stroke all the increases in excise duties on consumption goods of interest to the urban middle class, imposed in the previous budget by Charan Singh as deputy prime minister (finance) under the Janata regime. As Venkataraman slowly spelt out all these reductions one by one, he was wildly cheered by the House. After the House rose for the day, Prime Minister Indira Gandhi called him to her room and told him that the budget had been well received by her party men and would be well received by the country, too. In his very first foray into budget-making, Venkataraman had demonstrated that it was possible to be both fiscally responsible and politically imaginative.

Venkataraman lived up to his reputation as an institution builder by unobtrusively incorporating provisions for the establishment of appellate tribunals, for dealing with appeals by aggrieved parties against the orders of the executive under laws relating to excise duties, customs duties and gold control on the model of the appellate tribunals in respect of direct taxes. In carrying out this legislative exercise, Venkataraman consciously and in public interest overlooked the convention in vogue since 1967, that the annual Finance Acts should only enact changes in tax rates and that substantive changes should be effected through separate amending Acts. Separate legislation for setting up new appellate authorities would have meant considerable delay, of even up to two years. The setting up of appellate tribunals for indirect taxes was a long overdue reform and was warmly welcomed by all sections of trade and industry.

The severe drought of 1979–80 and the sharp escalation in prices of imported crude oil had led to a sharp deterioration in balance of payments. Without allowing the position to worsen further and compel recourse to drastic and destabilising measures later, Venkataraman took preemptive action by approaching the IMF in time with a carefully crafted 'Adjustment Programme'. The programme was successful. His timely action enabled the Indian economy to overcome its difficulties quickly. His successor as finance minister, Pranab Mukherjee, could leave about $1 billion out of the $5 billion IMF credit line unused, thanks to Venkataraman's programme. The country should be grateful that because of Venkataraman's prompt action, it avoided the kind of trauma which laid it low later, in 1991.

His second – and the last – budget will be remembered for the controversial but successful bearer bond scheme, which was launched through an ordinance later replaced by an Act of Parliament. It is relevant to mention that the constitutional validity of the bearer bond scheme was upheld by the Supreme Court. The budget for 1981–82 took credit for ₹1,000 crore, thus enabling the government to keep deficit financing at a relatively low level. The budget estimate was almost realised. In fact, Venkataraman called off the scheme as soon as the estimated amount was garnered. When Venkataraman mooted his scheme, he gave those of us in the finance ministry full freedom to express our views. We brought to his notice that only two years earlier the Public Accounts Committee, of which his cabinet colleague PV Narasimha Rao was chairman, had in its report advised against any tax amnesty scheme in the future on the lines of 'the Voluntary Disclosure Scheme of 1975-76'. Venkataraman, therefore, took pains to explain to Parliament that his scheme was not a tax amnesty scheme. He also made it clear that he alone was responsible for the scheme and that none of his officers should be held accountable for it. Venkataraman never passed the buck to the civil servant.

I would like to give an even more telling example of his readiness to assume sole responsibility for what are essentially political decisions, and shielding civil servants from the consequences of such decisions if they should go awry. Soon after Sanjay Gandhi's death, a wholly political and perhaps also emotional decision was taken to take over his venture, Maruti, and to develop it as a public sector unit. Venkataraman dealt with the relevant file himself and explained to me that the takeover of Maruti being a political decision, the politician alone should bear the cross for it. Fortunately, the political decision turned out to be a commercially sound one, thanks to the efforts of the highly competent team handpicked to implement it.

The civil servants also felt comfortable dealing with him because he did not fight shy of recording the reasons for his decision in the cases submitted to him. Even as bombs were falling all over London, Winston Churchill, working in his bunker, dictated detailed memoranda conveying instructions to his commanders and ministers with full explanation for his directives. Churchill believed that democracy was 'government by documentation'. Venkataraman, too, fully believed in documentation. Such documentation should be insisted upon at all levels, particularly at the highest levels of our government at the centre and in the states. It will provide safeguards against wrongdoing and promote transparency in our administrative system.

Venkataraman played an important role in the formulation of economic policies of the governments of which he was a member. He was development oriented and was a firm believer in a mixed economy in which both public and private sectors coexisted. Both would enjoy the support and patronage of the government and both would be subjected to regulation in public interest. He was all for free enterprise but not for freebooters. He was a centrist on economic issues. He was a fiscal conservative in so far as he believed that the government should pay its way. He was the last finance minister to present a budget without a deficit on revenue account. When he demitted office in 1992 as president of India, the economic reforms had just got under way. While he would have endorsed most of the reforms, it would be interesting to speculate on whether he would have disapproved of any of the reforms already implemented or those that are under contemplation. We can be sure that he would not have approved of any denigration, as is fashionable now among sections of our elite, of the role of government in economic development, nor would he have accepted that there are market-based solutions for all our problems. He would have cautioned that the 'invisible hand' on which some of our reformers place so much reliance could sometimes be that of a crook. He would have stressed the importance for our national well-being, of the small farmer, small and medium industry, and the street corner store. He would have emphasised the need to encourage, preserve and foster indigenous Indian talent and enterprise, and to not allow them to be overwhelmed by multinationals from abroad.

I began this article with a reference to Oliver Goldsmith. It will not be inappropriate to end with a couple of lines from Oliver Goldsmith's poem 'The Deserted Village' which, incidentally, Manmohan Singh had also quoted in one of his speeches in Parliament.

> Ill fares the land to hastening ills a prey
> Where wealth accumulates and men decay.

In a loud and clear voice, Venkataraman would have said 'I agree'.

Ramaswamy Venkataraman: A Personal Tribute

Lord Geoffrey Howe

> *R Venkataraman played an important role in the international arena, impressing all who came in contact with him, including the author.*

During the last twenty-two years, R Venkataraman and I renewed contact with each other on only three or four occasions. Each was very agreeable, however brief, because it enabled us to recall the years of partnership we had shared. Even so, it was a great surprise – and a great compliment – for me to receive from his daughter Lakshmi V Venkatesan an invitation to compose this tribute in her father's memory. And I do so with great pleasure, and with real pride. Not only was he sixteen years my senior in age, but as head of state for five years of the world's fourth largest nation, the Republic of India, he hugely outclassed my own fifteen months as deputy prime minister of the United Kingdom.

But our lives have indeed overlapped during the years in which we had both been responsible for managing our nations' financial and economic policies: myself as chancellor of the exchequer in Margaret Thatcher's cabinet, 1979–83, and he for two years as India's finance minister, 1980–82. So we found ourselves coming together in different global rendezvous. The most important was the Interim Committee of the International Monetary Fund, which met twice a year – every autumn in Washington, and otherwise, elsewhere. Another occasion was the meeting of Commonwealth finance ministers, which took place only once a year, always just ahead of the IMF Committee meet. I found myself regularly acting as chairman of the Commonwealth Meeting, and finally, in 1982–83, of the IMF Committee as well.

So we came to know each other very well, not least because our entire careers had been similar in many respects. We had, for example, both started as lawyers. I well remember his reply when I first asked him just how long he had been active in the legal profession. 'Almost fifty years,' he replied, 'if you count my two years of imprisonment by the British!'

No need, of course, for him to conceal this origin of his political career. He had been fascinated, at an early stage, by the irresistible draw of Mahatma Gandhi, and had quickly plunged into the freedom struggle as an active participant in the Quit India Movement. Years later, he had surprised one of Britain's high commissioners, who had asked for his view on Mountbatten's decision to advance the date of Indian independence (which so many Indians regarded as a cause of the bloodbath of Partition). He explained that he had lived through the period as an active supporter of the independence movement (and as one of the lawyers defending members of the Indian National Army), and that independence simply could not have been further delayed. Mountbatten, therefore, had no choice.

Many years, of course, had to pass before our paths came to cross, as finance ministers in the 1980s. His parliamentary career commenced some fifteen years ahead of mine, as a member of the first Lok Sabha (1952–57). He quickly won respect as an outstanding parliamentarian and an eloquent speaker, with keen interest in a wide range of subjects. No surprise, therefore, that he was soon being recognised as a formidable contributor to Commonwealth Parliamentary Conferences.

This reputation continued to grow, following the diversity of his experience as a cabinet minister, first in Tamil Nadu (Madras), with responsibility successively for industry, labour, cooperation, power, commercial taxes and transport. Subsequently in the Government of India, he looked after planning and defence, as well as finance. His experience quickly extended into the international field. Apart from the Commonwealth, he was India's representative at many levels of the United Nations Organisation – ranging from the International Labour Organisation and General Assembly to the honorary presidency for life of the UN Administrative Communal.

The fruits of this experience were extremely evident to those of us who had the privilege to serve with Venkataraman on the international financial bodies. I found him always ready to play the leading part in identifying the only possible solution to a complex monetary problem. I remember one of his achievements in this context, at an IMF interim committee meeting in Washington, where it became essential to put together a wide-ranging international partnership, which was necessary (and eventually able) to overcome a period of sustained resistance by the United States. He played a crucial role in securing the outcome which eventually prevailed.

One special feature of Venkataraman's performance on these occasions was his mastery of the English language (almost always the only option), which enabled him time and again to formulate the only possible form of words which could deliver an agreeable conclusion. Colleagues were often amused, as well as impressed, by his skill. Their Indian partner was a more competent draftsman than their English chairman! But that period in which we both enjoyed working together was not destined to last forever. For he was soon to be shifted, in August 1984, to the vice-presidency of the Indian republic. It was a measure of his eminence that he was a consensual candidate for this august office, which carried with it the ex-officio chairmanship of the Rajya Sabha. In this role, he proved to be an excellent moderator between the conflicting groups of parliamentarians, and established for himself a reputation of fair play and political even-handedness. Less than three years later, on 25 July 1987, Venkataraman achieved the pinnacle of glory when he was elected the eighth head of the Indian republic. This position he was destined to hold for five full years, which are described in great detail in his memoirs entitled *My Presidential Years*. Unsurprisingly, this is a most readable volume, with stimulatingly detailed accounts of a series of unusual political problems, arising out of a frequently 'hung Parliament', with the accompanying need to manage the emergence of unexpected coalition governments.

And in his typical style, Venkataraman gives vividly enjoyable accounts of his worldwide travels while visiting a diverse range of other heads of government. His visit to the Soviet Union, for example, coincided with the joint presence of on the one hand, the modern trailblazing chairman, Mikhail Gorbachev, and, on the other, the unfailingly sullen (as I had come to know him) Andrei Gromyko (the then Soviet president).

This is perhaps the note on which I should bring this essay to a close, for it enables me to also mention and acclaim the success of Venkataraman's visit to the United Kingdom itself. For this came at the end of a period of decided chilliness in our relations with the Government of India, over what the Indians perceived as our support for Sikh separatism. So it was agreeably surprising when, at the president's meeting with Prime Minister [Margaret] Thatcher, he was all praise for the UK: 'Between

India and Britain, there was more than a friendship, there was an affinity and a unique relationship.' He proclaimed his wish for Britain to be first in India's industrial investment, praised our aid programme and also, surprisingly enough, our efforts on Sikh extremism, and had no complaints about anything. Margaret Thatcher and he manifestly warmed to one another. It was a pleasure to be able to record that despite his earlier involvement in the Independence movement (including spending two years in a British jail), he showed no bitterness of any kind towards Britain or the British, but something of an affection and admiration for us.

It is a pleasure to be able to end on that note, which certainly set the tone for our last meeting together. I was in India (I think in 1994) to advertise the publication of my own memoirs, *Conflict of Loyalty*. And to my delight Venkataraman, still very active and alert, was ready to preside over the meeting in New Delhi at which my book was presented to the Indian press and people. The occasion was particularly pleasing to me, because of the characteristic kindness with which he conducted the event.

The Value of Decency

Gopalkrishna Gandhi

Would RV be an anachronism today? Perhaps he would. And yet, 'his' era was not some bygone age, it was yesterday. So near and yet so far.

Ramaswamy Venkataraman would have turned a hundred years old in 2010.

'Don't wish that for me!' he protested when I rang to wish him 'a full century and more' on his last birthday, in 2008. 'I have lost all desire to live ... .'

The former president was reflecting a widely-shared despondency about contemporary politics and public life.

In the Gandhi–Nehru years, of which RV was a part, politics absorbed hugely talented people. With thriving careers open to them in the law, in trained professions and callings, they yet devoted themselves to the free.

Between the 1920s and 1930s, new entrants joined the freedom struggle straight after school or college, often without completing their studies. By the time of the Quit India Movement, the full-time politician had well and truly arrived. But even in those politically surcharged times, politicians knew that life was larger than politics, politics was larger than the party, and the party was about more than one's own advancement within its ranks.

Today, the position is different.

'Anyone and everyone can join politics today,' RV rued not very long ago at a conversation with me in his sitting room in New Delhi. The day's newspapers were on the table in front of him. 'All he needs to do is to show enough money towards his electability, enough vote-bank numbers on his side, and he gets a ticket.'

His own electoral history was awesome. RV had fought altogether five elections to the Lok Sabha, winning four – 1952, 1957, 1977 and 1980 – and losing one, in 1967.

Standing for Parliament from Tanjore in 1952, in the very first elections held in independent India, RV had taken a huge risk. Was the seat selected for this Aiyar Congressman (or he for the seat) because the district had a fair number of Brahmins? Double-cropping deltaic Tanjore was tense with exploited agricultural labourers (prominently Harijan) asking for higher wages, and non-cultivating landowners (mostly Brahmin) of large paddy-acreages resisting the demand by importing labour and introducing tractors. In fielding RV from radicalised Tanjore, the Congress, in classical left-of-centre idiom, was making the statement that agrarian reforms must come, but must come constitutionally.

Leading the national campaign in 1952, Jawaharlal Nehru was a fit sixty-three. Leading the battle for votes in the state, K Kamaraj was an energetic forty-nine. And touring Tanjore in bullock carts, RV was an extremely young forty-two. Already valued as an exceptionally intelligent lawyer-turned-freedom fighter with a commitment to social equity, RV was known as one who had spent two years in jail for participating in the Quit India Movement, and on his release, had diligently taken up with cerebral passion issues pertaining to labour.

The Congress in Madras state was in for a tough fight and, with the rest of the South, did poorly. But RV won. He won the next election to the second Lok Sabha in 1957 too, from the same seat. Resigning from it to take up Chief Minister Kamaraj's call to join the state cabinet, the trade unionist politician with strong egalitarian views showed another mettle – economic planning, turning a state not known for industries into one that became a model for industrialisation at all levels, small, medium and large. And he did that with almost zero attention being allowed to focus on himself. He was a minister, a minister in Kamaraj's and later in M Bhaktavatsalam's cabinet, and that was that. 'We had a big team spirit,' he would say of that phase. Was that spirit smart because it was good or good because it was smart? If RV was asked that, he would probably have just smiled through his thick bifocals and said, 'You decide'.

The decade – 1957 to 1967 – that saw Kamaraj and RV becoming a politico-administrative duumvirate within the state also saw national politics shaken. The war with China and Nehru's passing away had demoralised the nation. The rise of regional parties coinciding with the formation of the Swatantra Party under Rajaji's formidable leadership had given democracy a new vigour, but the Congress, a jolt.

In the testy 1967 elections, RV contested the Tanjore Lok Sabha seat for Congress again. This time, not agrarian equity but ethnicity and incumbency dominated the universe of voters in the state, many of them 'first-timers'. Only three Congress contestants out of thirty-nine were elected, with the DMK trouncing the Congress comprehensively. Tasting defeat for the first (and only time), RV conceded victory to a DMK candidate, relatively unknown earlier and little known since. That is what waves, even tidal waves, do. It was just like RV to find no comfort in the fact that other Congress stalwarts like C Subramaniam, OV Alagesan, N Mahalingam and Maragatham

Chandrasekar had also lost by far wider margins in their home turfs.

One more decade was to pass before RV contested for the Lok Sabha again, in 1977. The intervening decade had seen Indira Gandhi's National Emergency, and his leader Kamaraj's death from a political site opposed to Indira Gandhi's. It is conceivable that if Kamaraj had lived, RV would have stayed by his side and either moved inexorably away with his leader from the Congress or – who knows – brought the titan closer to Indira Gandhi, for the good of the nation's greatness. But with Kamaraj gone, RV's 'intelligence' saw him back in the Congress fold, contesting and winning the Madras South against the DMK's Murasoli Maran. The Congress having been defeated resoundingly in the 'hinterland', RV sat in the opposition in the sixth Lok Sabha, respected by the senior Janata leadership. Had RV not contested the 1977 election, it is possible that he would not have been fielded at the elections in 1980, when he won by a thumping majority from the same seat, this time in alliance with the DMK, to become finance minister and then defence minister in Indira Gandhi's cabinet. He was seventy. The vice-presidency lay just ahead of him.

I happened to be secretary to the governor of Tamil Nadu when RV came to Chennai on his first visit as vice-president. After he had returned to Delhi, I was called by Governor Khurana. '*Upa Rashtrapatiji* wants you to join his staff as secretary ... I have said I will release you ... .'

The vice-president could have summoned me himself and said as much, but no. He asked my boss, his host, to do so. That is propriety. Seven years of intense work under a taskmaster lay ahead of me, first as his secretary, and then, in Rashtrapati Bhavan, as his joint secretary. Between those two transitions, came another remarkable occasion to see RV's sense of propriety at play. The Congress under Rajiv Gandhi nominated Vice-President Venkataraman as its candidate for the office being vacated by Giani Zail Singh. The Left fielded the esteemed Justice VR Krishna Iyer. 'Iyer v/s Iyer', the shallow wag commented.

Though the result was foregone, it was suggested to RV that he undertake a nationwide tour to campaign. He declined. 'I will have to speak for my candidature versus Justice Krishna Iyer's. That in itself will be unpleasant. But more importantly, when the country is plagued by so many divisions, what is the point of a future *rashtrapati*, going about dividing the country's Presidential vote ...? Let the electoral college decide on the basis of its knowledge of the candidates and a reading of the situation ... I will keep quiet.'

RV did not campaign, and he won. Any candidate of the ruling party would have. But RV's victory was won with a major propriety observed, life shown to be larger than politics, and a worthy opponent left free to lose the election – that was his prerogative, but not his prestige.

July 1987

Vice-President Venkataraman was to be sworn in the following day as India's eighth president.

Wanting to brief him on a few matters of procedure, I knocked at his apartment door late that evening. '*Yes?*' came his high-pitched voice. Mrs Janaki Venkataraman and he were putting some of their personal effects together. As we were talking, a bulb on the ceiling of the room exploded, scattering glass splinters all over the carpeted floor. Bulbs giving up the ghost due to long use was not uncommon, but I found the mishap most unwelcome. Not so the vice-president. As I made some silly noises about the quality of bulbs and Mrs Venkataraman looked mildly irritated, the president-designate's face beamed.

Beamed? Exactly that. 'Wait, wait,' he said, and with a few quick steps went to a chest of drawers and returned, smiling, with a tiny gadget in his hands. 'This picks up glass splinters,' he said, with the excitement of a child. And in no time, the seventy-seven-year-old was on all fours, the battery-operated instrument purring over the carpet, lifting the sharp pieces of shattered bulb. 'Careful of your hands,' Mrs Venkataraman cautioned, as I also joined the shattered glass vacuum-lifting exercise.

Neither the man who was to become India's First Citizen nor the woman who was to be First Lady thought of omens, signs, or any superstitious augury linking the tiny explosion to the induction the next morning of the eighth president of India.

Deeply pious, like his wife, RV had no time for superstition. Believing in a Supreme Power, RV had little time for astrology. The date he was sworn-in happened to fall in the Tamil month of Adi (Ashadha), when the orthodox do not commence new enterprises and do not move house. This consideration did not weigh with the couple. Although aware, as any Tamil would be, of the injunctions of Rahu-*kala*, the 'no-no' slot which slouches forward by one and a half hours every day of the week, when nothing important and nothing 'good' should be attempted, RV did not let his schedule be even remotely affected by that action-inhibitor.

RV was rooted in the philosophy of his faith, not in its ceremonials. He stood on a firm foundation of spiritual values, without the overlay of dogma. And his mind branched out in eclectically diverse directions, as befitted one from the Gandhi–Nehru–Kamaraj mould.

This also enabled RV to remain politically sited in the Congress but accessible, with the most natural ease, to non-Congress personalities. At a reception in the Chinese embassy to mark China's national day in 1986, EMS Namboodiripad was standing by himself in a corner. I went up to him and, offering my respects, asked if he would like to meet the vice-president (who, as per the demands of protocol, was seated at a fixed point and not 'mingling'). EMS immediately agreed and I had the privilege of conducting the living legend of India's Left to where RV was seated. On seeing EMS approach, the vice-president sprang to his feet and the two spent several minutes in pleasant converse. On our drive back to the vice-president's house, RV said in his typical accentuations, 'What are we before that giant of a man? He gave up *evvery-thing* for his cause, *evvery-thing*.'

This receptivity enabled RV as chairman of the Rajya Sabha to be equally cordial and equally firm with everyone across the benches, pulling members up for inadvertencies as much as for intentional misconduct during Question Hour, the 'hour' that he scrupulously spent in the House. Prolixity, additional supplementaries, 'irregular' Calling Attention Notices, Adjournment Motions would be summarily put down. 'Nothing will go on record, nothing ... .' was heard in the familiar high-pitched voice on the Chair whenever someone broke the decorum of the proceedings by speaking without authority. Members doing a 'walkout' would invariably hear the chairman saying with a smile, 'Walking out? All right, anyway attendance is optional ... .' making the MP look and feel utterly un-heroic. Predictably, RV earned the left-handed title of 'Headmaster'.

As president, seniority – the first attribute of a teacher – came to be nearly imposed on RV by virtue of him being a good deal older than most in the government and in the political class of the day. His strained eyesight, which required him to wear high-correction lenses, and his pure silver hair helped perpetuate the headmaster image.

The five decades' old Congressman in RV deeply rued the loss by Rajiv Gandhi of his office. But the president of India had to follow established procedures 'by the book', that too, transparently. RV did exactly that and over two elections to the Lok Sabha, he administered oaths of office to two prime ministers in quick succession, only to accept their resignations amidst political volatility until, after the 1991 elections, the Congress returned to power with PV Narasimha Rao at the helm and Manmohan Singh inducted as finance minister.

As with the exploded fragments of a bulb on the eve of his becoming president of India, RV had picked up the scattered shards of exploded mandates in a way that their jagged edges would not hurt our nationhood. And he installed a new one seamlessly.

The 'prefects' changed, the 'headmaster' remained in charge of the 'class'.

But a 'teacher' of the RV cast of mind, with whom propriety counts more than popularity, who does his own teachers' homework as diligently as he expects his wards to do the students', who mentors with all his being but evaluates stringently, who welcomes with warmth but expels without compunction, who advises and admonishes, cheers and checks, blesses and berates depending on the person's actions, and above all, *does not regard himself as above the law but governed by it*, is now a rarity.

What is more to the point, a mentor of that type is not really wanted.

RV was as fallible as any human being. He made his errors of assessment, of judgment, often in the way he reposed trust in people who deserved less. And, in the larger interest, sometimes 'looked the other way'. But in our times when *mala fide* intent exceeds 'honest error', he was something of an oddity.

Rarities are still to be seen, and exceptions remain. But these exceptions are becoming more and more exceptional. A 'standard politician' is now seen, unfairly to the exceptions, as someone void of ideals but replete of ambition, a pygmy in reliability but a giant in cunning, with almost no 'law' ruling him, no 'principle' governing him, save ruthless self-interest.

Politics is no longer the house of beliefs and the home of action, the field of honest elections fairly fought and gracefully won or lost, that we have known it to be.

We do have free and frank campaigning, free and fair voting. We have deserving candidates fighting clean, fighting hard, fighting to win honourably or to lose blamelessly.

But that, alas, is not the whole story. Our democracy is also about manipulation. It is also about undeserving candidates fighting dirty, fighting sly, winning dishonourably with a smirk or losing unsportingly with vengeance under the breath.

Leaders in the art and science of contrivance and improvisation that Indians are, we have managed to make our large democracy grow ever larger in size, but also become ever smaller, even petty, in the actual workings.

Politics cuts deals with masters of the herding method and with the mafiosi, whether for the success of rallies, for elections or for swollen egos to clash often with unashamed violence, for small-time scores to get settled and for money, huge money, to be spent to buy, seize, occupy turf or to retain a precarious hold on it. An estimate has it that a parliamentary election, to be fought seriously, requires a candidate to spend at least ₹8 crore. 'Bigger' candidates spend as much as ₹40 crore. Where are they to get the money from? Obviously from financiers outside the political universe. And they are bound to have some expectations from their 'investment'. And the 'return' can only come from favours, concessions and privileges bestowed by the victorious candidates. And where are those favours to come out of? From the natural resources of India, especially from land, and the ores and forest wealth that come with land. A far cry from the elections of the 1950s!

Law-making can hardly be a priority for legislatures elected thus.

It is no surprise, therefore, that if MPs schooled in the law like RV comprised thirty-five per cent of the first Lok Sabha, less than fifteen per cent of the law-makers comprising the present Lok Sabha have a law background. I will say nothing of the percentage of alleged law-breakers among them. There is another – surreal – fact that hits the eye. The number of male MPs who wore rings on their fingers to propitiate the gods, or strings around their wrists to ward off the evil eye, in the first Lok Sabha led by Jawaharlal Nehru and populated by men like RV (who, like his leader Nehru, wore neither), must have been no more than a handful. Invoking the Almighty for grace is natural. But He can be spared anxieties over politicians' personal prospects, or for security from the ire of those that have been hurt, harmed and made enemies of. Today, a huge number of legislators, across all party divides, bear those nervous adornments.

Can anything, anything worthwhile, be expected of so hugely compromised a person?

So, then, is this it?

Is there any hope for redemption?

There had better be!

Precisely for having known better, we cannot settle for less than redemption.

Politicians must be helped to see, and not through the mechanism of elections alone, but through responsible and calm public articulations, that they cannot afford to be seen as a byword for financial impropriety, administrative dereliction and valuational grossnesses.

But we cannot end with laying the blame squarely on politicians. They are artistes, many very gifted, many more, not.

Change has to come in the script of the play. It has, in other words, to start with 'We the People'.

We have to accept the inconvenient fact that if our politics has been debased, we have had a hand in the process. We have often chosen what we have regarded as 'the lesser of the two evils', have remained silent when politics has hijacked the law of the land, have condoned when we should have excoriated, looked the other way when we should have looked straight-in-the-eye. And we are as short-termist as any politician. 'What we are,' Jiddu Krishnamurti (who RV greatly admired and knew well) has said unforgettably, 'the world is.'

Is it too late for this cleansing?

It is late, but not too late.

Why do I say this?

I say this, for 'we the people' are not alone. Our constitutional authorities have made common cause with common sense and the common man to bring to justice great and palpable wrongs done by politicians and by those working under or with them. These authorities, headed by the Supreme Court of India, chief election commissioner, chief information commissioner, and the comptroller and auditor general of India, are there, edifices and instrumentalities, fashioned by the higher sense of our early law-makers, to be utilised in the national interest.

The RTI Act and the instrumentality of the PIL have brought the relief of justice to stricken people and causes. 'Civil society' and NGOs contain energies and means for political redressal that can be truly restorative if used with due care, non-vindictively and without generating its own counter-egoism.

And so, when our courts and our constitutional authorities speak harsh truths, I believe we must respect them as speaking in a voice that, going beyond the short-termist and the populist, the vindictive, and the sectionally selfish, seeks to find constitutional and legal remedies to the problems afflicting our body politic.

That voice is only a part-remedy. A full remedy has to come from within the body politic when it realises that India now needs, and deserves, a total break from the enervations of the last five decades and more. But until that 'full remedy' comes, we must respect, endorse and place our full trust in these authorities which, though not part of the architecture of an elected democracy, are yet striving to protect its spirit.

RV's Shining Services to India

Inder Malhotra

> *This essay explores R Venkataraman's career in high politics, first as a part of the government during the stormy, politically turbulent 1960s and later as president of India, when his mediating skills were once more called into action as he oversaw the country's transition to modernity.*

On the first day of the first session of Provisional Parliament in February 1950 – until then the Constituent Assembly used to double up as the central legislature – I had the privilege of first meeting R Venkataraman in Parliament's Central Hall. He was one of the new members who, at Jawaharlal Nehru's bidding, had replaced those in the Constituent Assembly that were chief ministers, ministers and MLAs in various states. I was then a young and raw reporter but RV, twenty years older, took me seriously and talked to me most courteously. This laid the foundations of a lifelong association, during which he was unfailingly gracious to me and, irrespective of whatever office he held and however busy he was, always accessible. Moreover, unlike many other friendly news sources, he was never pompously secretive but refreshingly communicative. Of course, if he did not want to answer a question about some sensitive and classified matter, he charmingly said: 'Ask me this some other time.' As time went by and he felt that I could be trusted to keep confidences, he usually gave me the information I sought with the proviso that it must not be published or whispered to others.

In the first general election in 1952, RV returned to Parliament. By this time, Nehru had obviously discerned his talents and potential, because year after year he sent RV to the UN General Assembly as a member of the Indian delegation. Once, after the nationalisation of the Suez Canal, when the Suez Crisis was on but the Anglo–French invasion of Egypt hadn't yet taken place, on his way back from New York, RV had stopped over in Cairo, met Gamal Abdul Nasser and found him 'calm and self-confident'. His performance in the Lok Sabha and its committees had also won admiration.

Though re-elected to Parliament in 1957, his services were needed in Madras, where K Kamaraj wanted him to be his industries minister. The yeoman services he then rendered are all too well known. Others have written eloquently about his role in industrialising Tamil Nadu and setting an example for other states to follow. I need not add to it except to recount a glimpse of it that I had. Travelling by train through Tamil Nadu one night half a century ago, I was struck by at least one electric light burning in almost every village we hurtled by. A South Indian travelling companion, seeing my expression that bespoke of surprise, said that people have to be grateful to Venkataraman for this. Electrification is essential for industrialisation, he added.

Around that time, this country was engaged in delicate negotiations with France for converting the de facto transfer of French possessions some years earlier into a de jure one. Kewal Singh, who later became foreign secretary, was deeply involved in these talks as consul-general in Pondicherry. Nehru told him to keep the Tamil Nadu chief minister fully informed of what was going on. 'But, sir, how do I talk to Kamaraj who speaks neither English nor Hindi?' asked Singh. Nehru replied that he need not go to Kamaraj. 'Keep R Venkataraman informed and the rest would be taken care of.' There could be no better clue to the close comradeship and mutual confidence between RV and his leader, Kamaraj. Gopal Gandhi aptly calls it a 'politico-administrative duumvirate'.

Beginning with the bleak border war with China in the high Himalayas in 1962, India was in turmoil for several years. Nehru died in 1964, his successor, Lal Bahadur Shastri, barely eighteen months later at Tashkent, a few hours after signing, with President Ayub Khan of Pakistan, an agreement to end the 1965 war between the two countries. Indira Gandhi's rise to the office of prime minister after defeating Morarji Desai in a contest brought about a virtual division within the party ranks that eventually ended in the Congress split in 1969, the year of the Mahatma's centenary.

In January 1966, Kamaraj, as Congress president, had backed Indira Gandhi's ascent to the hilt and persuaded other Congress leaders, collectively nicknamed the 'Syndicate', to do so. But then, as usually happens between the king and the kingmaker, the Congress president and the prime minister started drifting apart. This process was accelerated hugely by the devaluation of the rupee on 6 June 1966. Before announcing the government's decision, Indira Gandhi needed to consult Kamaraj. While inviting him to the prime minister's house, she took care to mention to him that the subject to be discussed was super-secret. So Kamaraj asked RV to accompany him, dispensing with his usual practice of taking with him as his interpreter a trusted journalist, R Rangarajan.

As is widely known, Kamaraj hit the ceiling the moment he was told that the rupee had to be devalued. What is not known is that taken aback by Kamaraj's vehement reaction, Indira Gandhi looked at RV and inquired what he thought. His instant reply was: 'It would be a disaster.' Let me add that RV vouchsafed this to me only in 2005, when I went to him at 5 Safdarjung Road in the course of my research for my second biography of Indira Gandhi.

In 1967, when the Congress was routed in Tamil Nadu (it looked as if for good) RV, like most other party candidates, was defeated in his constituency. But he was immediately persuaded to serve on the Planning Commission. When he returned to Parliament in 1977, the Congress had been bundled out of power primarily because of the Emergency. There was much despondency among Congressmen, but RV was composed and unperturbed. To talk to him was, as usual, a delight. In 1978, there were elections to the assemblies of some states. The Congress (I) and the Congress (O) were intensely hostile to each other. Yet, expediency demanded that in Maharashtra they form a coalition under the leadership of Vasantdada Patil, Congress (O) leader in the state. The Janata then ruling in Delhi and in several states lost little time in toppling the coalition ministry by winning over Sharad Pawar. In Congress (I) confabulations, RV told his colleagues not to waste their energy on saving the Maharashtra ministry because 'most of our MLAs are going with power and Pawar'.

Indira Gandhi returned to power spectacularly in January 1980. RV, who won his Lok Sabha seat, was her most senior colleague. Before being elevated to the post of vice-president in 1982, he held the crucial portfolios of finance and defence. In both he shone though his achievements as defence minister were arguably of critical importance. It was in his time that the Integrated Missile Development Programme was launched. Again, it was he who saw to it that the Indian Army got to the Siachen glacier ahead of the Pakistanis, who had been there the previous summer. Since Indira Gandhi had taken him into full confidence about the Indian nuclear programme, he played an important part in it, too, as also in strengthening the defence cooperation with the Soviet Union. And, next only to the prime minister, he bore the heaviest burden of Operation Blue Star at Amritsar.

On 31 October 1984, RV headed the array of dignitaries at the All India Institute of Medical Sciences (AIIMS) that mourned Indira Gandhi and planned what to do next. President Giani Zail Singh was away in Yemen. The consensus among the leaders at AIIMS was that Rajiv Gandhi should succeed his slain mother. RV had presided over the discussions. The decision to swear in Rajiv as prime minister was Giani's, however. What an irony it is, therefore, that the relations between the president and the new prime minister should have degenerated to such a low point that despite his four-fifths majority in the Lok Sabha Rajiv was rattled by reports that the president might dismiss him because of the storm over Bofors. No wonder, the prime minister heaved a sigh of relief when RV moved to Rashtrapati Bhavan in 1987.

Unlike his predecessor, Former President Venkataraman acted as, to use his own famous words, 'a copybook president'. Under the Indian Constitution, he used to say the president was like an 'emergency light' which came into play only when necessary. What he did not say was that he also did his duty to 'caution, warn and advise' his government, as Walter Bagehot had described it. For instance, during the 1989 general election that Rajiv Gandhi predictably lost, there was much agitation in the country, spearheaded by opposition parties, that the president must call upon their loose combination to form the next government if its numbers exceeded that of the Congress. RV firmly refused. He gave the first chance to Rajiv Gandhi, the leader of the largest single party in the new House, and only when the latter refused did he invite VP Singh to form the government and happily swore him in.

As it happened, VP Singh's rickety coalition fell in eleven months flat. His arch rival within the Janata Dal, Chandra Shekhar, in the best tradition of Indian politics, sought to become – and indeed did become – prime minister, with the support of the same Congress party he had vigorously opposed earlier. It is no secret that RV obtained from Rajiv Gandhi a promise that the Congress-supported Chandra Shekhar government would be allowed to last 'at least a year'. Unfortunately, this did not happen. Out went Chandra Shekhar in just 120 days.

K Subrahmanyam, the eminent strategic and security analyst, has already disclosed that at the time of the changeover from Rajiv Gandhi to VP Singh, a very serious and embarrassing problem arose. In 1988, when Rajiv authorised the weaponisation of the Indian nuclear programme, he decided to keep Singh, then defence minister, out of the loop. So, when Singh became prime minister, VS Arunachalam, then head of the Defence Research and Development Organisation (DRDO) and the man in charge of the project, was at his wits' end. On Subrahmanyam's suggestion, he went to RV, who solved the problem in his usual smooth manner. There are several other such instances.

In May 1992, a few months before retiring, RV paid an official visit to China. Very kindly he invited me, along with Nikhil Chakravarty, N Ram, KK Katyal, HK Dua, Saeed Naqvi and some other colleagues to go with him. To be a member of his party was a delight. The occasional briefings he gave us about his talks with his counterpart, Yang Shangkun, and other Chinese leaders were acmes of precision and clarity. What struck me even more was that he climbed the Great Wall of China more briskly than men half his age. At the cave of terracotta soldiers at Xian, onlookers were impressed by his dexterity with the camera.

For nearly a decade and a half after retiring he remained fit and active as always. Even after he became frail in his last years, his mind remained razor sharp and his memory prodigious, as I found during some meetings with him during this period. It is doubtful if we will see the likes of him in the years to come.

The Gentleman Politician

K Natwar Singh

The author remembers R Venkataraman's tenure both as the vice president and president of India against the backdrop of volatile political relations. He salutes RV for his unmatchable sagacity and wisdom.

The eighth president of the Republic of India did not worship unworthy causes. He did nothing unseemly or sordid. An untarnished man, he served his country well and for long. Venkataraman was a man of probity and virtue. In a polluted political environment, he strengthened and ensured the enhancement of civility. A man of sound judgement, steady nerve and commitment, he was uncomfortable with needless exuberance. A religious South Indian Brahmin, he was a judicious secularist. He did not allow his religion to stand in the way of his official duties.

He was, after S Radhakrishnan, the most effective vice-chairman of the Rajya Sabha. His authority was seldom, if ever, flouted.

I was elected to the Lok Sabha on 31 December 1984. Venkataraman was then vice-president. Once or twice he helped me when, as a novice, I got into a jam. In some ways he was of the Rajaji tradition, though not as austere or as learned. South Indian Brahmin politicians, in my opinion, score over their northern India colleagues. I have in mind the sensible, the sensitive and the sober, not those who, in the House, use their muscles, not their minds.

R Venkataraman worked with four prime ministers. Some lasted a few months, others longer. He dealt with them wisely, offered advice which reduced their burdens, and cleared their doubts. After the entirely unexpected assassination of Rajiv Gandhi, a very heavy and tragic fate befell him. But he handled it with calm self-assurance and was a source of strength to Sonia Gandhi and her family.

Having held the important finance and defence portfolios, Venkataraman was well-versed with the working of the central government. The obvious power centres are the prime minister and the president. It is, therefore, imperative that the two work in tandem. Nehru's relations with Rajendra Prasad were unevenly correct. They differed on the Hindu Code Bill, differed on the Somnath temple. Nehru was, on occasion, publicly impatient with the president. I remember one instance. The prime minister was leaving for Iran. Most ministers and diplomats had come to the airport to see him. I, too, had escorted the Dalai Lama. The president had, out of politeness, decided to see the prime minister off. Nehru was getting restless, walking up and down, swagger stick in hand. He kept badgering Tandon, the chief of protocol, who told him that the president had left the Rashtrapati Bhavan. After a few more minutes, the prime minister again enquired about him and Tandon said, 'Sir, he is half way'.

'Is he walking?' asked the momentarily petulant prime minister.

Nehru's relations with S Radhakrishnan were more than close. Both intellectuals and authors, they spoke the same language. However, Indira Gandhi fell out with Radhakrishnan. I was then working for her. She did not give him a second term. When Venkataramanji became the vice-president, Giani Zail Singh's relations took a nosedive. R Venkataraman's decisive, wise role as mediator saved an extremely serious and ugly constitutional crisis. Only a man of his sagacity and temperament could have succeeded in doing so.

In his presidential memoirs, I get more than one mention. The president, being a Tamilian and a friend of Tamil Nadu Chief Minister MG Ramachandran, took keen interest in relations between India and Sri Lanka, especially following the 29 July 1987 Indo–Sri Lanka Agreement. I, along with some of my experts, once met him to brief him regarding the difficulties in the establishment of an interim government in the northeast of Sri Lanka. As it happened, time proved us both wrong. The president did not accept our proposal, although with avuncular politeness.

I cannot claim intimacy with Venkataramanji. I did for almost two decades observe him from close quarters, read his speeches (mostly drafted by his scholarly secretary Gopalkrishna Gandhi). I, too, drafted one used half of a speech.

Like Radhakrishnan, he embodied what was best in our culture and civilisation. Our values pay homage to *vidya, tapa, dana, gyan, sheel, abhaya, dharma*. Our heritage respects *sahitya, kala* and *sangeet*. R Venkataraman concurred.

A True Statesman

K Parasaran

> *With his sharp intellect and deep understanding of all matters related to governance, R Venkataraman was much more than a politician.*

As R Venkataraman hailed from Tamil Nadu, we knew each other. I happened to be far younger in age than him. I came in contact with R Venkataraman on two brief occasions, when he was finance minister and defence minister.

Our contacts became closer and interactions more frequent when he became the president of India. My tenure as attorney general for India coincided with his presidency. He possessed a sound legal intellect with a deep knowledge of case law. This was complemented by his practical wisdom, sharpened through long experience. He used to call me frequently and extensively discuss matters with me. A remarkable aspect was his profound knowledge and appreciation of constitutional law. We freely discussed and debated on all aspects, despite his greater experience and years spent in practice of law. He was a typical example of *Vidya Vinayena Shobate* (Modesty adorns knowledge). As president, he would call me for discussions pertaining to important constitutional questions prior to taking a decision.

I also wish to recall a discussion that we had on the dissolution of Parliament. I drew his attention to a passage in the book *Theory and Practice of Dissolution of Parliament* authored by BS Markesinis, which impressed him so much that he asked for the book to be left with him for a thorough study.

The second half of his tenure presented him with challenges, and he used his experience and knowledge to create valuable constitutional precedents as to how the president has to go about the issue of dissolution of Parliament. He was particularly steadfast in maintaining true democracy. He set a convention of not rushing into dissolution when a party failed to command majority in the House and gave an opportunity to each party, in the order of its numerical strength, to form the government with the support of other party or parties. The credit for developing the convention of avoiding dissolution, if possible, should go to R Venkataraman, and it is his wisdom that led to political stability of governance through coalition government. He had foreseen that the country is bound to face formation of coalition governments.

It is said that 'The politician looks to the next election and the statesman looks to the next generation'. He was a true statesman, not a mere politician. He maintained high integrity with dedicated knowledge and his actions were actuated solely by consideration of national interest.

His wisdom invariably led to his taking fearless and correct decisions. On one occasion, when he was considering the Twenty-ninth Constitution (Amendment) Bill, he was under pressure form the media that counselled him to withhold his assent or return the Bill. He sent me a note on two points, as he was of the view that it was beyond the scope of authority of the president to go into the legal validity of a Bill duly adopted by Parliament and that if there was any infirmity, it was solely within the domain of the courts to pronounce upon it. I agreed with him. R Venkataraman made a fond reference to the said incident in his book *My Presidential Years*, when he wrote 'The Attorney General, K. Parasaran, whose erudition and integrity I greatly value, called on me and confirmed that on both these counts I was correct'.[22] It is a great solace for me to receive such words or compliments from his pen.

On occasions, we had divergence in our views. But the differences were resolved after discussion. On the occasion, the Supreme Court did not agree with the view of the president I am of the humble view that on this aspect, two views were possible. It related to the mercy petition filed before him by Kehar Singh. Venkataraman observed in his order that as the evidence had been appreciated by the Supreme Court, he should not re-appreciate the evidence. The Supreme Court did not agree with this view and held to the contrary. Unfortunately, the Supreme Court did not expressly dealt with the argument addressed by me, to the effect that in the UK, on facts it was a verdict of the jury, on appreciation of the evidence. Their verdict is binding on the judge. It is for this reason that in the United Kingdom, the home secretary re-appreciated the materials. However, in India, the judge decides the case both on facts and on law. This argument, though not dealt within the judgment, was rejected by the Supreme Court sub silentio and the Supreme Court held that the mercy petition invoking the power under Article 72 of the Constitution shall be deemed to be pending before the president and was to be dealt with and disposed of afresh by the president.

The president sent for me and told me that this was a rare occasion when we differed, and that my advice should have been followed. After remand, in his order, the president

---

[22]Venkataraman, R, *My Presidential Years*, HarperCollins, 1994 (p 146).

recorded no reasons and only held that on the appreciation of the entire material, it was not a case fit for exercise of his powers under the power of clemency. This order was upheld when it was challenged before the Supreme Court (of course, the president has to and did in fact act on the aid and advice of the council of ministers).

Even after I demitted the office of the attorney general for India, he used to call me and discuss legal issues, which continued even after he ceased to be the president.

He was a noble son of India who had great wisdom, sense of duty, high integrity and patriotism. He lived the Vedic age of almost a hundred years. He has left an indelible mark in the sands of history of the nation.

A Statesman and Manager

K Subrahmanyam

An astute manager, RV smoothly handled governmental affairs despite three prime ministers in two years.

As an IAS officer of the Tamil Nadu cadre, I had known Late R Venkataraman (popularly known as RV) personally since 1959, when I had joined the Tamil Nadu secretariat as deputy secretary (rural development). In the three years I served in Chennai, I had very little to do with him. I used to see him in the State Development Committee meetings. He was a highly respected minister, considered one of the pillars of the Kamaraj government, along with Kamaraj himself, C Subramaniam and M Bhaktavatsalam. I came into personal contact with him only when he became the defence minister in Indira Gandhi's cabinet in 1982, and I was the director of the Institute for Defence Studies and Analyses (IDSA). The institute was an autonomous body with PV Narasimha Rao as the president. The defence ministry was the funding body of the institute. Until the time RV took charge of the defence portfolio, the relationship between the ministry and the institute was strictly one of a fund-giver and recipient. He tried to change it. He knew about my work and reputation. He used to call me from time to time, just for a discussion on various defence issues and international politics. In the course of these discussions, we spoke about India exercising the nuclear option, acquisition of modern fighter aircraft, threat from Pakistan, Pakistan–US relationship, etc. He knew that Dr Ramanna, chairman of the Atomic Energy Commission, and Dr Arunachalam, his scientific adviser, were close personal friends of mine.

It was during his tenure as the defence minister that I was able to persuade the defence ministry to depute service officers to the institute. Since the institute was established in 1965, the chiefs of committee had placed it out of bounds for all service officers. RV broke that taboo and arranged to depute a brigadier from the army and a group captain from the air force for the first time to the institute. The brigadier, Amar Singh Kalkat, later became the commander of the Indian Peace Keeping Force in Sri Lanka, and an army commander, and the air force officer, Jasjit Singh, became my successor as the director of IDSA and led it with distinction for fourteen years. I owe a debt of gratitude to RV for his futuristic move.

RV had a reputation as a competent manager in all ministerial posts he handled. He had also been a member of the Planning Commission. It was no surprise to me when he asked me to explore the possibility of introducing institutionalised planning in the defence services. He wanted me to do it informally, without his issuing any direction. At that time, the defence planning was mostly a compilation of wishlists of equipment as determined by the chiefs. So I requested the defence secretary SM Ghosh, my batchmate in the IAS, to convene a meeting of the chiefs of staff to discuss the possibility. The chiefs were General AS Vaidya, Admiral OS Dawson and Air Chief Marshal Dilbagh Singh. I explained to them the imperative need for long-term defence planning to ensure the development of a defence production base and long-term R&D. But I failed to persuade them. Their stand was that they had to wait till an equipment got developed somewhere in the world, after which they could assess its performance in comparison with others in the same category elsewhere and make a choice. They did not accept that long-term technological forecasts could help us anticipate the performance parameters of an equipment in advance and attempt its development. After a couple of sessions, I had to report my failure to RV. He was not surprised.

The only time we had a difference of views was on an article that came out in the IDSA publication, critical of the annual confidential roll and promotion procedure in the army. The author of the article was a brigadier who had recently retired from the army and had joined the institute. I got a letter from the defence secretary saying that he had been directed to inform me that such articles should be cleared by the army headquarters before publication. Even during the Emergency, during the three months I was the director, I never submitted any article for vetting before publication, but cleared them on my own responsibility. I was also aware that RV himself, as the editor of *Swarajya*, went to court at the beginning of the Emergency against the pre-censorship. So I went to him and asked why such articles should not be published. He told me that the army was very upset that an officer, so soon after retirement, was so critical of the system and he could appreciate their sensitivity on the issue. I said I had been far more critical of the system, and did they expect that I should clear my articles with them? He said that my case was different. I was senior enough and had been in the field long enough to be treated with respect and taken seriously as a critic, but that did not apply to service officers who had just left the service. I said that if that was his decision, there would be no articles on such subjects in the IDSA publications, but I would never agree to submit any article for vetting before its publication. He said that that was up to me. We left it at that.

After his promotion to vice-president and thereafter, his becoming president, I met him twice or thrice at Rashtrapati Bhavan dinners. However, there was one episode which served to highlight his role as president, as the 'emergency light' (that was his own characterisation), in which I was marginally involved. In 1969, when Rajiv Gandhi demitted the office of the prime minister and VP Singh took office, India, under the decision taken by Rajiv Gandhi, assembled its first nuclear weapon. It would have been appropriate for Rajiv Gandhi to inform the incoming prime minister of the status of the Indian nuclear programme. There was such lack of trust between the outgoing and incoming prime ministers that Rajiv had reservations in getting VP Singh briefed on the same. This placed Dr Arunachalam, then scientific adviser to the defence minister and the coordinator of the progamme, in an awkward situation. He sought my advice and I suggested using RV, the president at the time, as the communicator. Rajiv agreed to have RV briefed in his presence. In turn, RV briefed VP Singh.

My last meeting with RV was as chairman of the Kargil Review Panel. He promptly agreed to meet the panel. We discussed with him the relations with Pakistan and the nuclear issue during his time as the defence minister. On both issues, he was fully forthcoming and his memory at his age – eighty-nine at that time – was very good. He told us about his visit to Pokhran in 1983 and his going down the shafts. He also told us about the race to Siachen Glacier in spring 1984, and how we got there ahead of Pakistan just in time. When we sent him the record of discussion, he signed and returned it. That valuable record lies buried in the seventeen volumes of annexures the government has not released as part of the Kargil Committee Report.

It was fortunate that the country had RV as the president, following the turbulent presidential years of Zail Singh. RV was a copybook president who was able to handle smoothly and sagaciously transitions through three successive prime ministers in two years. There have hardly been any statesmen or managers of his maturity and competence in the last fifty years.

The Harbinger of Industrial Growth in Tamil Nadu

KS Narayanan

R Venkataraman gave a major boost to the Tamil Nadu industry, with innovative reforms and policies.

I consider it a special privilege to recall my thoughts on R Venkataraman, whom I believe to be a legend of our times. R Venkataraman was a fascinating personality. His was not the mere story of an ordinary person from Rajamadam, an obscure village in Thanjavur district, to becoming the First Citizen of India and occupying the presidential chair, the highest office in the land. His rise to this position involved sacrifices and an unrivalled record of service in public life.

His academic background as a postgraduate in economics with a degree in law, his role in the struggle for freedom besides experience in the Bar, stood him in good stead in his distinguished political career, spanning over six decades.

It is not doing justice to simply describe R Venkataraman, fondly RV to many, as a politician. He was a thinker, a nationalist, a parliamentarian, a statesman and a world citizen. He was a Congressman throughout his life, but he had his own views on the policies of the party and voiced them openly, as he always believed in healthy debate. Even on government policies he encouraged public debate and dialogue, so that the government could accept legitimate criticism and change its stand wherever required, for the public good. He believed that the government was not the repository of all wisdom, and right suggestions from any quarter were welcome and acceptable in the overall interests of the country. There could not have been a greater democrat than RV in accepting debate and dissent.

Madras (now Chennai) boasted of several intellectuals, second to none as patriots who believed in national development and shared their concerns in public on the working of our young democracy, English as the national language, policies relating to agriculture, industry, taxation and economic policies, and several other serious challenges daunting the nation, including national security, defence and foreign affairs. This group included elder statesman CR, eminent educationalists, economists, leaders of the Bar, members of industry and trade. Whenever opportunities arose, RV consulted them informally for their views. He encouraged them to have a strong public platform to voice their views, to help the government in mending their policies. He was also an active participant. He believed in the vibrant voice of the citizens for democracy to succeed.

The thing that was cherished most in the state of Tamil Nadu, then Madras state, in the decade of 1957–67, was the extremely supportive industrial climate provided by RV the visionary, as industries minister, fully supported by K Kamaraj, a man of the masses, known for his common sense and pragmatism. RV, with his perceptivity and initiative, propelled industrial progress and economic development by enlisting the support of the private sector. It was a true partnership between the government and the private sector, which worked jointly to overcome obstacles in the path of industrial development. He was always scouting for entrepreneurial talent in the state and encouraging them to set up industries, offering suggestions on the opportunities beckoning them. During his frequent travels abroad, as a delegate to the UN General Assembly, as a member of the UN Administrative Tribunal and later as its president, he was also constantly looking at prospects of industrial and financial collaborations from abroad to partner enterprises in the State of Madras. This decade saw the promotion of a number of major industries in the state and covered a wide spectrum.

During his tenure as a minister in the State of Madras, and in the union government, there was bitter criticism on the licensing and taxation policies of the government. There was strong resentment from the opposition parties, trade and industry that the licensing policies of the government had resulted in severe shortages and were impediments to industrial progress. RV also shared this perception and used every opportunity to highlight the shortcomings of this policy in the party forum, even at the cost of some embarrassment that he was friendly to industry. It can be rightfully claimed that a reform policy was heralded by RV when he introduced dual pricing of cement in 1980, during his tenure as the union minister of finance, by liberating the age-old price control on cement.

It was during RV's tenure as industries minister in the state that most of the major industries – cement, chemical and petrochemical, fertiliser, aluminium, sugar, engineering, electrical, automobile, tyre, and shipping, besides traditional ones like textiles and leather industries, were established. Not content with the laying of foundation stones, he made sure that the industry was nurtured, constantly watching their progress and stepping in whenever government intervention was necessary. He was always looked upon as a friend, philosopher and guide to the industry. It was a 'golden era' in the industrial development of Madras state. Later governments acknowledged this achievement openly and emulated him. During this period, Madras state had done exceedingly well in all spheres of national activity. In fact, it led the rest of India in all important fields like education, electrification, industrial development and social development activities.

The state had its due share in the massive investments of central government undertakings during this period, largely due to the efforts of RV. Neyveli Lignite Corporation (Thermal Power and Fertilizer Units), Trichy Heavy Boilers, Surgical Instruments, Hindustan Teleprinters, Heavy Vehicles, Hindustan Photo Films, Madras Refineries (now Chennai Petroleum), Madras Fertilizers, and Salem Steel Plant were established during the 1960s.

I have to make a mention of RV's abiding interest in industry and its growth. India Cements, of which I was managing director, had its first plant in Sankarnagar in Tirunelveli district, and it was RV who encouraged us to set up the second plant in Sankaridurg in Salem and expand Sankarnagar plant, in the 1960s. He also laid the foundation and later inaugurated the Sankaridurg plant by lightning the kiln in 1965. India Cements was then producing about five lakh tonnes of cement per annum. He was constantly reminding us that we would become millionaires.

RV was also the spirit behind the setting up of a PVC plant by Chemplast in the 1960s. The sugar industry was on a fast growth track and with it was the problem of disposal of large quantities of molasses, a by-product of sugar manufacture and a pollutant, presenting a serious problem of disposal, unless put to proper use by converting it to alcohol. The state was then under Prohibition and there was no outlet for alcohol. RV learnt that the PVC plant was based on industrial alcohol. It was a different story when Prohibition was lifted in the early 1970s. Chemplast underwent difficult times, and RV was again there to help Chemplast tide over the feedstock problem.

As major enterprises were coming up in the state, he envisioned the need for setting up small and medium industries to meet their requirements of parts and ancillaries. RV was the author of the concept of industrial clusters. The two major industrial estates in Madras – Guindy Industrial Estate and Ambattur Industrial Estate – stand as testimony to his farsightedness. Industrial estates have also been established in twelve other places in the districts. He strongly felt that small and medium industries should coexist with major industries supplementing each other. This concept has found acceptance by all the governments that followed and spread to districts in the state. RV was always considered the benefactor of small and medium industries, which came up in a spectacular manner during his tenure as industries minister. The RV Tower in Guindy Industrial Estate bears testimony to his services to the SME sectors.

TS Narayanaswami, my colleague in India Cements, was the president of Hindustan Chamber of Commerce, Madras, during 1966–67. By coincidence, 2011 is also his birth centenary. RV was invited to address the annual meeting of the chamber in September 1966, and he had chosen to dwell upon the proposed fourth Five Year Plan outlay, estimated at ₹23,750 crore, which was made public by the Planning Commission. He referred to the all-round criticism that the third Five Year Plan had failed to yield the desired results and the massive deficit financing had accentuated inflationary pressures. He also drew attention to the unexpected Chinese aggression in 1962–63, the outbreak of the conflict with Pakistan in August–September 1965, which had upset all calculations, resulting in the diversion of resources for defence, and so on. However optimistic he was, he said, the country could not afford an outlay of nearly ₹24,000 crore, and he presented a strong case for downsizing the outlay to ₹18,000 crore, emphasising that a larger outlay might unleash further inflation. It was a stimulating talk, which received nationwide attention and editorial comments on his thoughtful, logical and passionate arguments.

RV was intensely associated with the Indian Education Society (now Indian Education Trust) which is managing two schools in south Chennai – Sri Sankara Senior Secondary School in Adyar and Sri Sankara Vidyasramam Matriculation School in Thiruvanmiyur. As the president of the Indian Education Society, RV nurtured the schools from their inception. He laid emphasis on character formation with our vibrant cultural identity. According to him, mere learning was not enough. He was also a benevolent donor to the society. He had supported the schools through thick and thin and helped the society overcome initial difficulties. In one of the meetings of the society, I had handed over a cheque to him as donation to the society for building a block. He formally received the cheque, but in a few moments he turned and handed over the cheque to me, announcing that henceforth I would be the president of the society and that I should receive this donation in the fitness of things. He greeted me and wished further growth for the educational institutions during my tenure. He then confided in me that he was joining the union cabinet and therefore relinquishing the presidentship of the society. Be it as union minister of finance or defence, or as the vice-president of India, or as the president of India, he ensured that his interest in the schools did not diminish a bit. He continued to visit the schools even while holding all these high offices, providing continuous guidance and encouragement. These schools owe a debt of gratitude to him.

K Kamaraj had a great influence on RV. Due to his immense faith and confidence, RV was entrusted with several important portfolios in the cabinet – industries, labour, cooperation, power, transport and commercial taxes. He was also the leader of the Upper House of the Madras Legislative Council. Even with tough and informed opposition leaders like AL Mudaliar,

RV had an easy way of presenting convincing facts. Focussed and constructive, he ably conducted the affairs of the Upper House. Kamaraj groomed RV for greater responsibilities, and RV always rose to his expectations. Kamaraj was his mentor and followed him faithfully until his end. Several like-minded admirers of Kamaraj felt that his statue should be installed in the national capital, as he played a crucial role in national politics at critical times. Some of us met RV and sought his blessings for this proposal. He spontaneously supported the move and a small committee was constituted with me, TT Vasu, Manju Bhashini and KT Kosalram. RV guided us at every stage, providing support of the government in locating a prime site for installing the statue. It was a proud moment for all of us, particularly RV, when the majestic life-size statue of Kamaraj was unveiled by the prime minister of India, Rajiv Gandhi, RV, as vice-president of India, presiding.

RV always felt at home whenever he visited Chennai, and his visits were not complete without his meeting the local industrialists in some context or the other. It was equally true that industrialists from Tamil Nadu ran to him for his guidance and advice at every provocation. He had a filial interest in the growth of industries in Tamil Nadu and during his brief visits to Chennai, he would update himself on the growth plans of individual industries, in the process ascertaining the details of the problems faced by them. This was not a casual exercise. Thereupon, as a follow-up, he silently persuaded the powers that be to provide necessary redressal, in his own inimitable style. People like me had some comfort when we talked to him about our problems, be it raw material, labour, tariff or any other. He was a father figure to the industry.

I must recall a particular occasion. This was in 1986, and RV was then vice-president of India. K Rajaram was the minister of industry in the Government of Tamil Nadu. During one of my meetings, RV expressed a desire to spend a few hours with the members of industry and trade during one of his visits to Chennai. Accordingly, a get-together was organised at Park Sheraton and he moved around with everybody informally, recalling old anecdotes. In his address, he said that, it was a homecoming for him, seeing so many known faces. He reminisced about the all-round development of Tamil Nadu and reminded the captains of industry to grab the ever-unfolding opportunities for growth to make India strong.

Another instance comes to mind. He showed great concern when he heard about the stranded Indian passengers in Kuwait during the first week of August 1990, due to sudden Iraqi invasion under Saddam Hussain's rule. The British Airways Boeing from London to Madras via Kuwait landed in Kuwait at 4.00 a.m. on 1 August, least realising that the airport was under siege. Passengers were told to run out of the plane into the terminal building. Madras-bound passengers included Mr & Mrs V Narayanan of Goodyear, Ramaswamy of TAFE and others. RV came to know that besides the stranded passengers, many Indians living in Kuwait were undergoing a horrendous time and hoping that the Indian government would provide immediate arrangements to evacuate them. As a sequel to this, the then foreign minister, IK Gujral, visited Kuwait, met the stranded passengers and brought back some of the women passengers and children, besides some two hundred more Indians from Kuwait in the first instance.

Uttara Swami Malai Temple, popularly known as Malai Mandir in Delhi, is a symbol of three (Chola, Pandya and Pallava) ancient and renowned styles of South Indian temple architecture and sculpture. RV totally identified with this temple construction from its inception and showed abiding interest at all stages of its development. He was the president of Sri Swaminatha Swami Seva Samaj when I was also associated with the *samaj* as a trustee for many years. RV later became its patron-in-chief. He will be remembered for generations for this spiritual service.

RV was one of the ablest administrators the country has ever seen. His success was due to his belief in delegation and trust in his officers. He allowed the bureaucrats who worked with him a free hand and they came up with excellent ideas and notings on files. He allowed them to take decisions on urgent issues in his absence from headquarters to avoid delays, and ratified their actions. Officers who worked with him had no fear or tension, and their working relationship was warm and cordial. One of his greatest virtues was his time management and punctuality, a lesson our modern-day politicians should learn.

I have many more happy encounters to narrate and my business contemporaries may have more to share. No one will disagree with me when I say that RV was known for his endearing personal qualities. He was simple and unassuming. Whatsoever high posts he held, he was easily accessible. A rare trait among politicians.

His smiling visage conjures up before my eyes whenever I ruminate on this personage who strode the world like a colossus.

Satyamurti – A Forgotten Patriot

KV Ramanathan

KV Ramanathan remembers a patriot R Venkataraman looked up to as the pioneer of parliamentary activities in the country.

Two outstanding leaders of the Indian National Congress in the Tamil-speaking part of the British Indian province of Madras from the twenties of the last century were Rajaji (C Rajagopalachari, to give him his full name) and S Satyamurti. Comrades in arms, and friends, they were very different from each other in their views of the manner in which the freedom struggle was to be waged. Till 1937, in any case, Rajaji was a total follower of satyagraha with a disinclination to take part in legislative and parliamentary activities, while Satyamurti, though a devoted acolyte of Gandhiji, was all for utilising the opportunities offered by the institutions established by the British to mount an attack on them. That these roles were reversed in 1942 was indeed the ultimate irony.

Satyamurti was born in 1887 into a poor family in the minuscule princely state of Pudukkottai in Tamil Nadu. When he lost his father at a young age, the responsibility of looking after the large family fell upon him. With great difficulty, he put himself through school and college, acquired a law degree and set up practice as an advocate in Madras. His heart, however, was then and always in public service and the struggle for the country's freedom. He joined the Congress party and was a volunteer in its Madras session in 1908. An eloquent speaker and fine writer, he wrote in the press on a wide variety of subjects. He came into notice in 1918 at a political conference in Kanchipuram, when he opposed most eloquently a resolution moved by the legendary Annie Besant calling upon Indian youth to join the British forces to help in the First World War. He was equally eloquent in his denunciation of the Rowlatt Act, and in 1919 he went to England as secretary of the Congress delegation to place the party's point of view before the Joint Parliamentary Committee that was then considering the Bill that later became the Government of India Act of 1919 (the Montagu–Chelmsford reforms). During the six months that he toured England and Ireland, he addressed a number of meetings on the nationalist cause and made many friends in British political life.

When, following the Rowlatt Act and the Jallianwallah Bagh massacre, Mahatma Gandhi, who had effectively assumed the leadership of the Congress party after the death of Tilak, launched his Non-Cooperation Movement (*satyagraha*), Satyamurti, by now fully devoted to Gandhiji, was in a fix. He was in favour of entering the legislative bodies constituted under the 1919 reforms and was against many elements of the *satyagraha* movement, particularly the call to professionals to give up their activities and to students of educational institutions to come out of them. He argued vigorously, though most respectfully, with the Mahatma on these issues, stressing his duties to his family and his unwillingness to give up his membership of the senate of the Madras University. Ultimately, he refrained from joining the movement and going to jail. Gandhiji suspended the movement in 1922 after the Chauri-Chaura storming of a police station and massacre of policemen, but was nevertheless arrested and imprisoned. While he was in jail, there was a vigorous debate in the party about the need for a change in policy. Matters came to a head in the Gaya Congress session of December 1922. President CR Das, Motilal Nehru, Vithalbhai Patel and Satyamurti led the campaign for change (to give up *satyagraha* and capture the councils and legislatures) – the pro-changers as they were called – but any change was opposed by Rajaji, Vallabhbhai Patel, Rajendra Prasad and others – the no-changers as they were known. The latter won the day and, while deciding to end civil disobedience, the party voted for a boycott of the legislatures established by the Act of 1919 and local bodies.

The pro-changers formed what they called the Swarajist party within the Congress, under the leadership of CR Das and Motilal Nehru early in 1923. Their constant agitation for fighting on the legislative front resulted in the mother party permitting those in favour of council entry to contest elections as the Swaraj party. The party contested the elections to the Central Legislative Assembly and the Provincial Councils in November 1923. Satyamurti entered the Madras Legislative Council (as it was then known) and began a brilliant career as a parliamentarian. In the six years he was in the council, he used his eloquence and expertise in parliamentary concepts and procedures to shake the diarchy to its foundations and to advocate the nationalist cause ceaselessly. He also entered the Madras Corporation and took great interest in civic affairs and problems.

In 1925, he went to England as representative of the Swaraj party of the Congress to plead the India cause, and again made a number of friends. The price he had to pay for all these activities was getting characterised as a power seeker who hobnobbed with the British, an impression sought to be created by some Congress members. In the Madras Legislative Council, there was no important discussion in which he did not participate with vigour, and no question where he did not torment officialdom with supplements. His speech on the ban on the songs of the poet Subhramania Bharathi was a fiery masterpiece. He was prominent in getting the Annamalai University Bill passed.

Meanwhile, the attitude of Gandhi and the Congress was hardening, and when the British government sent a commission to India under Sir John Simon in 1928, the party organised boycotts everywhere. This was followed by a demand for immediate grant of Dominion Status, failing which the party would fight for total freedom. When there was no response, the party decided, in its annual session of 1928, to give the British government a year to respond. When the required response was not forthcoming, the party decided to boycott the legislatures and gird up for action for Poorna Swaraj. This put an end to Satyamurti's career in the Madras Legislative Council, as the party did not contest in the 1929 election.

When Gandhiji started the salt *satyagraha*, Satyamurti held back at first, in the hope that the new Labour government of Ramsay Macdonald would be positive in its attitude, but was disillusioned and went to prison, following Rajaji. All this time, Satyamurti was in correspondence with the British viceroy and British ministers of the Labour party, pleading the Indian cause but to no avail.

When the Gandhi–Irwin pact of 1931 ended the *satyagraha* and Gandhi agreed to attend the Second Round Table Conference in London, Satyamurti was prompt with his suggestion to the Mahatma on the issues to be raised. The conference failed, and the new viceroy, Lord Willingdon, launched on a policy of repression, arresting Gandhi on his return from London. Satyamurti was by now a full-fledged *satyagrahi* and went to jail. Never in robust health, being highly diabetic with low blood pressure and piles, he was hospitalised and, after release, had to be operated on for appendicitis.

The Civil Disobedience Movement slowly slackened and was terminated. The voices of those like Satyamurti, who advocated capturing the legislative bodies, were becoming more persuasive. The Congress formed a Parliamentary Board and the party contested the elections to the Central Legislative Assembly in 1934. Satyamurti was elected with a thumping majority from Madras city, defeating his classmate, friend and future political foe, Sir A Ramasamy Mudaliar. The story goes that, when the two met in the streets of Madras while campaigning, Satyamurti went up to him and shook his hand. When his followers took him to task, he told them laughingly that he was actually feeling his opponent's pulse. Satyamurti continued in the Central Legislative Assembly till his death in 1943. He served first as secretary of the Parliamentary Party, with Bhulabhai Desai as president and Govind Ballabh Pant as deputy leader, and later succeeded Pant.

The Government of India Act of 1935, passed after consideration of the Simon Commission recommendations, provided for full autonomy in the provinces, with cabinets consisting of elected members, doing away with the earlier system of diarchy where power was divided between nominated executive councillors and elected cabinet ministers. It provided for a federation at the centre, which never took off because the princes, who had to be brought in, did not agree. Satyamurti argued vigorously for contesting the provincial elections and capturing power. Meanwhile, Rajaji had resigned his presidentship of the Tamil Nadu Congress Committee in 1935 and had inducted Satyamurti into that position. Satyamurti got elected in his own right in 1936. In this capacity, he had to deal with local problems such as infighting in the local party, including an outright revolt when a senior leader, TSS Rajan, set up a candidate to oppose the official nominee for the chairmanship of the Tiruchirapalli (then Trichinopoly) Municipal Council, who defeated the official nominee as well. All this, in addition to his work as secretary of the Central Congress Legislature party, corporation councillor and member of the Madras University Senate.

The Congress decided to contest the elections for the provincial assemblies under the new Act and on Satyamurti fell the responsibility of preparing for the battle. The Congress left the question of acceptance of office open. Satyamurti set about capturing the local bodies first and then mounting a campaign for the assembly elections. The electorate, while not based on adult franchise, had still been widened and the preparation of the electoral rolls had to be supervised. Rajaji, following the Rajan affair, had resigned from all Congress organisations. Meanwhile, Satyamurti had been defeated in the election to the presidentship of the Tamil Nadu Congress Committee. However, he continued to head the Parliamentary Board and exercised full responsibility for the campaign, as well as organised visits by Jawaharlal Nehru and Vallabhbhai Patel.

Satyamurti launched a vigorous election campaign, travelling up and down the province without regard to his health. He was asked by the high command early in January 1937 to file his nomination for election from the graduates' constituency and did so. But on 16 January came an announcement from Vallabhbhai Patel that Satyamurti had succeeded in persuading a hitherto reluctant Rajaji to take his place, and had withdrawn his own nomination. This created a tremendous sensation in every part of the province. The truth was that the high command sent a message to him through K Srinivasan, editor of *The Hindu*, asking him to withdraw and propose Rajaji's name instead. The disingenuous fiction that Satyamurti had voluntarily withdrawn was kept up by everybody, Gandhiji included. Sardar Patel had apparently concluded on the basis of his visit that Andhra

Congressmen would not take kindly to Satyamurti as a leader, not to speak of the possible hostility of the anti-Brahmin elements to the orthodox Satyamurti. It is a wonder that this did not occur to him when he asked Satyamurti to file his nomination. The latter took this in his stride and worked himself to the bone for an electoral victory. He achieved it too, the Congress securing 159 seats out of a total of 215. Rajaji gracefully acknowledged that the victory was really Satyamurti's. The effort sent Satyamurti to a nursing home for some time, but he continued to attend to all his party and legislative duties.

The Congress was initially unwilling to accept office because of the special powers given to governors to overrule their cabinet. Satyamurti argued vigorously for office acceptance and wrote to the viceroy to relent on this question. Ultimately, a statement from the viceroy, that the governor would avoid any clash that would lead to a breakdown of government, mollified them, and the Congress formed ministries in the provinces where it had secured a majority. Rajaji had been elected leader of the Congress party in March 1937, and he formed the government in Madras in July. There had been hopes that Satyamurti would be included in the cabinet, but that did not happen. All this had long-term effects. K Kamaraj, a long-term acolyte of Satyamurti, could not forgive Rajaji for what had happened, and much of the later coolness between the two began then. Satyamurti concluded, perhaps rightly, that Rajaji felt that the cabinet was not big enough for both of them.

Satyamurti now turned his full attention to the central legislature. He became the deputy leader of the Congress party in place of Govind Ballabh Pant, who had moved to the United Provinces as premier after the 1937 elections and had proceeded to dominate the legislature through his eloquence and mastery of parliamentary practices and procedures. He was a master of repartee and supplementary questions, and came to be known as

'Supple-Murti'. Five consecutive budgets of Sir James Grigg, the then finance member of the executive council, were defeated and could be brought into effect only by certification by the viceroy, a procedure that Satyamurti castigated. In division after division, the government was bested, but Satyamurti and his party did not withhold cooperation on progressive legislation like the Insurance Bill. The bitterness of debate did not affect personal relations and the treasury benches were his admirers and friends. One of the British members of the viceroy's council, in a letter to him when he was absent from the House while ill in Madras, said, 'Come back soon. The House is not the same without you. We are missing you'.

The Second World War started in September 1939 and India was declared to be on the Allied side. The Congress felt that the Central Legislative Assembly should have been consulted and there should have been an assurance about freedom for India. It asked its ministers in power in the seven provinces to resign. It also asked its members in the central assembly not to participate in the proceedings, except to the extent to avoid disqualification, and not to participate in government functions. Satyamurti protested against this blanket ban, but to no avail. This effectively ended his activities in the central assembly.

In 1939, Satyamurti, a long time councillor and alderman of the Madras Corporation, was elected mayor for one year under the then system of communal rota, by which it was then the turn of a Brahmin. He grasped this opportunity to perform in a public office requiring administrative skills. His most notable achievement, for which he will always be remembered with gratitude by the people of Madras, was to start the Poondi Reservoir scheme to augment the supply of drinking water to Madras city. The foundation stone was laid in August 1940 by the governor and an effort was mounted, principally by the Andhra Congressmen of Madras led by T Prakasam, to get the High Command to prevent Satyamurti's participation. When Maulana Azad, then Congress president, agreed with this view, Satyamurti argued vigorously that, as the mayor and the father of the scheme, he could not keep away from a corporation function. He did attend, but received a mild rap on the knuckles. Satyamurti maintained his interest in the scheme through 1941 and 1942, with letters to the advisers to the governor who were in power during governor's rule. The corporation later demurred from naming the reservoir after Satyamurti, which provoked Kamaraj on a later occasion into rebuffing a welcome address from the body. It was, however, later named Satyamurti Sagar.

Throughout 1939 and 1940, Satyamurti kept up correspondence with the viceroy and Gandhiji with a view to finding a solution to the political stalemate. While Gandhiji, true to his credo of non-violence, was opposed to the war, the Congress in the mid-1940s offered cooperation to the government if Britain would accept India's right to independence and the formation of a national government. Satyamurti was himself in favour of taking back the state governments and fighting in the central and provincial assemblies. When the government rebuffed the Congress offer, the latter turned again to Gandhiji, who started an individual *satyagraha* movement demanding freedom. All leaders, including Rajaji and Satyamurti, were jailed.

After the release of the leaders, Satyamurti again campaigned for fighting within the legislatures, but Gandhiji was inflexible on this issue. Satyamurti pointed out that, after Japan's entry into the war in December 1941 and its victorious march through southeast Asia, total non-violence was not a practical policy of self-defence. Events moved quickly after the fall of Singapore and Churchill sent Sir Stafford Cripps, a labour minister of the war cabinet, to India to find a satisfactory solution. The British continued to uphold the 'minority problem' as they called it, and the views of Jinnah. The Cripps mission failed, and there was an impasse again.

In April 1942, Rajaji got the Madras Legislature Congress party to pass two resolutions, one, that the formation of Pakistan should be agreed to if Jinnah insisted on it as the price for freedom, and two, that the Madras Legislature Congress party should be allowed to take back power in Madras. The Congress rejected both ideas and Rajaji left the Congress. Satyamurti adhered to the orthodox Congress attitude and led the campaign against Rajaji's views in Madras and elsewhere.

Gandhiji now decided that the solution was to ask the British to quit India. On 8 August 1942, the AICC passed the famous Quit India resolution in Bombay. The government struck at once and arrested Gandhiji and the Congress leaders. Satyamurti was arrested in Arakonam while on his way to Madras and taken to Amravati Central Jail in conditions that damaged his spine and endangered his life. He was then brought to the General Hospital in Madras, where his condition worsened. He was released from custody but could not be moved from the hospital, where he died on 28 March 1943.

It may be noted, in passing, that the Quit India Movement in 1942 drew into its fold a large number of people from all over India and had its quota of heroes, Jayaprakash Narayan being the most notable. Two young advocates, R Venkataraman of Madras and C Subramaniam of Coimbatore, who threw themselves into it, rose to high positions in independent India. Venkataraman, an ally of Kamaraj, occupied the highest constitutional position of the president of India. Subramaniam, who was responsible for persuading Rajaji to come to the rescue of the Congress in Madras after the 1952 elections and becoming the chief minister, distinguished himself most of all as the architect of the Green Revolution.

Satyamurti was a man of wide and varied interests. He was a member of the Senate and Syndicate of Madras and the Annamalai University for a long time. He was a scholar in Tamil, English and Sanskrit, deeply immersed in the literature of all three languages. He was a lover of Carnatic music and was associated with the Madras Music Academy, being its vice-president for some time. He was an amateur actor and played important roles in plays staged by the Suguna Vilasa Sabha. This naturally led to the patronage of cinema, and he was the first to realise its value for nationalist propaganda. He was the president of the South Indian Film Chamber in 1937–38 and presided over the All India Motion Picture Congress in Bombay in 1939. When broadcasting was introduced in India, he took to it and spoke over the radio in both English and Tamil. Ironically, his view of the helpfulness of the stage and the cinema for propagation of political ideologies was adopted successfully by the DMK, which displaced the Congress in Madras thirty years later.

His place in Indian history – and there can be no doubt that he deserves one – is as the pioneer of parliamentary activities in the country. Gandhiji is reported to have said, 'If there had been ten Satyamurtis in our legislature, the British would have quit long ago'. The irony was that he never held a ministerial office, having had to be content with the mayoralty of Madras. The irony of the route the careers of Satyamurti and Rajaji took, given their views in the political struggle, has already been noted. The crowning irony was his nomination as a member of the Congress Working Committee in the Bombay AICC session of August 1942, but even the announcement could not be made before his arrest. The Satyamurti statue in Parliament, the Satyamurti Sagar in Madras (an almost forgotten usage) and the Congress office being named Satyamurti Bhavan in Madras are the only reminders of this great patriot. He did not live to see a free India.

It is said that Satyamurti's ambition was to be free India's ambassador to the court of St. James. And a fine ambassador he would have been too, with his mastery of the English language and wide circle of friends in British political life. But that was not to be either.

A sad postscript: When the proposal to put up his statue in Parliament was mooted, a leading Congressman, who had been speaker of the Lok Sabha and a member of the central cabinet, supposedly asked, 'Who was Satyamurti?'

The True Spirit of Democracy[23]

M Hamid Ansari

> *R Venkataraman embodied the correct spirit of 'political virtue', and his conduct, both personal and public, is worthy of emulation by today's leaders.*

It is a privilege to attend a function commemorating the birth centenary of a great son of India. The late President Ramaswamy Venkataraman had an extraordinary career in public life as an eminent lawyer, trade union leader, parliamentarian and statesman. The journey from Rajamadam village to Rashtrapati Bhavan is an example of dedication, perseverance and concern for public interest.

Ramaswamy Venkataraman contributed to the strengthening of the institutions of our republic. He was a practitioner of virtue in the classical sense, a stickler for propriety and decency, for doing what was right in accordance with his conscience and convictions. He believed that the incumbency of public office necessitated decision-making, and that doing right was more important than catering to personal preferences or seeking popularity.

---

[23] Address during the birth centenary celebrations of Late R Venkataraman on 30 July 2011 at the India International Centre, New Delhi.

It is a truism that the Indian reality is reflected in contrasting images. We have witnessed in our own times significant strides in economic growth, technological innovation and social change. We also see societal and regional inequalities, widespread poverty and disease, and unrealised aspirations for a better life. Change has generated hope; the challenge to our political process is to transform this hope into reality.

Venkataraman believed in the Gandhian dictum that 'self-government is not a substitute for good government'. He noted in the opening lines of his presidential memoirs that he viewed his role as one where the ideals of Lord Krishna, taught upon the battlefield, were tested. He believed that while the observance of one's dharma, and right conduct, was necessary for the efficient functioning of our democracy, it was nevertheless insufficient since the test of good governance lay in delivery of justice.

The key to the twin imperatives of observance of dharma and delivery of justice thus lies in adherence to propriety in public and personal behaviour and practice. Venkataraman's life and conduct is a fitting example of such propriety. He remains a shining example worthy of emulation.

The question of propriety in politics, of political morality, is a perennial one. Kautilya dwelt on the perils of flouting the Dharmashastras and the *Arthashastra*. Others accorded differing priorities; Confucius stressed the primacy of virtue; Machiavelli espoused the 'virtue' of the ruler in terms of success and sustainability; Ambedkar spoke of 'the paramount reverence for the forms of the Constitution'.

It is necessary to elaborate on this matter since it goes beyond ideals and touches the very core of public behaviour.

While political virtue is important, it can neither be pursued in isolation, nor can it be the sole guide for political action. Political virtue, combined with idealism and activism, can degenerate into political anarchy, even tyranny. A classic case is

Robespierre's famous oration on political morality, wherein he argued that in revolutionary times the mainspring of popular government is both virtue and terror.

In any structured society and polity, therefore, especially in a republic such as ours, it is paramount that political virtue be wedded to the grammar of constitutional morality.

What are the ingredients of constitutional morality? We can do no better than to go back to the description relied upon by BR Ambedkar. It involved, as he put it:

> A paramount reverence for the forms of the Constitution, enforcing obedience to authority acting under and within these forms yet combined with the habits of open speech, of action subject only to defined legal control, and unrestrained censure of those very authorities as to all their public acts combined too with a perfect confidence in the bosom of every citizen, amidst the bitterness of party contest, that the forms of the Constitution will not be less sacred in the eyes of his opponents than in his own.

In other words, freedom with self-restraint, recognition of plurality, consensus on constitutional processes, and absence of a claim to singularity in representation, are absolutely necessary. Constitutional morality, in the words of an eminent political scientist, requires that allegiance to the Constitution is non-transactional, not premised on specific outcomes. It was conceded even by the Constitution framers that such an outcome was not to be a natural process and required the development of healthy conventions.

How successful have we been in developing such conventions and adhering to them? How vibrant is our democratic process in the periods between elections? Has our democracy tended

R Venkataraman: A person extraordinaire

RV (third from left) with Jawaharlal Nehru at the Avadi Congress Session, 1955

With Vijayalakshmi Pandit

With his mentor K Kamaraj (left) in the former German Democratic Republic

RV and Mrs Venkataraman next to K Kamaraj's statue in New Delhi

With Edmund Hillary, the high commissioner of New Zealand

RV and Mrs Venkataraman with Richard Weizsäcker (extreme left) and his wife (extreme right)

With Lord Geoffrey Howe

With Nobel Laureate and Palestinian leader Yasser Arafat

(L-R) Rajiv Gandhi, Sonia Gandhi, Mrs Venkataraman, Sri Lankan President JR Jayawardene, RV and Mrs Jayawardene

With the king of Bhutan

With Prince Charles of UK

With MG Ramachandran

With Field Marshal Sam Manekshaw

Presenting the Sangeet Natak Akademi award to Ustad Amjad Ali Khan (right). Girish Karnad is standing behind

RV and Mrs Venkataraman with Morarji Desai

to become progressively non-deliberative? Is there a suggestion of disenchantment with the state and its institutions?

It is essential that there be public debate on these issues.

Today we witness, across the length and breadth of the country, political activism at the grass-root level. In some instances, such activism has sought to utilise Gandhian approaches, both in tactical and strategic terms. These socio-political movements coexist alongside mainstream politics, represented by the political parties and related electoral dynamics at the national, state and local government levels. Their causes vary from environment, farmers' issues, land acquisition problems, disputes regarding natural resources and mining activities, and public policy goals such as improving public service delivery and combating corruption.

Instead of focussing on solving socio-political problems through established constitutional processes, the search for solutions is increasingly moving towards quasi-legal, perhaps, extra-legal arenas. This has longer term implications. De-legitimising political processes is unlikely to solve our problems. Likewise, seeking to erode the careful in-built balance between the executive, the legislature and the judiciary as contained in the Constitution, either through under-reach of one or overreach of another, could lead to chaos.

We were fortunate that many of the founding fathers of the republic were not only freedom fighters, but were deeply committed to putting in place institutions, systems and processes. They had idealism, were endowed with political virtue, and were deeply committed to the constitutional morality of the republic. Venkataraman was from that political stock, and hence imbued his public life with such an approach. There is merit in rejuvenating that spirit, and the commitment that went with it.

The Copybook President

MK Narayanan

Drawing a parallel between the early 1990s and the present, the author feels that the need of the hour is for another Venkataraman, to handle the political situation adroitly.

I am indeed grateful to Lakshmi Venkataraman Venkatesan for inviting me to participate in the birth centenary celebrations of R Venkataraman, former president of India. I have been privileged to be associated with Venkataraman, and count myself among his legion of admirers.

Millions of Indians within the country and abroad still revere his memory. From his humble beginnings in Rajamadam village of Thanjavur district of the then Madras Presidency, he rose to become India's eighth president – a philosopher-statesman of the rarest of the rare variety. He has been universally acclaimed as a great humanist, a practical idealist, a sagacious human being and much more. To me, however, he was a gentle and caring human being, and a most balanced individual – someone who possessed a steely determination to achieve what was required in the interest of the country, but never swerving from the path of righteousness.

Among President Venkataraman's many distinctions were: his being a member of the Constituent Assembly that drew up India's Constitution; his role as the principle architect of industrialisation of the then composite Madras state (now renamed Tamil Nadu); the miracle he wrought by bringing electricity to every village in the state; and enabling Madras state to emerge as India's premier state in those days. In the process, he caught the attention of the visionary Former Prime Minister Jawaharlal Nehru.

After Panditji's (Jawaharlal Nehru) demise, Former President Venkataraman came to be closely associated with both Prime Minister Indira Gandhi (1966–1977, 1980–1984) as well as her son Prime Minister Rajiv Gandhi (1984–1989). In 1980, Venkataraman became finance minister (1980–1982), steering the country through a very difficult period, and thereafter took over as the defence minister in 1982. It is widely acknowledged that he was the guiding spirit behind the Integrated Guided Missile Programme for which the engineer-scientist and later president of India, APJ Abdul Kalam, has been widely acclaimed. His spells in the Ministries of Finance and Defence were, however, only stepping stones to further stages of elevation – to the post of vice-president of India (in August 1984) and next to the office of the president of India in July 1987 – the crowning glory of his years in public life.

It was while he was president (1987–1992) that I got an opportunity to closely interact with him. My admiration for the way he looked at problems, the kind of solutions he proffered and the kind of sage advice that would follow was unbounded. Today's title – RV: The Copybook President – brings vivid memories of the many tutorials I was privileged to receive from him.

It may not be out of place here to mention a few instances of President Venkataraman's understanding of men and matters, to which I am privy. One instance was his advice to me when I had gone to brief him in mid-1988 under instructions from then Prime Minister Rajiv Gandhi, on a proposed operation against Sikh extremists in Amritsar. The prime minister was anxious that the president should have a clear idea of the nature and extent of the operation, and wanted his advice on the matter, if necessary. With his sharp intellect, ex-President Venkataraman quickly came to grips with the finer points of the operation, putting forward his views, without in any way violating constitutional propriety.

Another instance that I recall with gratitude was his advice on the dangers of predatory capitalism. This, he said, was becoming more manifest after India had begun to usher in economic reforms and economic liberalisation. He was concerned that predatory capitalism would have greater sway in the period ahead, and that it was extremely important for those in authority to understand and appreciate the fundamental complexity of managing the affairs of a large country such as ours.

The third instance that comes to my mind was the emphasis that he constantly laid on the importance of those in authority adhering closely to the principles underlying Article 14 and Article 19 of the Constitution. He would say that Article 14 – Equality before the Law – was a fundamental right and that India would be effectively demolished in the eyes of the people and the world at large if she and her agencies did not strictly adhere to it at all times. Likewise, on Article 19, he would emphasise that the Indian State should uphold the rights relating to Freedom of Speech and to assemble peaceably at all times, and must not overreact to such incidents.

The nation is currently passing through a turbulent phase, essentially concerning internal developments. My mind goes back to 1990–91 (especially the last couple of months of 1990 and the early months of 1991) when the nation was wracked by a violent agitation against the implementation of the Mandal Commission recommendations. There was a minority government in office for most of this period, headed by the late Chandrasekhar. It was fascinating to see how a sage president helped steady the situation. I was particularly taken up by the president's sense of timing, for the best advice can prove unproductive if not made available at the appropriate time. Despite the depth of the crisis, and his deep involvement, Venkataraman remained the 'copybook president', never stepping beyond the *lakshman rekha* of constitutional propriety.

We face another kind of emotional upsurge today. Our problems appear magnified as of now, and it is not my intention to draw any parallels between what is happening today and the situation that the country faced in 1990–91. Nevertheless, there are some similarities in mood between today and during that period. Factors such as perceptions of deprivation and alienation existed even then. Left-wing extremism, which thrives on the perception that the state is unable to protect the poor and the weak who are victims of exploitation, was quite active at the time, as also other mezzanine forces who often employed violent means. Long-standing problems such as indigenous and externally directed terrorism, and separatist movements in Jammu and Kashmir and the Northeast still remain. Today, the ambit of violence is increasing because of the growing numbers of sub-state actors. Corruption has become an overweening concern at present, which, however, was not the case then.

Wise counsel is the key to dealing with such situations. We do miss at this time people like President Venkataraman. In the 1990–91 period, he helped focus attention on the deep social imbalances that existed at the time to improve the situation, as also steps to overcome the weakness of some state institutions.

India is a shining example of democracy. We do have men with both wisdom and probity, and with deep insights on how to handle situations of varied kinds. Venkataraman was one such individual, but we need many more of them. He straddled the political domain with principle and integrity. We were lucky to have produced a Ramaswamy Venkataraman, but surely (and certainly) a 5,000-year-old civilisation and a nation of 1.2 billion can produce a few more good men like him to steer the ship of state into safer waters.

An Able Achiever

MK Venkatachalam

> MK Venkatachalam remembers his long association with R Venkataraman and elaborates on Venkataraman's important achievements during that time.

KP Singh Deo has rightly observed that 'while the country's political life was the site of his major activity, his impact ranged over a spectrum of social issues, encompassing its cultural mores, its legacies of philanthropy and social integration, its intellectual tradition, its administrative evolution, its diplomatic method, economic and technological insurgence and the large and continually growing field of human well being.'

All the activists of the Indian independence movement and the historic Quit India Movement of 1942, the celebrated non-violent resistance to the mighty British Empire, were my heroes. R Venkataraman was indeed one of them. He suffered detention for two years under the Defence of India Rules in 1942. On his release from prison in 1944, he took up the organisation of the labour section of the Tamil Nadu Provincial Congress Committee. He had an abiding interest in law, having practised law first in the Madras High Court from 1935, then in the Supreme Court from 1951. The law pertaining to labour-related trade union activity attracted him towards politics. His sympathy for the poor and the downtrodden was also reflected in his approach to national problems during his entire political life.

When the transfer of power from the British imperialist government to Indian hands was imminent in 1946, the interim government of undivided India included RV in the panel of lawyers sent to Malaysia and Singapore to defend Indian nationals charged with offences of collaboration during the Imperialist Japanese occupation of those two places. RV was a Renaissance man of the Gandhi–Nehru tradition. He was a true patriot – true to his nationalistic feelings and having sympathy for the underdog. The first assignment given to him by the emerging free India in the international arena, appropriate to his energies and focus, was to defend the hapless victims of colonial imperialism of the East or the West variety.

He was the member of the Constituent Assembly that drafted India's Constitution. He was elected to India's provisional Parliament in 1950 (1950–52) and consequently was a member of the first Parliament (1952–57). The members of the Constituent Assembly who had drafted the Constitution of India and who were present at the midnight hour of 14 August 1947, adopted it and signed it, were truly a galaxy of patriots – the gifted ones who heard the historic 'A Tryst with Destiny' speech of Pandit Nehru. R Venkataraman was one of them.

Although re-elected to Parliament in 1957, he resigned his seat to join the State Government of Tamil Nadu as minister of industries, labour, cooperation, transport and commercial taxes from 1957–67, during the premiership of K Kamaraj and later of M Bhaktavatsalam. His abiding interest in labour and labour-related issues always energised him in his handling of the various political offices held by him. The well-being of people was his forte. He tried to find solutions for any problem of the general public according to the *aam junta*'s preference. He was indeed sensitive to well-informed public opinion on any issue placed before him.

As Minister of Industries for Tamil Nadu, he gave a tremendous fillip to the industrial development of the state, under the controlled economy of those days, by innovating what is known as 'Single Window Clearance', by which an entrepreneur could get government clearance for his project at one place instead of approaching different departments for the different aspects of his project. This was a great boon. Tamil Nadu owes a deep debt of gratitude to R Venkataraman for his innovative efforts in ensuring the state's orderly industrial growth.

It was my good fortune to be associated closely with R Venkataraman in the following areas:

First, as a member of an official committee, set up by the Government of India, of which he was the chairman, while he was a member of the Planning Commission. Then, after my retirement from the government in 1980, as a senior executive of the newly established Housing Development Finance Corporation Ltd (HDFC), Mumbai, when he was the union finance minister (1980-82). Last, as a member of the Board of Management of Sree Swaminatha Swami Seva Samaj from 1999 to 2009, while he was its respected patron-in-chief, till his demise on 27 January 2009. I will now elaborate on some path-breaking achievements by R Venkataraman during the times I was associated with him.

As Member, Planning Commission (1967–71)

Fourteen major Indian commercial banks were nationalised on 19 July 1969 and the state's economy assumed commanding heights. 83.32 per cent of the deposits of the banking system – the said fourteen banks with the eight banks of the State Bank of India group, already in the public sector – came to be held by the twenty-two public sector banks. Former Prime Minister Indira Gandhi called her nationalisation policy of the fourteen major banks 'an engine of economic growth'. One of the measures taken as a sequel was the appointment of a high-powered committee under the chairmanship of R Venkataraman to classify and identify industrially backward areas to qualify for concessional finance from the financial institutions and the newly nationalised banking system, thus achieving balanced industrial growth for the entire country. I had the good fortune to be nominated as a member of the committee, representing the newly created Department of Banking. The committee used to meet every alternate Saturday (the day was a working day at the time). We, as members of the committee, used to admire Venkataraman's vast vision, how methodically, meticulously and judiciously, without any discrimination, he used the several economic parameters – such as demographic pattern of the population (tribal versus non-tribal), consumption of electricity, rural composition of the population, road and rail communication infrastructure network, and so on, for determining the industrial backwardness of the several districts or segments of districts. The classification and grouping of the different districts received wide appreciation from all the state governments, the Reserve Bank of India, the banking and the long-term financial institutional system, and the public. The policy of taking banks which provided concessions as well as institutional finance to the small, medium and tiny sectors of industry in the backward areas all over India was put into operation during his time.

As Union Finance Minister (1980–82)

With the Indian National Congress coming back to power, after a brief interlude (1977–1980) during which there was a Janata Party coalition government, R Venkataraman became the union finance minister in January 1980, in the cabinet of Indira Gandhi.

I would like to digress here for a moment and refer to the life of another great soul whose birthday centenary fell on 10 March 2011 – Late Hasmukhbhai Thakoredas Parekh (10 March 1911 – 19 November1994) – a good friend of Venkataraman. HTP brought about a revolution in the field of housing in 1977. On his own initiative, he floated the first ever housing finance institution in the private sector as a public company with participation of the general public in its share capital, for a modest sum of ₹10 crore. Eminent men before him might have thought about the problem, but he alone gave practical shape to provide the common man his own house during his active earning period – security in its most fundamental form – that would enable him to lead a life with dignity. This was no mean achievement. His thinking was crystal clear. He would not expound any theory if it could not be given practical shape in a simple and economical manner. Indeed, he was a visionary who built institutions, as well as sustained and nourished them. The magic wand he wielded was his team of dedicated men and women whom he personally chose and delegated duties to. The personality of Parekh and his Catholic outlook was similar to that of R Venkataraman.

Venkataraman had known Parekh prior to this development. The Housing Development Finance Corporation Ltd (HDFC) had just been floated by Parekh. He did not need any help from the government in the shape of resources. HDFC, the first ever housing finance institution, wholly in the private sector, was specifically advised by its promoters to exclusively help the individual borrower directly, and create a retail market of mortgage housing finance for the first time in the country. With housing finance being a long-term proposition, it was not easy – rather, impossible in the 1980s – to raise matching long-term resources from the market. The response of the banking industry, despite nationalisation of fourteen major banks, was lukewarm. The response of the open market was practically negative.

Parekh, however, had an excellent relationship with the international banking and finance system. But his successful initiative in exploring foreign sources for the housing finance sector in India could not secure the needed government approval at the official level under the controlled economy of those days. The issue had to be taken up by Parekh with the union finance minister, Venkataraman. Housing represents the large and continuously growing field of human well-being – shelter being next only to food and clothing in the basic needs of man – *roti, kapda aur makaan*. Human well-being was the forte of Venkataraman as well. Without any hesitation, he directed that HDFC might be permitted to borrow from abroad and devise means of repaying the amounts. This was a landmark decision at the time. Over the years, it became government policy to borrow from foreign institutions, with subsequent liberalisation of the economy. HDFC is today a household name. Other institutions have entered the field and commercial banks also have commenced lending affordable housing loans to the common man. The real-estate sector has grown by leaps and bounds, provides excellent investment and is poised for huge capital appreciation. The National Housing Bank in the public sector was established by an Act of Parliament on 1 July 1988 as the apex institution of housing finance. A small opening in 1982 through a new policy enabled by R Venkataraman has resulted in phenomenal growth. A well-coordinated and well-meant effort of two noble souls acting in unison for human well being!

As an architect of Uttara Swamimalai (Malai Mandir) of Sree Swaminatha Swami Seva Samaj (Regd) New Delhi (1968-2009)

As an architect of the Uttara Swamimalai Temple, popularly known as 'Malai Mandir' R Venkataraman combined the contemplation of God with the service of man, naturally and creatively. In his own words:

> The Samaj has an interesting early history. A few young men, in their early twenties, who had come to Delhi for their official careers in 1944, more than sixty years ago, commenced celebrating Sree Skanda Shashti in their households, by turn. The tiny seed of devotion to the Glorious Lord Swaminatha Swami, sown by them at that time, has since sprouted and grown giving shape to the sacred Uttara Swamimalai complex, in the national capital of India, complementary to Dakshina Swamimalai in the South.

The evolution and construction of the temple complex has a long and chequered history. It took nearly thirty years to come up, from 1944 to 7 June 1973, the day of consecration of Lord Sivaskanda Murthy, son of Lord Shiva, worshipped as Lord Swaminatha Swami.

In 1961, a small mound was noticed by the devotees in the then undeveloped Ramakrishna Puram housing colony of government servants on the outskirts (at the time) of New Delhi metropolis. The devotees felt that the mound could be a suitable location for building a temple. His Holiness the Paramacharya of the sacred Sree Kanchi Kamakoti Peetam blessed the commencement of the temple project in principle. His benediction in 1961 proved an augury for the subsequent course of events, over the years.

An unexpected coincidence, hitherto unknown, also came to the notice of the devotees at that time. Ramachandra Dikshitar, the deputy director-general of archeology, Government of India, checked the map of Delhi to see whether the mound could have some religious significance or historicity from the heritage point of view. He found that there was a mark, 'RP', on the map, to indicate that the area was once a religious place. It should be noted, in this context, that the proposed location of the new temple for Lord Swaminatha on the top of the hillock in North India admirably conforms to the traditional practice of building temples for the Lord on hillocks or elevated places in the South. Thus the homogeneity – religious and cultural unity – of India was maintained. Appropriately, it came to be named Uttara Swamimalai, complementary to the Dakshina Swamimalai in the South, referred to earlier by Venkataraman. Its name in popular parlance comes from *malai*, a Tamil word meaning mountain, and *mandir*, a Hindi word meaning temple – therefore, a temple on a hill.

A team of office-bearers proceeded to the South to solicit the blessings of His Holiness Jagadguru Chandrasekharendra Saraswati Swamigal (Venerable Paramacharya) of the holy Sree Kanchi Kama Koti Peetam and of His Holiness Srila Sri Kasi Vasi Arul Nanda Thambiran Swamigal of the Sri Kasi Mutt of Tiruppanandal for the project. The Kasi Mutt made a land endowment of ₹1.50 lakh. Various temples of Tamil Nadu contributed, providing assistance to the pioneering efforts of the pioneer *bhaktas*.

His Holiness the Venerable Paramacharya had been watching with concern the trials and tribulations of the young *bhaktas* and monitoring their progress in building the edifice. At this very crucial stage, R Venkataraman arrived on the scene. He was deeply devoted to the Sree Kamchi Matam and had very high regard for His Holiness. His Holiness advised R Venkataraman to assume the presidency of the samaj and extend his leadership and help to the young *bhaktas*. R Venkataraman, who had held high profile offices in Tamil Nadu, had just arrived on the all-India arena. The subsequent methodical progress of the *samaj* in building the temple complex and in enhancing its religious sanctity and dignity, as an ideal place of worship over the years, would show beyond all reasonable doubt that R Venkataraman's assumption of office of the president of the *samaj*, at that crucial stage, was actually in response to a divine message to him, as it were, from Lord Swaminatha Swami himself, conveyed through His Holiness the Paramacharya. Truly speaking, Venkataraman's thoughts and ideals laid the foundation of the *samaj* as an institution. Viewing his invaluable and dedicated services to the temple and the *samaj*, one is tempted to quote a saying of venerable Swami Vivekananda:

> Religion is the manifestation of the natural strength that is in man. A spring of infinite power is coiled up and is inside this little body and that spring is spreading itself. And as it is spreading, body after body is found insufficient: it throws them off and takes higher bodies. This is the history of man, of religion, civilisation or progress.

After the *kumbhabhishekam* in 1973, a code for the conduct of rituals and pujas in the temple was compiled, in consultation with competent Sivacharyas by two of the founder *bhaktas* who had been vice-presidents for religious affairs for long periods. The precious printed code contains the Puja Vidhis and Utsava Paddhadis for the benefit of the present and future generations of Sivacharyas and members of the Board of Management of the temple. It has become an invaluable guide and reference handbook. In the words of R Venkataraman: 'The compilation will serve as a guide to the future generations to continue the conduct of the four *kaala* pujas, festivals, etc., in accordance with ancient Agama Shastras without departing from their religious significance.'

R Venkataraman continued as president of the *samaj* till the end of January 1980, when he assumed the office of the union finance minister. After a gap of three years from 1980–83, when the temple was under a chairman of the Board of Management (T Swaminathan), Venkataraman requested RV Subrahmanian to assume the office of the president. RVS, as he was affectionately called, assumed office on 8 May 1983 and served with dedication until 2 April 2006. R Venkataraman agreed to take up the office of patron-in-chief which he held with unique distinction till his demise on 27 January 2009.

Over the subsequent years, construction of other temples for Lord Sundareswarar, Goddess Meenakshi and Lord Karpaga Vinayakar were planned and completed. Under the guidance of Venkataraman, RV Subrahmanian brought to bear on his office his long administrative experience to consolidate the gains so far achieved and carry forward the good work of his predecessors. A well-modulated administrative system was built, based upon broad consensus among the members of the board of management that included the illustrious 'young men in their early twenties – *bhaktas* who had come to Delhi for their official career in 1944 and subsequent years'. Constant emphasis was laid upon improving the infrastructural base, following an enlightened labour relations policy towards the employees, thereby enabling the *samaj* to provide a host of services to the general devotees of all classes. This process has continued till date. With increasing number of devotees thronging the temple complex everyday, its sanctity and dignity are also heightened.

From the year 2006–07 onwards, Venkataraman felt somewhat weak in health. Thinking that the call from the Lord might come for him, he began to engage himself feverishly in bringing about some desirable changes in the *samaj*. The Board of Management of the *samaj*, at his behest, organised the *eka koti archanas* – one crore recitals of the holy *Namavalis* of Lord Swaminatha Swami – in the months of June–October 2007. This was highly appreciated by all.

While Venkataraman was engaged in organising and conducting the sacred *eka koti archanas* for Lord Swaminatha Swami, a proposal for the construction of a flyover or an underpass right opposite Malai Mandir was suddenly placed before the management of the *samaj* by the project authorities of the Commonwealth Games 2010, to widen the Olof Palme Marg. That would have involved cutting the protruding rocks of Malai Mandir, which supported the Moolavar's temple on top of the hill. The proposal caused apprehensions in the minds of R Venkataraman and the board of management that the stability of the entire hill would be jeopardised. It also created doubts in the devotees' minds, bordering on offending their religious sentiments. The matter was taken up immediately by Venkataraman with Delhi Chief Minister Sheila Dikshit. Unhesitatingly, she gave an assurance that the location of the underpass or the flyover would be suitably realigned so as not to disturb the Malai Mandir in any manner. No formal communication was, however, received to this end for more than a year. In the meanwhile, Venkataraman passed away on 27 January 2009.

With the protective canopy of Venkataraman no longer available, the board of management was very apprehensive that the old proposal of construction of flyover might be revived at the official level. The matter was broached gently with the chief minister on 7 April 2009. Her spontaneous reply was that she would not go back on her assurance given to Venkataraman just because he was no longer with us. After some developments, she also made an official statement on the floor of the Delhi Legislative Assembly on 3 July 2009.

Appreciating the spirit of service of the devotees, R Venkataraman's message to the devotees, a few months before his demise, was, 'I hope this spirit (the spirit of benevolent services, large and small, of all the devotees present and future), helped by Lord Swaminatha Swami will continue as long as the hills stand and the rivers flow, like Ramayana in this holy land.'

We, the devotees, solemnly state that we will be true to his ideals and expectations and serve the *samaj*, as ever, to grow on the lines shown by our beloved RV.

Epilogue

Throughout the forty years of his leadership of the samaj, his love for his fellow workers and the employees was deep. From the second half of the year 2008, he started getting a sinking feeling, despite his alert mind. He was, however, quite regular in visiting the temple for worship. On Saturday, 10 January 2009, he made his usual visit to the temple after informing some of us. As he was leaving, he peeped out and looked up towards the top of the *gopuram* and, in our hearing, uttered, as if addressing the Lord, 'When will I come again?' We felt almost as if he was making a farewell call, as it were, to the Lord, pouring out his heart as his car moved away.

Helping India Scale New Heights
RV's Contributions Towards India's Defence Sector

MM Pallam Raju

R Venkataraman made immensely significant contributions to India's missile programme during his tenure as defence minister, propagating self-reliance.

As I write this article, I feel proud that my family, for three generations, was fortunate to have been associated with R Venkataraman, former president of India. A freedom fighter who actively participated in the Quit India Movement and a great parliamentarian, he served with distinction in various capacities in public life, with commitment to the highest principles and standards all his life, and ultimately rose to occupy the highest office in the country.

My grandfather, the late Pallam Raju, was in jail with him during the freedom movement. My father MS Sanjeevi Rao was his ministerial colleague in Indira Gandhi's team and had the highest regard for his administrative abilities and knowledge. As a young parliamentarian in 1989, I have had the privilege of interacting with Former President Venkataraman and still cherish the gift he gave us when my wife and I called on him after our marriage.

Venkataraman's contribution to India's strategic security, as the defence minister, is very significant. In my capacity as the Minister of State for Defence since 2006, I have had the opportunity of visiting various defence establishments all over the country. In my interactions with scientists and officers there is an air of reverence while remembering him, and glowing tributes are paid to him for the many successful programmes that were initiated during his tenure as the defence minister of India. APJ Abdul Kalam has acknowledged that Venkataraman, as defence minister, was responsible for shaping the country's missile programme. A number of Western countries at the time attempted to restrict India's weapons programme by introducing the Missile Technology Control Regime (MTCR). Venkataraman understood the country's security needs, and to defend India adequately he realised that India had to focus on building her own missiles, where the principle of self-reliance would be attainable. Any project, to be successful and completed in time, needs a capable and dynamic leader. So he persuaded Kalam and brought him from the Department of Space to the DRDO as a director.

Venkataraman, on his mission to speed up the missile programme of the country, set up a committee consisting of the three service chiefs, senior bureaucrats and top scientists. The initial proposal submitted to the defence minister was a row of unrelated projects to be implemented consecutively, one after another. Venkataraman, the visionary that he was, insisted that they combine all these projects to cover the entire missile systems needed by the nation, with the assurance of getting the necessary budget, and thus the Integrated Guided Missile Development Programme (IGMDP) took shape. He pursued and secured expeditious cabinet approval for the programme, with a sanction of ₹3.88 billion. The programme consisted of five major projects which were scheduled to be completed in a time frame of ten years: 1. Nag – an anti-tank guided missile. 2. Prithvi – a surface-to-surface missile 3. Akash – a swift medium range surface-to-air missile 4. Trishul – a quick reaction surface-to-air missile with a shorter range and 5. Agni – an intermediate range ballistic missile. As the defence minister, Venkataraman monitored the programme closely and gave his full support to all those involved. Agni established the indigenous capability towards self-reliance in defence preparedness. This programme has been India's most successful research task to date, and credit should be given to Venkataraman for his vision and leadership. Very few people know that the idea of acquiring a nuclear-propelled submarine from Russia was floated by him. Several other initiatives taken by him in the defence ministry have paved the way towards self-reliance.

The economic liberalisation started in 1991 by then Finance Minister Manmohan Singh and Prime Minister PV Narasimha Rao has resulted in the tremendous economic growth of India in the last two decades. Venkataraman was the president during those crucial years when the reforms were initiated. The economic situation in the country in 1991 was grave, with the foreign exchange position precarious, and India was struggling to secure an IMF loan to tide over the crisis. Venkataraman, who had earlier worked as union finance minister, actively supported the government in its financial and austerity measures. His advice on various financial issues were solicited and his suggestions were taken seriously. Venkataraman was so concerned about the economic situation that he persuaded the government to cancel his state visit to Chile, Italy and Turkey that year.

Venkataraman was the president of India from 1987 to 1992, during which time the country saw four prime ministers in office, with three of them being appointed by him. Those years were a critical period in our history with contentious issues looming, such as Sri Lanka, Punjab, and the tragic demise of Rajiv Gandhi. Venkataraman was a man of high intellectual integrity and absolute probity, and always acted according to his beliefs. Credit should be given to him for steering the country in those difficult times towards peace and economic progress. India, over the past decade, has been one of the fastest-growing economies of the world. It is thanks to the foresight of leaders like him that we may emerge as one of the three largest economies of the world in the coming decades.

Venkataraman firmly believed that India would overcome its problems and regain its past glory. He asks us in the epilogue of his book *My Presidential Years*, 'Are we contributing to that resurgence?' He will be remembered for generations to come as a leader who significantly contributed to the resurgence of India.

I salute the great man who made the nation proud!

R Venkataraman's Role in the SSI Success Story

MS Parthasarathy

RV was a staunch supporter of industrial growth. His support and encouragement towards small-scale units laid the foundation for India's future economic growth.

It is a great tribute, that eminent people of India are celebrating the birth centenary of our Late R Venkataraman. Former president of India, R Venkataraman has been the beacon for the small-scale industry of our country, particularly in southern India. We are proud that all small-scale units have got RV's blessings.

My contact with RV truly changed my life. The Government of India had issued a licence to me to start a factory, but could not allot a suitable place at Madras. I requested RV for an interview at his office or at his home. He replied, 'I am always available for any person getting into industrial work.' His representative took me to meet the director of industries, who allotted me an industrial shed in Guindy. RV graciously agreed to inaugurate the factory in 1958. Even the heavy rains did not deter RV from giving an excellent address to SSI units and its holders. The smile on his face brought happiness to everyone who attended the meeting at the venue.

Under RV's guidance and direction, I became the president of Guindy Industrial Estate Association and other national-level governing bodies. This in turn strengthened RV's means to help many aspiring small-scale entrepreneurs of our nation with full courage and confidence.

RV attended all industrial exhibitions, seminars and factory visits. In Guindy, RV wanted to visit a glass factory but his security advised him not to go ahead as the unit had glass articles. RV replied, 'This is a factory allotted to a minority community and I am visiting the factory to know the progress, so do not worry about security process.' This showed his involvement with small-scale industrialists, who were all encouraged to run units independently.

In all the SSI meetings he addressed, he made fervent appeals to bankers, government officers, etc., to support small-scale industrialists in all their aspirations, as they are the backbone of our country. At the same time, he would give advice openly and even chide them if any mistakes were reported. His advice and support resulted in the rapid growth of small-scale units. RV was unbiased with both industry and government, which increased the appreciation from state and central governments towards small-scale unit associations.

Now, India is indeed well-placed, with a GDP growth rate of 9 to 10 per cent. In 1970, it was 2.8 per cent, 1990 – 5.5 per cent, 2000 – 7.6 per cent and in 2010 – 9 per cent. This growth trajectory is a classic example of RV's vision of developing industries from infancy since we achieved Independence. The seed for GDP growth was planted in Indian soil by RV. He is indeed a commendable person, one to be remembered forever.

RV moved from state affairs to central at Delhi, but still people associated with small-scale industries made a beeline for him, to discuss their progress and problems, and I had the great opportunity to utilise his ideas and put them into action when I became the president of Federation of Association of Small-Scale Industries of India.

An incident is worth quoting here. A group of SSI units under my presidency visited Delhi, and a question was raised by a member as follows, 'Sir, you seem to be so well informed and you are fully knowledgeable about every aspect of an industry, why did you not, sir, become an industrialist?' Pat came the reply from RV, 'I am happy in creating many industrial units in a sincere way and [in the] right direction. So I request all of you to contribute for the healthy growth of industries in our country.' Such was RV's greatness in motivating and inspiring all the small-scale units of our nation.

RV championed the growth of small-scale units to the jubilant community of the small-scale industrial sector. Even as the vice-president of India, the stream of SSI units did not decrease, which continued when he became the president of our country. In their hearts, millions of tiny, small-scale entrepreneurs of our country wish that the government would bestow the Bharat Ratna posthumously upon RV, the highest honour, which would inspire them towards greater work and commitment to build India.

In achieving his objective of rapid industrialisation of our country, RV was assisted by brilliant officers, namely, PC Alexander, Padmashri Nanjappa, Abid Hussain, P Murari, P Shankar and SL Kapoor, who relentlessly worked for the purpose of industrial growth of the country.

The people of our country acknowledge with gratitude RV's dedication, devotion and goodwill towards the industrialisation of our country. RV's life of purpose and determination is an excellent example for generations to emulate. We already have 'Father's Day' 'Mother's Day' 'Teacher's Day' and our small-scale associations would like to celebrate an 'SSI Day' on his birthday, which would be a great fillip to all small-scale industries of our country.

RV was a truly religious person. Shri Kanchi Mahaswamigal respected all religions and prayed for peace and prosperity. RV followed Shri Mahaswamigal's path and inspired millions of people to follow the same. RV was a true philanthropist too. He was associated with an organisation for special children, and his concern for healthcare to reach all the people of our nation paved the way for many self-help organisations to do humanitarian service.

RV, apart from industrial development, was equally interested in encouraging and developing women's education. He had been the chairman of Meenakshi College for Women and also the chairperson of Shri Meenakshi Sundararajan College of Arts, Science and Engineering Faculty. RV's initiatives for the right of women's education have helped the women of India reach great heights in all sectors of our country.

Nothing matches the rush of blood to the brain when you read the success stories of great celebrities. RV was a born leader, and created more leaders to lead India at par with mighty countries. He was an exemplary, inspirational role model, a strategist, and an effective motivator. I congratulate Rupa Publications for bringing out articles in commemoration of the birth centenary of R Venkataraman, our former president of India.

The Karmayogi of Raisina Hill

Meira Kumar

R Venkataraman was the 'emergency lamp' who guided India through politically sensitive times with sagacity and vision.

Ramaswamy Venkataraman stands out as one of the most eminent presidents India has had in its six decades of Independence. The seed of his remarkable and prolific public life was perhaps sown at his birthplace, Thanjavur, where his father Ramaswami Aiyer, a respected scholar and lawyer, inculcated in him a moral grounding that would help him in his long and distinguished career.

An incident is often recalled where a young Venkataraman, practising law at the Madras High Court, took up the defence in 1935 of a group of young men accused of killing a British officer during a mob frenzy. The court sentenced all of them to death. However, Venkataraman filed a petition with the Privy Council challenging the sentence. As a result, the hanging was suspended. It was perhaps this incident that became a precursor to his joining the freedom struggle, during which he also spent two years in jail. It was because of his legal acumen that the interim government chose him in 1946 to go to Malaya and Singapore to defend members of the INA charged for collaborating with the Japanese during the Second World War.

Venkataraman's foray in politics began in right earnest with his election to the Provisional Parliament in 1950. When the country went to polls in 1952, he was elected to the first Lok Sabha. He returned to the Lower House in 1957, then again in 1977, and finally in 1980. In 1957, he went back to Tamil Nadu to become a minister in the Kamaraj cabinet. It was during this time that he came to be regarded as the Father of Industrialisation in Tamil Nadu. He also held other important portfolios in the state, such as labour, cooperation, power and transport.

Ramaswamy Venkataraman, 'RV' to close friends, worked hard towards setting a personal example in a career that spanned four long decades, culminating in the highest office of the land. From his home town Rajamadam in Tamil Nadu to Raisina Hill, he travelled a long and arduous distance like a true *karmayogi,* always conscious of his actions. 'Parliamentarians have a great responsibility,' he once said, 'in that they have to discharge their functions under several constraints, sometimes act according to popular opinion; sometimes even against the popular opinion where the popular opinion is not correct.' There is no doubt that Venkataraman was a parliamentarian of the highest order. Being aware of the human tendency to get impatient with contrary opinions, he felt that Parliament should be a platform where members could articulate the voice of the people freely. 'It would, indeed, be a sad world,' he used to say, 'if everyone agreed with everyone else.'

As chairman of the Rajya Sabha, he presided over the House of Elders with great aplomb and earned the respect of one and all. It was at that time that I personally had the honour of coming in contact with him and was impressed with his views for improving the lot of the underprivileged. He held in great regard our system of adult franchise whereby parliamentarians were obliged to seek the support of the less privileged and vulnerable sections of society and in the process become the 'watchdogs of public interest'.

When Venkataraman took over as president, he was more than aware of the responsibility that destiny had entrusted him with. In his address to members of Parliament following the oath-taking ceremony on 25 July 1987, he said: 'I am deeply conscious of the honour bestowed on me by the people of India. I, however, look upon the Presidentship of India not as an office of pomp and pageantry, but as a post of duty that calls for the highest standards of honesty, sincerity and objectivity ... I will neither fail to exercise the duties and functions attached to this high office, nor stray beyond the powers enshrined in the Constitution by the founding fathers.' Five years later, at the time of demitting office, he redeemed that pledge as only he could.

He was the only president in the history of our republic who worked with four prime ministers in a five-year term. The era of coalitions had just begun, following the general election in 1989, and precedents were yet to be made. And he made a mark on the nation's polity with his unquestionable sagacity, taking bold decisions in what were truly politically sensitive times. The split verdict of 1989 put before our young nation some very daunting challenges. But the man at the helm of affairs put the country at ease by explaining the new paradigm of coalitions to the people. In his almost prescient Republic Day address of 1991, he noted: 'We in India may have to adapt ourselves to such a situation and learn to work together in the common cause, shedding in the process, rigid party positions.'

His own role as president also became much more important in the absence of conventional bipolarity. Like a true political scientist with finely honed legal instincts, he threw new light on the president's role. 'The President under the Indian Constitution is like an "emergency lamp". When the power fails, the "emergency lamp" comes into operation; when the power is restored, the "emergency lamp" becomes dormant.'

It is not easy for a Constitution to foresee how the future will unfold. Hence, the onus of interpretation lies on the operators of the system, people with the gift of intuitive understanding and the boldness to stand by what they see. President Venkataraman's understanding of our Constitution was outstanding. It was our nation's good fortune to have had such an enlightened soul leading us in times of far-reaching change.

It was also my good fortune that I always enjoyed his affection and blessing. More so in the later years, when he would sit in the drawing room of his New Delhi bungalow and recall with sparkling clarity the important and not-so-important but certainly interesting incidents of days gone by. At my request, he also headed the Babu Jagjivan Ram Centenary Celebration Committee in 2008.

As we celebrate the birth centenary of this visionary leader and statesman, I wish that more people like him may come into public life and take the country forward to its deserved place in the comity of nations. Those aspiring for a career in public life must read and assimilate his progressive ideas and thoughts. I do sincerely hope and pray that his legacy continues to grow and illuminate our path.

A Stickler for Propriety

Najma Heptulla

> *As chairman of Rajya Sabha, R Venkataraman ensured that everyone had his or her say, without undue wastage of time or unruly behaviour.*

I was deputy chairman of the Rajya Sabha when in August 1984, R Venkataraman was elected as the vice-president of India and chairman of the Rajya Sabha. On 18 January, when Venkataraman came into the House for the first time to preside over it, he was felicitated by the members. All sections of the House praised his administrative acumen and referred to his vast political and parliamentary experience. In answer to the sentiments expressed by the members, Venkataraman thanked them and assured them that he would protect the interests of all sections of the House. He said: 'I was told that I should not lend my ear but lend my eyes to this side. I have proposed doing both, not only lend my ears but also lend my eyes to all sides of the House. If in the exigencies, I am not able to do so it is not for want of goodwill but only because of the pressure on time in parliamentary proceedings.'

The Rajya Sabha has, over the years, evolved several healthy traditions and one of them is that chairmen, during session days, come to their chamber at around 10.30 a.m. and then confer with the deputy chairman on all matters important to political and procedural developments. As deputy chairman, I met Chairman Venkataraman daily and we used to discuss the strategy to deal with any knotty situation likely to arise during the course of the day, knowing the political stand taken by the government and the opposition. During these meetings, some very senior party leaders belonging to the ruling party and the opposition also used to be present, to place before the chairman their viewpoints. I was really impressed by Venkataraman's political astuteness and legal acumen. He often guided both members of the ruling party and the opposition to arrive at some consensus on the mode of discussion on contentious issues.

There has also been another tradition in the Rajya Sabha that the chairman, barring a few exceptions, mostly presides over the House during Question Hour and thereafter, at noon, the deputy chairman goes to preside over the House. Question Hour is the most important time in the forenoon, when executives' accountability towards Parliament is enforced by the members, by asking questions on various aspects of the functioning of government departments, their programmes, policies and other related issues. Since the time available for the members to ask questions and the minister to answer is limited to one hour, it has always been the endeavour of the presiding officers to see that this hour is optimally utilised. Managing the time of the House efficiently by ensuring opportunities to members to make the government accountable to Parliament, as also allowing ministers to explain government's policies and programmes, is indeed a ticklish task, but I had noticed that Chairman Venkataraman skilfully used to intervene while a member was asking a long-winded supplementary. He could even tell ministers to be precise in answering the supplementary questions. In order to make efficient use of time available during Question Hour, the chairmen have introduced an informal rule of limiting the time of asking and answering a question. VV Giri allowed a maximum of ten minutes for an important question and five minutes for an ordinary question. M Hidayatulla later reduced this time limit to eight minutes. Chairman R Venkataraman was still not satisfied with the arrangement and he, therefore, reduced this time limit to two minutes, meticulously applying this informal rule, as a result of which more questions were taken up in the House.

While presiding over the House on important debates, Chairman Venkataraman gave landmark rulings, which reflected his in-depth understanding of constitutional and procedural matters. On 18 July 1986, the chairman permitted P Upendra to make a reference to matters pertaining to centre-state relations. NKP Salve raised a point of order, saying that matters impinging on the question of federalism in the Constitution should not be allowed to be raised through the use of special mention. Such matters, according to him, should be raised through a substantive motion.

The chairman allowed the members to make their observations on the point of order raised by Salve. Having heard their views, the chairman gave the following ruling:

> Hon'ble members are aware that in the past, I have allowed special mentions of this kind whenever [a] minister made statements relating to affairs connected with the State.
>
> This is the Council of States and, therefore, matters relating to relationship between the Centre and the States can appropriately and legitimately be discussed. Since Mr Salve has raised a point of order, I am bound to give my thought to this point of order and give a ruling which will put at rest this point for eternity; at least till it is changed by [some] other Chairman.

> I am now faced with two options. One, whether I allow special mention or number two whether I allow a substantive motion that is a more special mention. And I, therefore, say that there will be substantive motion on this subject and parties may give a notice of substantive motion.

He zealously guarded the right of the member to free speech. On 6 May 1987, Dharam Chander Prashant was highlighting the need to provide assistance to Sanskrit scholars wishing to participate in the World Sanskrit Conference at Laiden, Holland. He said that Sanskrit is the mother of all Indian languages. At this point, V Gopalsamy refuted this by saying that he did not accept Sanskrit as the mother of all Indian languages.

Disallowing the refutation by Gopalsamy of the views of Dharam Chander Prashant, the chairman observed: 'What is happening is the negation of democracy. Every member is entitled to express his opinion. You may disagree. Merely because you disagree, you cannot shout him down. Then there will be no Parliament.'

He was of the view that without discipline and decorum, Parliament could not discharge its mandate efficiently. The government had to listen to the viewpoint of the opposition and the opposition could always exercise the option of offering policy alternatives and criticise the government when they perceived that the government has either failed to act or has not acted adequately. For running the House smoothly, both the government and the opposition were equally responsible.

Venkataraman always saw to it that the prestige of Parliament was not compromised. If a minister had erred he could, on the floor of the House, ask him to apologise. On 2 August 1985, after the Question Hour, the chairman called upon the minister of state in the Ministry of Finance, Janardhan Poojari, to lay the papers mentioned against his name on the table of the House. Poojari was not in the House at the time. The chairman took serious note of the absence of Poojari and also that of the minister of parliamentary affairs in the House.

Thereafter, when Poojari came to the House, the chairman observed: 'Now I would call upon Mr Poojari to first of all apologise to the House for not being present in the House at the appropriate time … .'

In my long political career, I have for about seventeen years been the deputy chairperson of Rajya Sabha, and have worked with R Venkataraman, Shanker Dayal Sharma, KR Narayanan, Krishan Kant and Bhairon Singh Shekhawat. Every chairman had his unique qualities. Venkataraman was a great statesman and had an abiding faith in democratic values. He always saw in Parliament a great potential to bring about social change.

I had many occasions to interact with him other than while conducting the business of the House. One such occasion, which I fondly remember, was in 1986, when he released my book *India's Progress in Science and Technology – Continuity and Change* at his official residence, 6 Maulana Azad Road. He appreciated my effort and expressed surprise that despite being in politics, I had still maintained my interest in science and technology.

On the occasion of the centenary celebration of R Venkataraman, I pay my humble tribute to him.

Entrepreneurship Development Through Small-Scale Industries in India

PC Alexander

> *R Venkataraman played a crucial role in mentoring a newly independent India's journey to economic self-sufficiency, always analysing a policy from every conceivable angle before it passed into legislation. In this way, he harnessed the best talent and resources available in the country.*

I had the privilege of knowing R Venkataraman closely from the mid-1950s, when he was a minister in the government of Tamil Nadu and I was deputy secretary in the Ministry of Commerce and Industry on deputation from the IAS cadre of Kerala. In the central government, I was mainly looking after work relating to the newly started programme of small-scale industries development, and this position gave me ample opportunities to be in regular contact with the ministers and senior officers in charge of industrial promotion at the state level. Venkataraman was the minister for industries, cooperative, power, commercial taxes, and transport in Tamil Nadu during 1957–67, and had made valuable contributions to the growth of entrepreneurship in India through programmes for the development of small-scale industries. These are remembered with great admiration not only by the people of Tamil Nadu, but by all Indians familiar with the history of the evolution of entrepreneurship in India. I have chosen the subject of 'entrepreneurship development' for this article in tribute to his memory as a pioneer in this field.

Judging by the criterion of industrial development, India was quite a poor country in the mid-1950s. At the time, we had few modern industries in the small-scale sector of the type we see now, and imported even simple consumer goods which could be easily made in the country. Most of the existing small industries still followed the old techniques of production and catered to very limited markets. Still, the people of India were in a euphoric mood because of their implicit faith in the enlightened leadership of their government. They had great expectations that India would be able to emerge as a strong industrial power in a short span of time.

Great programmes were being launched to make India self-sufficient in foreign exchange resources, or at least to reduce its over-dependence on imports. In the early stages of our Independence, we could draw on the sterling balances which had accumulated in Britain in our favour during the Second World War years; but these balances lasted only for a short period. Unlike some other developing countries, we had no oil, no gold, no diamonds for generating foreign exchange. It was most important, therefore, to establish a network of small industries which could help in import substitution, besides providing new avenues of employment, thus ensuring more balanced regional development. The government also recognised that in order to encourage new industries in the small-scale sector it had to give a helping hand to those interested in starting new industrial ventures, as well as modernise the existing ones. These objectives were clearly enunciated in the second industrial policy resolution announced by the government in April 1956. It described the role of small industries as follows:

> They provide immediate large scale employment, they offer a method of ensuring a more equitable distribution of the national income and they facilitate an effective mobilisation of resources of capital and skill which might otherwise remain unutilised. Some of the problems that unplanned mechanisation tends to create will be avoided by the establishment of small centres of industrial production all over the country.

The most important step taken by the government in pursuance of the above objectives was the inclusion of import substitution policy in the Import Export Control Act of 1947. The Act originally had its main thrust on conservation of foreign exchange rather than promotion of new entrepreneurship. The strict use of tariffs and quotas in the Red Book (the import control policy used to be printed every six months in a book with a red cover, hence the name Red Book) was the main tool with the government to ensure that imports were allowed only if they satisfied the strict criteria of essentiality and indigenous non-availability. It used to be said in those days that small-scale industries in India were born out of the pages of the Red Book!

In the early stages of entrepreneurship development in the country, this policy led to the production of some low-quality goods in the small-scale sector. But due to acute shortage of foreign exchange, it was inevitable that some of the goods produced in the small-scale sector would fail to satisfy the desired levels of quality. However, as industrialisation progressed, the quality of goods in the small-scale sector also improved substantially, and many of the products by small entrepreneurs from India are now able to find foreign markets through exports.

Next to the change in the policy on imports, the most important step taken by the government for entrepreneurship development was liberalisation of credit. In the pre-Independence days, the one factor lacking the most among all the factors of production was capital. Those who wished to start new businesses had to have their own capital, or had to be in a position to generate capital on the security of their own land assets. Banks would not lend money to anyone merely on the viability of the project or the marketability of the products. They were interested in knowing how solid his or her assets were, not how sound his or her proposal was. Bank loans in those days were the monopoly of a few families, and those outside this privileged circle had very little chance of raising funds, however deserving their projects were. The joke in those days was that the banks would lend money only if the borrower could convince the bank manager that he really had enough capital of his own to need a loan from a bank!

The bank nationalisation programme introduced by the government proved to be a great blessing for the success of the entrepreneurship development programme in the small-scale sector. It facilitated the entry of a new class of entrepreneurs who would otherwise have never thought of starting industries of their own. A number of graduates from engineering and technical institutions opted to start new industries of their own instead of seeking employment in other establishments. Many of them started manufacturing ancillaries and components required by large industries, as the nationalised banks found such ventures quite eligible for financing.

Within a short period after liberalised credit proved to be successful, the government introduced two new schemes which proved to be of great assistance to small entrepreneurs – schemes for supply of machinery and equipment required by the small entrepreneurs on hire-purchase basis, and provision of factory accommodation in industrial estates with facilities like power, water, technical guidance, etc., on rent.

In order to give technical guidance to start new enterprises and help in modernising existing industries, the central government established a network of service institutes under the development commissioner for small-scale industries, one each in every state, manned by experts in subjects of direct interest to small industrialists. Very soon, extension centres for special subjects of interest to small industries were established in places where such industries were concentrated, and by the middle of the 1960s, about fifty such centres were providing technical advisory services to small industries all over the country. Extension services provided by the Small Industries Service Institutes included not only advice on technical matters, but also on business management, participation in government purchase programmes, marketing, and so on. Several model schemes of production were prepared by the small industries organisation and distributed widely among those interested in starting new enterprises.

Mention must also be made of another important development relating to the growth of small industries, which was the inflow of several special skills bought in by refugees from Pakistan after Partition. The new places where these skilled workers settled down in India became flourishing centres for entrepreneurship development, thanks to the assistance extended to them by the government under the development programme for small industries. The growth of the sports goods industry in Jallandar and Meerut, the shoe industry in Agra, glassware and scientific instruments in Ambala, and foundry in Batala, are examples.

An encouraging feature of entrepreneurship development in India is that a large number of small industrialists could progress towards becoming medium or even large industries through the success of their small-scale ventures. The success story of entrepreneurship growth in India through small industries attracted the attention of several developing countries, which secured the services of experts from India for their small industries development programmes through the assistance of the United Nations and its agencies, and also through bilateral agreements with India.

An important reason for the success of the small industries development programmes in India was that these programmes were evolved after detailed discussions in the forum of the Small Scale Industries Board which had as its members the ministers and directors of industries of all the states, the representatives of the Reserve Bank, Planning Commission and other such institutions, besides the representatives of the concerned ministries of the central government. The meetings of the board were held frequently and the merits as well as shortcomings of various programmes were discussed in great detail at these meetings. I remember with great pleasure the highly practical comments and suggestions given by Venkataraman at these meetings, based on his experience in Tamil Nadu.

Venkataraman indeed played a pioneering role in both the designing and implementing stages of these programmes.

My Recollections

P Murari

> *The author, remembering his long association with R Venkataraman, provides an overview of Venkataraman's different aspects and categorises him as a constitutional president, rather than a copybook president.*

R Venkataraman, former president of India, passed away on 27 January 2009, just a year away from his hundredth birth centenary. With his passing away, India lost one of its greatest sons, a unique amalgamation of a statesman, administrator *par excellence*, a *savant*, a towering political leader, an unparallelled labour administrator and above all, a warm human being. With his demise, the light was extinguished for many of us across the length and breadth of this country.

It was my wont to wish him personally along with my wife on 4 December every year after our retirement, over phone in the early hours of the morning, both during our sojourn in Delhi and subsequently, after my relocation to Chennai post-2006. Strangely, when I wished him on 4 December 2008 and informed him that my wife and I would like to come and seek his blessings on the hundredth year of his birth, for the first time he stated that if I had any love and affection for him I should not wish him so and should be happy if he passed away quickly and peacefully, without being a burden on anyone. Perhaps it was an early intimation of his mortality. Be that as it may, it still reflected another great and positive facet of his character; he always had a lot of consideration for all human beings, extending to the fact that he would not like to be a burden on all those who cared for him. Such was the sterling nature and outstanding character of the man who lived and died for all the exemplary ideals which he admired, cherished and followed strictly to the letter till his dying day.

I was fortunate to come in contact with him and blessed to have such a great human being as my boss and mentor in the formative years of my service. It was in the year 1963, six years into my service, that I was selected by him to take over as the chairman of a cooperative sugar mill in Udumalpet, a dormant unit which he wanted to revive. I was totally new to the sugar industry and told him so. He brushed aside my apprehensions and stated that I had it in me to take up this challenge. I am today proud to say that I did not let him down, and when I left that post in 1966, I had not only revived the mill but also placed it on the road to prosperity.

Based on that experience, he next asked me to take up the extremely important post of Director of Handlooms and Textiles, to look after not only the handloom industry, which had immense potential for exports to foreign countries, but also to bring about a synergy between the cooperative spinning mills and handloom weavers.

At this stage I would like to mention that Venkataraman was not only the architect of Tamil Nadu's industrialisation, who attracted many budding industrialists from far and wide to invest in the state, but he also established industrial estates for the benefit of the micro, small, and medium industries. Today, these clusters are a byword for efficiency and have been established all over the country. He was also the first to negotiate with Japan and set up fourteen cooperative spinning mills in the state, something no one had ever contemplated earlier. There were a number of sceptics who gloomily forecast failure for this bold venture but as industries minister, Venkataraman not only successfully established these mills, which are running even today in an outstanding fashion, but also ensured that the yarn produced by these mills met the demand of both the handloom and textile sectors. These twin initiatives of Venkataraman, I think, suffice to place him permanently at the top of the list of those who were instrumental in the industrialisation of Tamil Nadu. Accordingly, for the next two years, I had the honour, privilege and opportunity to work with R Venkataraman, until the political situation changed and I was sent out on deputation to the United States of America by the Ministry of Commerce to work as general manager of the Handicrafts and Handloom Export organisation. In this post too, R Venkataraman's initial mentorship stood me in good stead during my four-year tenure.

As a result of the changed political situation in Tamil Nadu, Venkataraman moved to higher positions in the Government of India, apart from the most prestigious position of the chairman of the UN Administrative Tribunal. In Delhi, at different points of time, he served as the minister for industry, finance, and defence, before being elevated to the post of the vice president of India.

As Shakespeare noted, there is a tide in the affairs of men, which taken at the flood, leads on to recognition and good fortune, something I enjoyed when I had the occasion to get the unique opportunity and privilege of serving Venkataraman again in his capacity as chairman of the committee set up by the government of India to celebrate the fortieth anniversary of India's independence and later, Jawaharlal Nehru's birth centenary. I consider this assignment, spread over a period of two years, to be one of the most rewarding ones I had ever experienced. I got first-hand knowledge as to how Venkataraman operated, bringing together diverse elements with differing views and getting them to sharply focus on the objective at hand, namely, to successfully conduct the Jawaharlal Nehru centenary and the fortieth anniversary of India's independence. As member secretary of the committee, I was amazed to learn the speed at which he could separate the grain from the chaff and hit upon the correct solution in no time, but above all, I really learnt the nuances of man-management, since the committee consisted of ministers, eminent politicians, academicians, journalists, cultural icons with Former Prime Minister Rajiv Gandhi as vice-chairman.

It was indeed a red-letter day for me when I was appointed secretary to the president of India in November 1989, halfway into the tenure of President R Venkataraman. Later, I learnt that he had asked for me to man the post, which added to my pleasure, yet made me feel very humble that I was given an opportunity to work alongside such an outstanding personality.

I still recall my first interaction with the president in this new capacity of mine. I approached him with great trepidation and informed him that since I was totally new to the post and the swearing-in ceremony of the prime minister and the cabinet was just two days away, I did not know what my role was in the whole exercise. With a smile, he enacted the entire ceremony for my benefit, which reassured me quite a lot. When I told him tongue-in-cheek that it was a wonderful piece of acting, he quietly mentioned that politicians have to be actors at some stage or the other.

The years 1989–91 were indeed highly turbulent years. Both VP Singh and Chandra Shekhar were at the helm of minority governments. Coalitions, at best, were unsatisfactory political arrangements and the president had at all times to provide his wise and sane counsel to keep things on an even keel. Even after the fall of the VP Singh government, the president was absolutely correct in his approach. Notwithstanding the fact that Rajiv Gandhi had indicated his support to the minority Chandra Shekhar group, he consulted a number of legal luminaries and met all the coalition partners who had extended support before he called upon Chandra Shekhar to assume the reins of government. Such was his intimate knowledge of the Constitution and his commitment to discharge the onerous duties and responsibilities as a head of state and to eliminate any whisper of criticism in all decisions taken. It was indeed sad that the Chandra Shekhar government was short-lived because of the withdrawal of support by the Congress. Yet again, the president consulted a number of legal pundits, including the attorney general, before he took what I know was the most painful decision – to dissolve Parliament and call for fresh elections.

Against the backdrop of the political and economic turmoil of those two years of 1989–90 and at the beginning of 1991, a number of political stalwarts and others considered Venkataraman to be a copybook president. Having worked intimately with him for three years, I can unequivocally state that he always considered very carefully the pros and cons of an issue before arriving at a decision which was almost invariably correct. Under those circumstances, I would characterise him as truly a constitutional president. He once told me that only the president takes the oath to honour, defend and protect the Constitution.

The year 1991 was truly a horrendous year. It saw the assassination of our most beloved Prime Minister Rajiv Gandhi while he was campaigning in Sriperumbudur, Tamil Nadu. It was impossible to even imagine the magnitude of that irreparable loss or what the aftermath would bring. The president took charge of almost everything since there was only a lame-duck government. All of Rashtrapati Bhavan worked on a war footing to counter a possible repetition of what had happened in 1984 after the assassination of Indira Gandhi, the then prime minister of India. The strong sentiments aroused against South Indians in general and Tamilians in particular in New Delhi and its surroundings led the president to order the chief of army staff to organise flag marches throughout areas where Tamilians were concentrated. Thanks to him, not a single drop of blood was shed. I think more than anything else, this act should be etched in golden letters when the history of those times is chronicled. He also took the bold step, perhaps the first in independent India, of dividing the elections into two parts, something no one had envisaged earlier. In retrospect, it seemed the best course the country could have adopted.

His knowledge of the Constitution was truly legendary. I recall, when the union cabinet recommended the dissolution of the Tamil Nadu Assembly in 1991, I put up a note against the background that the governor of Tamil Nadu had not sent his report against the government and hence, based on the Supreme Court judgment in the SR Bommai, case it might be imprudent to accept the union cabinet's decision. The president then called me for a discussion, pointed out the relevant features of the Constitution regarding the dissolution of the state governments under Article 356, and brought to my notice that even without the governor's adverse report one could still accept the Cabinet's decision, since the founding fathers had thought it fit to add an alternative clause to this effect. Truly, a lesson for me, to my discomfiture, with regard to the provisions of the Indian Constitution.

I do not know whether anyone is aware of Venkataraman's delightful sense of humour. Suffice to quote two instances. When the president of a small Pacific island state called on the president, he stated that he had problems handling a population of 9,000 in his island nation. With a twinkle in his eyes, our president remarked that he could understand the travails of his guest, since his own Rashtrapati Bhavan, covering an area of 450 acres, had over 13,500 people to be looked after and administered properly!

On another occasion, during our first ever state visit to the Philippines, the Philippines president asked Venkataraman whether a parliamentary form of government or a presidential one would be best suited to her country. Again, with a smile, our president replied 'Madam, the grass is always greener on the other side.'

The First Lady, whom we all called Amma, was the perfect foil to His Excellency and meticulous in attention to every detail. She supervised not only the arrangements in the guests' suites in the south wing of Rashtrapati Bhavan, which housed VVIPs, but would also instruct the staff on every occasion, checking menus, flower arrangements, etc. Above all, she was a very warm human being, caring intensely for the underprivileged, the poor and the needy. In fact, in Rashtrapati Bhavan, during the five years of their stay, all birthdays and anniversaries were always celebrated amongst children, particularly the visually challenged, physically disabled and those otherwise in need of care and consideration. I recall, she once called me to her room to display an article which had appeared in *The Times of India*, regarding the pathetic condition of the widows of Vrindavan. She directed me to immediately have an inquiry conducted and to ensure that some measures were put in place by the Government of Uttar Pradesh to look after these widows. I had to report to her from time to time regarding the action taken in this matter, both by the centre and state governments. Such was her intensity with regard to care for the poor and the needy. In fact, during their years in Rashtrapati Bhavan, the president took the unprecedented step of sitting for group photos with all the Class III and Class IV staff at the time of their retirement, so that they would possess a photograph with the president. This was something which had never been done before.

The First Lady took firm steps to help the wives of the staff and with my wife, set up Kalyan Kendras for training women workers in tailoring and allied activities, and organising other social service activities for the benefit of the staff of Rashtrapati Bhavan.

Perhaps, apart from what the president achieved in the political and economic fields, what deserves equal mention is what he did for the promotion of fine arts, music and dance. During his stay in Rashtrapati Bhavan, every fortnight the auditorium reverberated to the sounds of dance, music and drama to which all the top political dignitaries and other special guests were invited. This provided an opportunity to eminent musicians and dancers, as also budding artistes, to display their talents and gain recognition. His doors were always open to eminent personalities like MS Subbulakshmi, Ustad Bismillah Khan and so on, who would stay at Rashtrapati Bhavan and enthrall with their vast repertoire of music and dance.

Perhaps one of the greatest contributions R Venkataraman made lay in the preservation of priceless works of art in Rashtrapati Bhavan, and in ensuring that these were displayed in museums so that people could view these valuable items. My wife was requested to undertake this task, and in the course of a year, four museums were set up. The first, the *toshkana,* contained all the gifts and other precious items which were gifted by heads of states to the president and his family, the second, called the Marble Hall which contained marble sculptures and portraits of all the viceroys and others representing the British Raj, a third one with special artifacts, and finally the one at No. 2 Willingdon Crescent, with several rooms containing articles and paintings relating to the lives of the former presidents. In fact, these museums attracted worldwide attention.

As supreme commander of the armed forces, Venkataraman was sensitive to the needs of this critical sector. He never declined an invitation or opportunity to interact with all the wings of the armed services. Be it the passing-out parade at the Indian Military Academy at Dehradun, interacting with the National Defence Academy at Kadhakvasla or presenting the colours to the regiments at Bangalore, he always accepted these assignments. Interacting with the armed forces from top to bottom made them feel that the supreme commander was highly receptive to their needs and requirements. I had the privilege of accompanying him in all these interactions, during which I also visited Tawang in Arunachal Pradesh and the highest point where our forces were stationed, Nathu La. I still recollect with nostalgia an incident reflecting his great concern for those who had served the country with courage and bravery. He broke protocol in calling on the severely ailing Field Marshal Cariappa, who was undergoing treatment at the Bangalore military hospital. This grand old man was deeply touched by this gesture and insisted, in spite of the objections from doctors and nurses, on receiving his supreme commander in full military uniform.

On demitting office in July 1992, the president and his family moved out the very day his term got over, from Rashtrapati Bhavan to Chennai. I personally escorted them. The president wanted to live in his own house at Kotturpuram, but the IB objected from the point of view of security, so he had to move to a more secure accommodation on Greenways Road. But since there were some stray comments on him getting government accommodation he finally relocated to Delhi and made it his permanent home where he lived till his last days. Till his last breath, he was mentally and physically alert, sharply focussed, and even after his retirement he attended functions and provided sane counsel and advice to all. It can be said of him that all the finest elements combined in him so that nature could proudly say, here was a man. Albert Einstein stated on Mahatma Gandhi's death that such a man will never walk again on the face of this earth. The same could also be said of the late R Venkataraman.

The Father of Industrialisation of Tamil Nadu

PR Ramasubrahmaneya Rajha

R Venkataraman prepared Tamil Nadu to compete on the global stage, by encouraging the development of industry as well as the most important resource of all – manpower.

It is my privilege to have been asked to write an article about respected R Venkataraman for the commemorative volume being brought out on his birth centenary celebrations. If he could have lived another three years, maybe it would have been our great privilege to celebrate his centenary along with him.

I used to meet RV in Chennai and Delhi periodically even after his retirement as the president of India, offer my respects and seek his blessings, which inspired me to take up more and more projects. Our respected and beloved 'Bharat Ratnas' K Kamaraj and RV, were solely responsible for the growth of our Ramco Group of Industries as seen today. My revered father PAC Ramaswamy Raja in his advanced age of nearly sixty-five years was encouraged to take up the cement industry, even though traditionally he had been the pioneer in establishing the spinning industry in backward and agricultural areas in 1937.

Kamaraj and RV were very confident that my father had the vision and the courage to take up this seemingly impossible task. They encouraged my father in the gigantic task of establishing a cement factory near Virudhunagar, the birth place of Kamaraj. My father reluctantly accepted that challenge. He was also encouraged by his cousin PS Kumarasamy Raja, former chief minister of Madras Presidency and then governor of Orissa. My father relied on his support and guidance. Unfortunately, Kumarasamy Raja passed away in 1957, leaving a vacuum in my father's efforts in putting up the cement factory. But RV, who was the industries and labour minister in the Kamaraj cabinet then, filled the void. RV rendered all his moral support to see that the cement factory was established.

The reason why RV supported this venture so much, in my opinion, was not only to give the cement factory to my father but also to oversee Tamil Nadu's march towards industrialisation by starting such a core industry. The people of Tamil Nadu are extremely lucky to have had an industries minister like RV. Kamaraj gave RV a free hand in this matter as he knew RV's integrity and capability to work. Kamaraj and RV took the unprecedented step of investing ten lakh rupees at that time in Madras Cement Ltd as capital, in order to encourage people to invest in this company. By showing the confidence the Tamil Nadu government had in my father thus, they helped promote this industrial venture.

My father had to sacrifice his health and put in nearly twenty hours of work a day to raise the capital of two crores without going to the capital market. As he had built a strong reputation for himself among the investors of our spinning mills, he could approach many friends personally and request them to invest in Madras Cements Ltd. He succeeded in his attempt. He had to encounter many difficulties like getting a mining license for limestone, obtaining a power connection, railway siding and so on. RV personally got involved to sort out these difficulties and expedited the approvals, for which we are ever grateful to him. He was not merely an industries minister legislating rules and regulations. In fact, he was acting as a public relations officer for industrialists to obtain various approvals.

Businesspeople in Tamil Nadu were generally shy in taking risks, as compared to North Indians who were leading industrialists at that time. It is RV who encouraged Tamil Nadu industrialists and advised them to come forward and seize the opportunities available in the growing Indian economy. He practically handheld them and made their ventures successful. In fact, whenever he had the opportunity to bring new industries to Tamil Nadu, he selected the right industrialists, invited them to his office, and advised them on the right projects, assuring his moral support and guidance. That created a conducive atmosphere in Tamil Nadu for establishing many industries, particularly the automobile auxiliary sector which came up in and around Chennai, using technical collaboration with leading companies from German, England and USA.

This paved the way for several leading automobile manufacturers from Europe, Korea, Japan, England and America to eagerly choose Tamil Nadu for setting up their ventures. They believed that they would get assured supplies of quality automobile parts tailored to their specifications. I can confidently say that RV has made Tamil Nadu the Detroit of India. Thousands of young Tamilian engineers got placed in automobile and other industries near Chennai.

The people of Tamil Nadu should also be grateful to RV, among other things, for having encouraged young people to study, so as to get good jobs and remuneration. This has boosted the purchasing power of the middle class in Tamil Nadu, which in turn has directly improved India's GDP growth.

As far as politics is concerned, RV was basically a Congressman, having made a lot of sacrifices as a freedom fighter, besides being a successful lawyer. In the early days, he fought for the rights of labourers, which indirectly helped industries increase their productivity. Kamaraj had also given the portfolios of electricity and technical education to RV. He made the best use of these opportunities for the benefit of the people of Tamil Nadu. As the minister for technical education, he granted permission to establish a state polytechnic in the name of my revered father, who was very keen to promote technical education in Rajapalayam. The permission given to us was a mark of his respect for my revered father. He was also responsible for starting many engineering colleges, as well as the IIT in Madras.

In spite of his great contributions towards the welfare of the people and his initiatives to give them the chance to earn and live in a dignified way, he was defeated along with Kamaraj in the Tamil Nadu State Legislative Assembly election in 1967. But that did not discourage him in any way. Fortunately, Indira Gandhi chose to utilise his services and talents in the centre, giving him the opportunity to exhibit his talents for the benefit of the entire nation. Here I must admire his political manoeuvreability in central politics. He worked as a member of the Planning Commission, he was the industries minister, finance minister, defence minister, vice-president and then finally the president of India. I don't think any other politician has had such widespread opportunities to serve the people of our nation. He brought out many worthy changes in industrial policy and taxation, modernised defence equipments and ensured that debates in the Rajya Sabha were disciplined. He is, therefore, a proud son of Tamil Nadu whom we miss today.

After my father's demise, he encouraged me, as a young man, to continue my father's tradition, and helped me to improve upon the various industries initiated by my father. He advised me on many important matters, and helped me come out of several difficult situations in my efforts to expand these industries. I am greately indebted to him forever. He was kind enough to participate in my father's centenary celebrations held at Rajapalayam and made it a great success. My family will always remember the love and affection he showered on us.

In Service of the Services

Admiral (Retd) RH Tahiliani

> R Venkataraman's close connection with the defence services extended well beyond his tenure as defence minister of India. He embodied the qualities instilled in the forces.

It was my great good fortune that I got to know R Venkataraman rather well when I was flag officer commanding-in-chief (Southern Naval Command) in 1982 and later as flag officer commanding-in-chief (Western Naval Command) in 1983 and the first half of 1984. Venkataraman, as defence minister at that time, had visited these commands. During his first visit to Cochin in 1982, I accompanied him to the Lakshwadeep Islands. He was a gentleman to the core and always wore a beautiful smile on his face. He had been a great asset to whichever organisation he had led till then.

I got to know from reading about him that in his younger years he had been the minister for industries in the erstwhile Madras state. If that part of the country is today well industrialised, a good deal of the credit must go to Venkataraman.

During his first visit to Cochin, at a function in his honour, I introduced him to all the ladies present and asked the ladies to tell Venkataraman, the defence minister then, what difficulties they were facing. They were quite frank. The Chiefs of Staff Committee had, a couple of months earlier, proposed to the government that officers in the armed forces should be given some perquisites to cater to the hardships which are implicit in being part of the armed forces, particularly for the families. R Venkataraman had said that he would look at the problems when he got back to Delhi. True to his word, during his next visit to Cochin, he told us all that he had discussed the problem with then Prime Minister Indira Gandhi, and that the government was about to sanction free school transport for school-going children and free rations up to the rank of full colonel and equivalent. This was implemented in early 1983, before I was transferred to Western Naval Command.

In August 1984, he became vice-president of India. I became chief of naval staff in November the same year and hence did not have a chance to serve the country under him directly. But from all accounts, he was very down to earth as defence minister. He was much more than just a politician; he was a statesman par excellence. He had a reputation of being very thorough in going through the files. In fact, some affectionately labelled him a good bureaucrat.

He was obviously fond of the armed forces and all that they stood for. Whenever there were any functions, like a musical evening, in the vice-president's house, the three chiefs of staff were invariably invited. I have checked with a couple of my seniors who were chiefs of the other two services, and they are full of praise for Venkataraman in the discharge of his duties as defence minister. He preferred to stay in the WNC Mess' VIP suite on the seventh floor, which had a great view of the Arabian Sea, rather than Raj Bhavan, even when he came for purely political work. I would receive him at the airport and drop him at the WNC mess. He would invariably invite me for lunch before I went to see him off at the airport.

In 1989 he had become president of India, and sometime during his presidential tenure he paid a visit to Sikkim, when I was the governor of that beautiful, peaceful state with happy and affectionate people. An easier and gentler guest would be difficult to find. Janaki Venkataraman was an equally gracious and gentle soul. I would like to record an instance about my mother and her failing memory. Although she knew that the president of India was visiting Sikkim and would be staying with us at Raj Bhavan, she had forgotten this fact when she was actually introduced to him on his arrival. So she asked me in Sindhi, 'Who is he?' I explained in Sindhi that he was the president of India about whom I had mentioned before his arrival. My mother was obviously not too impressed with this fact! So her next question was, 'Where does he live?' I explained to her that he lives in the Rashtrapati Bhavan in Delhi. President Venkataraman, who understood this exchange, had a big smile on his face throughout!

I have in my career come across many politicians, but I can honestly say that I have not found another who had the same qualities of head and heart that R Venkataraman had. Most politicians do not pay interest outside their own spheres of work. Not so with Venkataraman. Although he did not wear a uniform, he had the same qualities which are instilled in the uniform fraternity – country first, our subordinates next and ourselves always last.

India's Youth and the Challenge of Sustainable Development

RK Pachauri

RK Pachauri discusses the pressing environmental issues of the day as he highlights the importance of taking cues from R Venkataraman's approach to conflict resolution and balancing competing interests – mediation, moderation and sustainable development.

Venkataraman was one of the tallest leaders we have had in this country. He was not only a part of the freedom movement, but had a prominent role in guiding the destiny of Indian society after Independence. He represented not just a high level of intellectual leadership, but strength of character, symbolised by his active participation in the Quit India Movement of 1942 and detention by the British government for two years under the Defence of India Rules.

Venkataraman was a person of global vision, deeply sensitive to the challenges that a developing society had to face. His awareness of how national and international challenges could be dealt with by a newly-independent India was actually sharpened by the exposure he had had in 1946, when he was included in the panel of lawyers to go to Malaya (as it was then known) and Singapore to defend Indian nationals charged with offences of collaboration during the Japanese occupation of both these societies. This was the period when Indian society was clearly divided between the bravery and nationalistic aggressiveness of Netaji Subhas Chandra Bose and Gandhiji's non-violent and peaceful approach to fighting for independence. Venkataraman realised the importance of resolving these conflicting choices, and as a follower of Gandhiji in the Quit India Movement, he apparently also found defending those who had sympathies and support for Netaji and the Indian National Army (which fought the British through armed action) an important duty.

India later became an independent country, but organised economic activities were still a very small part of the national economy. Management of industrial units and other sectors was characterised by a feudal approach that often denied the working class requisite freedom and rights by which they would get a fair deal. This prompted Venkataraman to take deep interest in labour issues, as a culmination of which he took up the organisation of the labour section of the Tamil Nadu Provincial Congress Committee in 1944. In 1949, he founded the *Labour Law Journal*, which published important decisions on the subject of labour laws and practices. As a result, he became closely involved with trade union activity and was seen as a leader by plantation workers, dock workers, railway workers and even working journalists. His journey into politics was, therefore, inevitable, and he distinguished himself not only as a member of Parliament but also as a minister in the state government and at the national level. In view of his intellectual capability, he served in the Planning Commission as a member and, of course, in several positions in the Government of India, including as union minister of finance in 1980.

It is of utmost importance for the young people of this country to be acquainted with the lives and work of outstanding leaders like Venkataraman, because these provide inspiration and guidance to the leaders of tomorrow in tackling challenges that are now coming to the surface and which perhaps did not get early attention soon after Independence. It is also important for the youth of today to understand the functioning of global forces and constraints on our development choices which have a profound impact on the growth and development of Indian society. We are living in a globalised world, and as the Indian economy grows, so would its trade with several countries of the world and its dependence on harnessing global forces for the benefit of human society at large, at the global level and, of course, in the interests of Indian society, which our government is primarily responsible for. Of particular relevance to India is the growing challenge of sustainable development, which clearly is not in evidence in those countries of the world which have led the race towards rapid and large-scale industrialisation. While industrial growth and development have provided human society with a large number of tangible benefits in the form of multiplicity of goods and services, to which a large part of the population today has access, this has not been achieved without a number of negative impacts.

First, the disparity between rich and poor has grown much wider in most countries of the world. In a country like India with a population of about 1.2 billion, which is likely to increase significantly before it levels off, it is important to remember that the growing prosperity of a few and continuing stagnation of a large number is clearly not a sustainable condition. At the same time, industrial growth worldwide has led to major impacts on the global commons, most crucially exemplified by the increase in the concentration of greenhouse gases (GHGs) in the earth's atmosphere, which is leading to climate change with all its ill-effects in different parts of the world. As far as India is concerned, this is a country that is and will become increasingly vulnerable to the impacts of climate change, including the problem of sea level rise for a country that has an extensive coastline. India also has the largest number of farmers among all the countries of the world who are dependent on rain-fed agriculture. The change in precipitation patterns is, therefore, likely to affect water availability for this group of farmers, and in those areas where the impacts would be negative, it would further exacerbate the stresses that agriculture, dependent on rain, is being subjected to on account of a range of other factors. Climate change may also result in higher frequency and intensity of floods, droughts, heat waves and extreme precipitation events.

The effects of climate change on health are also likely to be serious, not only because of the threat of higher morbidity and mortality on account of floods, droughts and heat waves, but also on account of increase in vector-borne diseases. Future generations would bear the brunt of these, and clearly they could adversely affect opportunities for development, with serious consequences for those yet unborn. Indian society would have to adapt to the impacts of climate change, because even if there is a sharp reduction in emissions of GHGs at the global level, a certain level of climate change will continue for several decades.

As a major economic power on the global stage, India would also be under a great deal of pressure to modify its path of development such that it can limit the emissions of GHGs in the future. Mitigation of emissions would, therefore, have to become an important part of India's development policy. However, for important reasons of equity and common but differentiated responsibility, India cannot forgo opportunities for development purely to reduce emissions of GHGs under pressure from other countries. Yet, India cannot also afford to blindly emulate the example of the developed world, which has pursued a highly energy-intensive and therefore, emissions-intensive path of development. For India, the co-benefits of a low carbon and low GHG intensity path of development are substantial. These co-benefits are in the nature of higher levels of energy security, larger health benefits because of lower levels of air pollution at the local level, greater employment opportunities and higher levels of agricultural production. Agriculture is one sector where the impacts of climate change are showing a negative trend in terms of yield of certain crops in India. With a growing population, higher incomes and limited land available for agriculture, issues of food security are of enormous concern to Indian society. Overall, therefore, India would have to devise a pattern of development which would be distinctly different from that pursued by the industrialised nations. It was perhaps in view of this impending challenge that Mahatma Gandhi saw the benefits of a path distinctly different from that established by Britain for instance. An interesting anecdote brings this out. Mahatma Gandhi was once asked if he expected India to attain the same standard of living as Britain. He replied, 'It took Britain half the resources of the planet to achieve this prosperity. How many planets will a country like India require?'

Taking into account the challenge that India faces at the global level, the youth of today must take the lead in defining a path which ensures sustainable development of Indian society and the Indian economy. To understand the powerful appeal of such an approach, we must remind ourselves of the simple definition of sustainable development, which essentially is that form of development which allows the present generation to meet its needs without compromising on the ability of future generations to meet their own needs. Continuing degradation and damage to the earth's global resources and ecosystems, and changes in the earth's climate system, are likely to impact unfavourably on opportunities for India to continue on a path of growth and development and at a rate that it would need for wiping out widespread poverty.

To the arguments of major co-benefits for India from a low GHG intensive approach must be added the arguments for protecting the environment at the local level as well. Already, we in India have polluted the air that we breathe, the water that flows in our rivers, and the soil on which we cultivate essential crops, to an extent that is imposing huge costs on this society. TERI's GREEN India 2047 project clearly documented the high cost, even in economic terms, of pursuing a business-as-usual approach. The consequences of such an approach if pursued unchanged up to 2047 would create a totally unacceptable condition with very high costs in the form of environmental damage and degradation. One sector in which we must deviate rapidly from business as usual is in the consumption and production of energy. The rate at which the transport sector is growing, for instance, with overwhelming dependence on private vehicular transport, is detrimental to prospects of energy security, given the fact that Indian imports of oil are growing at a very rapid rate to meet the demand imposed by this sector. On the supply side, since Indian coal reserves are proving inadequate for meeting even today's needs, a shift to renewable sources of energy and much more efficient use of energy of all forms is an economic and strategic imperative that India cannot ignore.

The term 'demographic dividend' is used glibly in a number of contexts in this country today because India has now become an overwhelmingly young society with almost half the population under the age of twenty-five. We, therefore, have a very large number of people who have a greater stake in the future than at any other time in the history of the country. We have to take into account the aspirations of these hundreds of millions of India's youth. This should, therefore, entitle the youth of this country to become involved in setting the development agenda of this society. That, of course, will not happen immediately in terms of their involvement in formal decision-making structures. Hence, we need to mobilise them for action outside the system so that through the articulation of appropriate choices by civil society, youth can influence decisions and strategies that would ensure a secure future for all of them. It is in this regard that the lives of fearless, intellectually driven and dedicated leaders like R Venkataraman can inspire action by focussing on the future far beyond what one sees today as a preoccupation with conforming to the consumerist trends in evidence. If Indian youth were to bring about such a shift, this would not only provide a powerful model for the rest of the world to follow, but would also be a solution to the global problems of climate change, unsustainable development and threat to the earth's ecosystems that we are facing today.

The Trade Union Movement as a Political Force

TS Sankaran

A man of vision whose words remain relevant even today, RV was the consummate professional when dealing with matters official.

One of the labour ministers under whom I worked in the Ministry of Labour of the Government of India asked me, soon after he became my boss, what is meant by labour policy and what is the Government of India's labour policy? I had no direct answer to that question, and so prevaricated by saying that Part III and Part IV of the Constitution of India dealing with such issues as Freedom of Association (Article 19[1] [c]), Prohibition of Forced Labour (Article 23), Prohibition of Child Labour (Article 24), Equal Pay for Equal Work (Article 39[d]), Right to Work and Social Security (Article 41), Just and Humane Conditions of Work and Maternity Relief (Article 42), Living Wage (Article 43), Participatory Management (Article 43-A), et al., add up to what may be loosely described as labour policy. At the same time, I added that quite a few of the above, more particularly matters relating to conditions of work and welfare, wages and social security, and so on are in

Part IV of the Constitution and hence not justifiable. Even more importantly, the labour policy of our country as it had evolved in (then) recent years had become restrictive and suspicious of labour, for the very simple reason that labour policy if anything was only a handmaid of economic policy, which was more concerned with GDP, rate of growth, fiscal deficit and so on. That labour policy should be an essential part of social policy, dealing with employment, wages, and living conditions, and that Article 39 of the Constitution of India mandates the government of the day to follow the principles incorporated in it, were matters of no avail; the workers and their issues became secondary to all other issues.

All these thoughts and more came to my mind when my good friend Gopal Gandhi requested me to write a piece for the publication that is planned to be brought out in the centenary year of our former president R Venkataraman. RV, as we knew him and referred to him in our working years, was truly a civil servant's dream of a perfect minister, who was able to keep his political loyalties and compulsions aside when dealing with civil servants and the matters that came to him for decision in his day-to-day work as minister. Above all, he was a 'professional' in the full sense of the term, whether he was attending the United Nations General Assembly as a member of the Indian delegation in the late fifties, as a member, and later chairperson, of the UN Administrative Tribunal, or while dealing with industrialists in giving that enviable boost to the industrialisation of Madras state (now Tamil Nadu), or as a minister dealing with matters of high state policy and interacting with his ministerial colleagues and civil servants, or as a connoisseur of fine arts – in each and every one of these and other roles, he was professional to the core and protean in the best sense of the term.

It was in 1958, when RV was Minister of Industries (MI) in the Madras government, that I joined duties as director of handlooms and reported to him through the secretary ILC (industries, labour and cooperation). Right from then till the mid 1980s, I had been interacting with RV off and on. In the mid 1980s (1985 to be exact), he, as vice-president of India, accepted the invitation of the National Labour Law Association (of which I then was the executive president) to inaugurate a fairly important high-power seminar-cum-workshop in Delhi on constitutional law, industrial jurisprudence and labour adjudication. We thought of him not merely because of the high office he held then, but because of his past association with labour, including his starting the labour cell of the Congress party in the then Madras state and also his having been the founder-editor of the famous *Labour Law Journal*, to which I subscribe even today, uninterruptedly from 1976. He readily agreed to the invitation and I am devoting the rest of this paper to some of the thoughts he expressed in his inaugural address.

Referring to the increasing role of the Supreme Court of India, particularly through Article 32 in labour matters, RV said that it 'would appear to an orthodox trade unionist like myself who has greater faith and reliance in collective bargaining rather than on judicial process, as a symptom of sagging faith in recourse to bipartite settlement and of the weakening of the Trade Union Movement as a political force'. There are two significant thoughts in the above quote, one about collective bargaining vis-à-vis compulsory adjudication, and the other about the weakening of the trade union movement. Both are interrelated and merit some detailed examination, and that is what I will do now.

According to the ILO, 'collective bargaining is a process of decision-making. Its overriding purpose is the negotiation of an agreed set of rules to govern the substantive and procedural terms of the employment relationship as well as the relationship between the bargaining parties themselves'.[24] It is thus a rule-making process and markedly different from individual bargaining. As Prof. Allan Flanders says, one of its great achievements has been the promotion of rule of law in employment relationships.

The above is collective bargaining in the full sense of the term. More narrowly, we can construe it as an arrangement by which the employer and his workers enter into agreements periodically over terms and conditions of employment, more particularly on wages and allowances. This is the level of collective bargaining that RV perhaps had in mind, as the rest of the rule-making aspect of collective bargaining was, in India, by and large legislated in the form of acts and rules and standing orders/regulations. Even this limited collective bargaining process was vitiated in India, again by law, in the matter of strikes and lock-outs. The Indian law, to wit, the Industrial Disputes Act, 1947, treats collective bargaining and strikes (and lock-outs) as though they have no inherent relationship. If collective bargaining has not made much headway in India, it is essentially for two reasons – one, the overarching role of the state in industrial relations, and the other, the stultifying provisions in the ID act in the matter of the restrictive nature of bipartite settlements and of strikes. Above all, there has been the failure of the state to provide in the law for a procedure and mechanism to define and identify the bargaining agent on behalf of the workers in a bargaining unit.

Let me elaborate. The legacy of the Defence of India Rules, particularly Rule 81-A, which provided for prohibiting strikes and referring labour disputes to compulsory adjudication – a provision then considered necessary by the British colonial government to ensure uninterrupted war production – was incorporated into

---

[24]ILO, *Collective Bargaining in Industrialised Market Economies* (1974), p. 7

the ID act with all the consequences. It was a pre-Independence act. That it was brought into force on 1 April was not without its quirk. While agreements entered into between employers and their workmen, represented usually by a trade union, was recognised under the law, it was understandably binding only on the parties to the agreement and not on all the workmen of the employer; this was so because the trade union did not have all the workers as their members but only a part of them, and sometimes only a minor part of them. Thus was the occasion created for a settlement, entered into between the employers and representatives of workmen in the course of conciliation by a conciliation officer; such a settlement was binding on all the workers, irrespective of whether or not they are members of the trade union(s) which entered into the settlement on behalf of the workers. This was on the basis that the conciliation officer was expected to ensure that the settlement was just and fair, more particularly that the employers did not take advantage of the relative weakness of the workers and trade unions and thus impose an unfair and unequal settlement on them. *Prima facie* this appears to be a fair and equitable dispensation. But the effect of such a provision on the growth of the trade union movement and on collective bargaining can easily be imagined. And, when we find that the Government of India had even gone to the extent of enacting a legislation, namely Life Insurance Corporation (Modification of Settlement) Act, 1976, to nullify a settlement entered into by a representative union with a leading public sector employer (LIC) of which the Government of India is the owner, we realise the extent to which parties were allowed to settle matters between themselves directly. That this act was later on declared to be void by the Supreme Court of India in 1978 is not relevant here. Let us also remember that RV's mentor in labour matters in earlier years, VV Giri (another former president of India) resigned from the office of labour minister in 1954 as the Government of India persisted in tinkering with an award of the Labour Appellate Tribunal in the bank employees' case.

All these reveal the overarching role of the state in matters relating to industrial relations. Though the government (both in the centre and the states) is the largest employer in our country, both directly in departmental undertakings like railways, post offices, ordnance factories, hospital, educational institutions, public works, civil services and so on, and indirectly as the sole or the biggest owner of public undertakings, it finds itself in a difficult situation trying to balance the role of both employer and government. The tendency, therefore, gravitates towards a negative and repressive attitude as far as workers and their organisations are concerned. Maybe this is an over-simplification of the issues involved, but it cannot be denied that the state as the largest employer has driven itself into a corner, and is, in the process, falling between the two stools!

How do these developments affect the workers and their organisations? In the quote mentioned above, RV had referred to the 'weakening of the Trade Union Movement as a political force'. How true it is even today, twenty-five years after RV had said that. One of the reasons that led to this is the absence of a law regulating identification on behalf of both the employers and workers – more so on behalf of the workers – of the bargaining agent and the bargaining unit in respect of an enterprise, an area or an industry. This is a matter that has been under discussion and 'under consideration' literally for decades. Commissions and committees have examined the matter and made their recommendations, but somehow the central government seems reluctant or even afraid to enact a law in this regard. One can only guess the reason for this – is it that once this is legislated upon and things settle down after an initial period of doubt and distrust, it will strengthen the collective bargaining process and lead increasingly to the unification of the trade union movement, and as a corollary, increase in the power of trade unions as a political force? Obviously, not a consummation to be wished for devoutly!

In the face of an unfriendly, if not a hostile state, what do the workers and their organisations do? Of course, they have grown in numbers; their organisations also seem to have done likewise over the years. That the majority of the workforce is self-employed does not militate against the fact that the size of the workforce is huge enough to be greater than the total population of any other country in the world, other than China. Apart from the fact that experts think that we have a 'demographic dividend' vis-à-vis social security programmes, bulk of the workforce is in the unorganised sector, and the workers in the organised sector who can lay claim to some improvement in the matter of their living and working conditions account for only about eight per cent of the total workforce. And of this eight per cent, how many are members of one or other of the myriad registered trade unions, the bulk of which are affiliated to one or other of the dozen or so central trade unions? I don't have the numbers, but it will be no more than thirty per cent, that is, representing about two to three per cent of the total workforce. Nor do I have any figures or information of the recently enacted Trade Unions (Amendment) Act, 2001, which seems to have been directed principally for reducing the number of primary trade unions. Whatever be the outcome, surely, in terms of trade union density, we, as a nation, must be somewhere at the bottom. What with the attitude of employers towards trade unions and unionisation and the sort of sanctuary against 'trade unionism' in the IT and ITES sectors, in SEZs and so on that is being encouraged by governmental policy, or at least 'benign neglect', the trade union movement has been weakened as a bargaining power, not to speak of it being a political force as RV had wanted. The near hundred per cent unionisation in sectors like banking, ports and docks, coal mining, railways and so on seems to be a thing of the past. The prestige and maybe even 'fear' of the trade unions and their leaders seem again to be things of the past.

While one does not want anyone, least of all the state, to be in fear of the trade union movement, it is time that the legitimate place of the trade union movement in the total scheme of things was recognised and things ordered accordingly. Then and only then will the trade union movement become, as RV desired, a political force. And that is good for the country, the people, and for democracy. And this can and should predominantly be the outcome of the efforts of the movement itself, not as a splintered and competing entity but as a unified force capable of speaking in one voice about the interests and demands of the working people, who, with their dependants, constitute the bulk of the population, and whose political strength in terms of numbers isn't and has never been in doubt or dispute.

The Minister and the Mandarin

VS Arunachalam

> R Venkataraman's contribution towards defence and technological innovations was immense. He is responsible to a great extent for India's technological superiority today.

I moved to Delhi in February 1982, as scientific advisor to the defence minister of India. This also coincided with ministerial changes in the central government. R Venkataraman, affectionately referred to as RV by his colleagues and close friends, moved from the finance to the defence ministry after negotiating a major loan for the country from the gnomes of the International Monetary Fund. The ministry, at last, had a full-time minister. Until then, the prime minister (Indira Gandhi), in addition to her other portfolios, was also looking after the defence ministry. I had not met RV before this, and was hesitant about his attitude towards a department that was known more for spending money than for revenues. I need not have worried.

With a warm smile, he welcomed me to the ministry and told me that I had been specially selected to ensure that science and technology became a major determinant in the country's defence preparedness and policy-making. 'Come out with some major programmes,' he said, 'that will make our country stronger and self-reliant.' I pleaded for time to prepare a plan and used that meeting to enlist his support for modernising the administrative procedures of the Defence Research and Development Organisation (DRDO). Some of these were remnants of the Second World War colonial vintage. He asked me to meet the cabinet secretary Rao Sahib Krishnaswamy, who would help in reorganising the administrative setup. In parting, he also suggested that I dress more formally as he wanted me to participate in all high-level meetings of the ministry. My tailor Bakshi quickly took care of this requirement!

When I met Rao Sahib a few days later, I found out that the minister had already spoken to him and he was all ready to help, though he warned me of the many pitfalls ahead. Thanks to the earlier contributions of my predecessors, Prof. MGK Menon and Dr Ramanna, some of DRDO's administrative and recruitment procedures were getting modified along the lines of the Department of Atomic Energy and Department of Space. These changes were not always smooth, and occasionally I had to seek RV's help in smoothening the ruffled feathers of one administrator or another. But the real excitement in working with RV was in getting many of DRDO's path-breaking programmes sanctioned, all within a short period of a year or so.

For decades, with notable exceptions, DRDO confined itself to projects on indigenous substitution of systems and components and other services. The scientists were discouraged from addressing major programmes. I encountered a feeling of insecurity among scientists in every laboratory I visited. Naipaul's criticism of Indians preferring 'anything foreign' seemed almost true. The hesitation to trust DRDO with large projects was so pervasive that the more indigenous aircraft designs were shot down on the drawing board, than in the sky. There were so many conceptual designs, Advanced Strike Aircraft (ASA), Advanced

Strike Fighter-300 (ASF-300) and Hindustan Fighter 25 (HF25), but all were abandoned at the design stage itself.

C Subramaniam, a former minister of defence, was so concerned with the import dependence that he headed a committee, which suggested a number of radical initiatives to change the face of aeronautics in India. One of the suggestions was building a modern indigenous fighter aircraft. DRDO initiated a series of meetings, both with the air force and with the manufacturer, Hindustan Aeronautics. But everywhere we went, there was scepticism. The meetings were endless, with foreign deputations seeking numerous partnerships, and opinions were many. But there was no convergence. We had lost the collective memory of running a major aircraft programme after three decades of inaction – following HF24, a fighter that was designed and built in the late 1950s.

It took RV only two meetings to understand the challenge and its implications. He sought the advice of a senior technologist from Bangalore before making up his mind. But that technologist spoke despairingly of our technological competence and inability to pool resources and work together. He was also not sure whether the production agency would be interested in such major projects, when license production of foreign designs was the norm. As soon as that technologist left his parliamentary chamber, RV asked me to go ahead with the aircraft programme. He said he was not afraid of failure. He felt confident that the mood of the country was ready for starting such a major programme and was getting tired of unceasing imports and political compromises. It was heady working with RV then.

Every request I made to him for that project, he approved readily, including the setting up of an independent and innovative organisation, the Aeronautical Development Agency (ADA) for executing the programme. He realised that a few hundred crores was grossly inadequate for the whole programme, but suggested that I should come back to the government later for more funding. He joked about not wanting to frighten his old colleagues in the finance ministry in one go, but suggested my persuading them gently for a few hundred crores as a first shot that could be followed by more such requests. A few hundred crores!

I remember an incident while the aircraft programme was being discussed. The Soviet Union's Defence Minister Marshall Dimitri Ustinov was visiting the country. He was totally against indigenous programmes as India was a major importer of Soviet fighters, starting from MIG21 to MIG29, and he did not want to lose the political and economic power these imports leveraged. He first tried to persuade me to abandon the Light Combat Aircraft (LCA) programme by sending his ministers for aeronautics, Ivan Silayev and A Systov, to argue against it. When these meetings proved futile, he chided me angrily in a meeting where RV and all the senior officials and ministers were present, saying that he would have thrown me out of the job if I were his advisor. RV heard him out patiently through a translator, and with a smile, responded that he considered me a valuable asset for the ministry. I was saved from a dismissal! I had an occasion to mention this incident to Rajiv Gandhi, who was then a secretary of the Congress party. Rajiv jocularly responded that RV should have taken up that suggestion!

There was another occasion when RV's foresight saved the LCA programme. Rolls Royce, which had promised to supply the engine for the programme, demurred, complaining that it and its partner Germany could not supply to a country that had not signed the Nuclear Non-Proliferation Treaty. It was against all the promises the company had made earlier. It appeared as though our programme would be badly delayed, if not abandoned. But RV wasn't discouraged one bit, and suggested my approaching the Americans for the engine. It was the early

1980s and our country's relationship with the US was just then coming out of the freezer, and I wasn't sure whether I would be well received. But he was confident of his understanding of international relationships, and more specifically, the USA, and encouraged me to go there and negotiate. The Americans were also surprised by our audacity in asking for the engine that was then powering their front-line jet fighter F18. But we were able to reach an agreement and thanks to RV's foresight, we were able to prove our aircraft design with a well proven engine. While I can think of a few heroes who transformed LCA into reality, I would definitely place RV on that list for enabling DRDO to break away from a minuscule project mentality that was stunting the country from realising its full potential.

Guided missiles programme was another area where RV made a major impact. In the early 1980s, India was only manufacturing, under license, anti-tank missiles. A major indigenous reverse engineering programme for developing surface-to-air missiles was floundering as the air force wasn't interested in it. But that programme, under the inspiring leadership of an air force officer Air Vice-Marshal (Retd) Narayanan, built excellent infrastructure and laboratories for the development of missile technologies. That was also the time when APJ Abdul Kalam joined DRDO.

On the advice of RV, we formed an inter-service team, along with DRDO and manufacturing agencies, to prepare a long-range plan for the development of guided missiles. The programme aimed at identifying missiles for four roles, from low-level quick reaction surface-to-air (SAM) missiles to very long-range surface-to-surface ones. A technology demonstrator for Agni, a long-range missile, would come later. The programme as envisaged was an ambitious one, integrating design, development and manufacturing of all critical components. This was also the first programme where we integrated private manufacturing agencies into the projects.

The study team recommended a sequential development of missiles, starting from surface-to-air and surface-to-surface. But when we presented the recommendations to RV, he suggested that DRDO should embark on a simultaneous development of all four classes of missiles. He felt that this would keep the programme going even when it encountered some hitch in any project. His advice proved to be prescient, as one of the early developments of SAM encountered radar problems. But the Prithvi programme was racing ahead. RV's advice on becoming self-sufficient in all stages of development, and his financial approvals in the midst of bureaucratic objections, came in handy when India had to face embargoes and technology denials. The decade of denials was painful. Even access to scientific meetings was denied, commercial and committed orders were cancelled and political pressures were applied to abandon the programmes. But our scientists never lost heart. It took time and effort, and often we were able to develop indigenous substitutes that performed as well as the imported ones. The culture of building competence in critical technologies would come to our rescue later, especially after the Pokhran tests, when some of our scientists were abruptly sent back from the United States without even allowing them to collect their notes and personal belongings. This denial, however, proved futile, as the scientists, on return, built the indigenous fly-by-wire system in record time, and it has performed so well for over a thousand flights and is well on the way to becoming a workhorse.

RV was not connected with the first Pokhran experiment, but soon after my moving to Delhi, my predecessor Raja Ramanna and I briefed him on the status of the programme and of the subsequent developments. Some of the innovations we developed at that time for increasing efficiency and miniaturising the system were exciting, and called for a few more underground experiments. When we briefed RV about our our plan and sought permission, he persuaded the prime minister to attend a meeting in the defence ministry, where Ramanna and I presented a case for further testing of nuclear weapon systems. Apart from the two of us, RV invited only the cabinet secretary Krishnaswamy Rao and the prime minister's principal secretary PC Alexander. Indira Gandhi heard us patiently for a full hour and felt that we could go ahead with the tests. We were excited with her decision, and Ramanna rushed back to Bombay to prepare for the tests, while I flew to a defence laboratory to assess our preparedness. But within just two days, RV called me back and informed me that the prime minister had changed her mind and there would be no further tests. We were disappointed, and pleaded for a change. When both Ramanna and I requested for a meeting with the prime minister, RV smilingly refused and did not want to discuss it further. But he allowed us to continue with our research work and the digging of deep holes at Pokhran. These would come in handy later. While narrating this incident in his book, RV attributed Indira Gandhi's change of mind to American pressure. I learned later, after a few brief conversations with Rao sahib and Alexander, that at that time the prime minister was keener on economic development and did not want that pace to be stunted by denials and embargoes from Western nations and global financial institutions.

But briefing RV on the developmental status of strategic systems would help me later when I had to keep prime ministers periodically informed of the developments. With the permission of Rajiv Gandhi, who was then the prime minister, I kept RV informed of the project. He was the president then. Only one other member of the government, BG Deshmukh, was then in the know and approved our work at every stage. When Rajiv lost the election, I did not know the protocol for briefing his successor. Rajiv Gandhi agreed to my briefing VP Singh in the presence of the president. This meeting was held immediately after the farewell tea at Race Course Road. RV formally introduced me to VP Singh and informed him that I would be briefing him on the developmental progress of the strategic systems. A similar situation would recur later when Chandra Shekhar was to be briefed. But Chandra Shekhar politely suggested my continuing the briefing to the president as he was not sure how long he would remain prime minister, and he was not ready to be briefed with top-secret information involving some amount of technical details. When PV Narasimha Rao became the prime minister, he wanted to be briefed and I followed the precedent of going through RV, as other cabinet members and senior officials were yet to be briefed. Thanks to RV's foresight, I was saved, especially in times of political transitions, from carrying the heavy burden all by myself, of information related to the status of technologies and our preparedness in the area of strategic systems.

RV was the first minister I worked for, and our association was for less than two years. But I was able to establish a rapport that was friendly, though formal, which continued even after he became the vice-president and later, president of the country. RV was the ideal minister one could have wished for. He was always accessible, and ready and willing to discuss all the issues before reaching a decision. Even though he was a lawyer, and I am sure this brought about clarity in his arguments, he was willing to be briefed on technological issues. His love for science and curiosity to know things scientific, perhaps reinforced by his closeness to his daughters and sons-in-law, who were competent scientists, permeated in every technical discussion on weapons and weapon systems I had with him. I specially remember an instance when on a state visit to Italy, he overwhelmed the Italian Defence Minister Giovanni Spadolini with a masterful analysis comparing the operational performance of a European jet fighter Italy at the time had, with a MIG-29 our country was then acquiring. The Italian defence secretary, who was sitting next to me, quietly enquired whether RV was a military technologist. Later that evening, Signor Spadolini got his own back by ordering exquisite Italian vegetarian dishes for dinner that our minister had never heard of!

RV was a great sports fan. In the summer of 1983 I was with him while he was visiting the shipyard in Riga, then in the Soviet Union. It was also the day the Indian cricket team was playing the World Cup final against the West Indies at the Lord's. Unfortunately, the BBC cricket broadcast did not reach Riga for us to know the state of play. Our military attachés, who were accompanying us, installed a vital communication bridge with our high commission in London, who were periodically informing me of the progress of the innings. In turn, I would write the score as a note and pass it on to the minister. Our Russian hosts did not know what was happening, and imagined the worst, fearing that we were planning to haggle on the price of the frigate that was then under negotiation. When Kapil Dev took that incredible catch, sending the legend Viv Richards back to the pavilion, RV beamed and wrote a note saying that the match was as good as won. On seeing our minister smile, the Russians were relieved and the frigates were as good as sold! We celebrated the victory that evening in a Latvian restaurant with our Late Defence Secretary Pratap Kaul trying unsuccessfully to explain the intricacies of cricket to our Latvian friends; even many flutes of champagne did not help much.

My years in Delhi were coming to an end. It was more than ten years ago that I reported for duty to RV, and all the projects that RV had helped sanction were flourishing. DRDO had grown into a formidable organisation. I sought his advice about leaving for an academic assignment abroad. He was not happy but understood my longing. I explained that Abdul Kalam was ready to take over from me. But RV felt that he

(RV) was already beyond the retirement age and it wasn't wise to burden him with heavy responsibilities. But he understood the compulsions of the organisation and agreed with my recommendation. Just before I left, he graciously hosted a dinner for my family at Rashtrapati Bhavan. That was the last I saw him as our president.

Science and technology have enriched our nation with major achievements. The Green Revolution has replaced the begging bowl with a bread basket. The embracing of information technology has created millions of jobs and transformed our country to become technically savvy. Our scientists and technologists have broken the technology denial regimes and embargoes imposed on us by the Western countries and multilateral institutions, enabling us to explore the opportunities that atomic energy, space technology and information technologies provide. The heroes for these achievements are many. But among the politicians who encouraged and sustained these efforts through unflinching and inspirational support, RV's name stands out. The country was fortunate to have had him at the helm of affairs, especially at a time when it needed a visionary leader the most.

A PATRON OF THE ARTS

A Constant Source of Support

Amjad Ali Khan

Ustad Amjad Ali Khan recollects how R Venkataraman always provided support and encouragement to performing artistes.

India has had many presidents, but the contribution of Late President R Venkataraman will always be remembered. He was very fond of art and artists and always encouraged the traditional classical arts.

I still remember when we invited legendary singer, Late Semmangudi R Srinivas Iyer to be honoured with our annual Haafiz Ali Khan Award in Delhi. Venkataramanji hosted him in Rashtrapati Bhavan. On my request, Venkataramanji also hosted a tea party in honour of the Haafiz Ali Khan awardees in the year 1985–86. The awardees included, besides Semmangudi R Srinivas Iyer, Ustad Vilayat Khan, and two Russian musicians, Igor Frolov and Givani Mekhailov.

On UNICEF's fortieth anniversary, I had composed for an orchestra of children, which included my sons Amaan Ali Khan and Ayaan Ali Khan, called Ekta Se Shanti and Ekta Ki Shakti (International Day of Persons with Disabilities, 1987) and Venkataramanji graced the occasion and encouraged the young participants.

During several of my concerts, Venkataramanji was present in the audience and our entire family – my wife Subhalakshmiji, Amaan and Ayaan – received the blessings and love of Venkataramanji and his wife Janaki Venkataramanji.

I am sure most of the musicians and dancers of India can speak volumes about the love and encouragement they received from President R Venkataramanji. We will always miss his presence, but I am sure we can feel his presence while we are performing even now.

May his soul rest in peace.

The Epitome of Graciousness

Kapila Vatsyayan

R Venkataraman, a patron of the arts, occasionally even supported 'crazy' plans to ensure that cultural events took off successfully.

It was my privilege to know R Venkataraman over many years. I cannot recall where I met him first, in Chennai or in Delhi. However, I definitely recall his spacious house in Chennai where one would always be served filter coffee with *idli* or *upma*, where we talked about many things – the Music Academy, Kalakshetra, and specially, his concern for Rukmini Devi. In Delhi, there were numerous occasions to meet him, both at an official level as also at a personal level. I had the privilege of walking into his house when he was minister of defence, when he was vice-president, and then of course when he was the president of the Republic of India. He was always affectionate, loving, full of humour and with incisive commentary on the happenings of the day. All this was a learning experience. It was also an extremely enriching experience to have the privilege of knowing and talking to someone who held such high offices. At this moment, I can only pay my humble and sincere tribute to him.

But the occasion which I will never forget and which needs re-narration is the exhibition entitled 'Masterpieces of South

Indian Bronzes', held at the National Museum in Delhi as a special programme to coincide with the holding of the Non-Aligned Conference in 1983. It was not abnormal for then Prime Minister Indira Gandhi to call upon me directly. I was told, 'Kapila, we want to organise an exhibition to coincide with the Non-Aligned Conference.' I was thrilled. I replied spontaneously: 'Will you give me a free hand?' She said, 'All right, free hand; what free hand?' I said that I will put up an exhibition of material which has never been seen before. She said, 'All right, go ahead.'

For years I had visited practically every nook and corner in South India, especially Tamil Nadu, including small and great temples, be it in the vicinity of Kumbakonam, Tiruvarur, Chidambaram, Thanjavur or elsewhere, particularly in the company of R Nagaswamy, then director general of archaeology in the Tamil Nadu government. I knew he had registered many great pieces of sculpture, particularly bronzes, for the Religious Endowment Department. I was fascinated by some of the material that I saw. All these were in the custody of the temples of the region, but were kept in storehouses, in cellars. They were there because they were all considered to be, in the words known in traditional language, *khandithmurthis*, because there was some blemish or the other in them and they could not be worshipped! I thought this was the best opportunity to bring out these rare, magnificent bronzes and display them in an exhibition.

Nagaswamy and I worked very hard, going to each temple, trying to persuade the priests, especially Dikshitars, to loan these. They were at times reluctant, and at others, openly hostile to the idea of taking them out. Nevertheless, we succeeded by persuading, cajoling and entreating them. We did have the backing of the Government of Tamil Nadu. MG Ramachandran was the chief minister then.

It was an exhilarating experience to go through this treasure house of some of the most outstanding bronzes which lay neglected, having never seen the light of the day. We persevered and ultimately made a selection from the bronzes, naturally and understandably revolving around the Shiva theme mostly. These were largely drawn from the storage collections of the temples of Singaravelar, Sikkal, and Vadakkalattur. They also included bronzes from Thiruthuraippundi and the villages of Koilpattu, Paruthiyur and from the Vadavir temple. Some bronzes were borrowed from the Art Gallery, Thanjavur, and from the Madras Museum.

It was not so easy cleaning them and making them fit for an exhibition – some of them were full of oil and soot; some with green patina; others were covered in mud and silt. We did whatever we could, but the main problem was how to transport all these, without making them public, to Delhi. It is here that I will never forget the graciousness and the spontaneity with which R Venkataraman responded to my absolutely crazy idea.

I rushed into his room in the Ministry of Defence one day without an appointment. He was surprised, but certainly welcomed me. He asked me what brought me there. I said, 'Sir, I have a mad idea and I want your help.' He asked what idea. I said that I wanted an air force plane! He said, 'What? What do you want an air force plane for?' I said that I had a secret to share with him. I told him about the proposed exhibition, a rare and outstanding exhibition appropriate for the Non-Aligned Conference, about how Nagaswamy and I had chosen the outstanding bronzes, but transporting them to Delhi without making a fuss would be a problem. Therefore, could he very kindly give me an air force plane to transport these bronzes in? He smiled, he laughed, then said, 'You are crazy, but let me see.' He did order an air force plane to be put at our disposal to ensure that these bronzes were transported to

Delhi. Sculpture after sculpture was loaded onto the plane and brought to Delhi, unloaded, and the exhibition was held in the National Museum. This extraordinary and generous gesture of R Venkataraman I shall never forget.

The exhibition was an outstanding success. These bronzes were not put inside glass cases. It was a very different type of exhibition, and none other than the all-gracious, all-knowing and all-encouraging Grace Morley was our guide. The exhibition of South Indian bronzes held at the National Museum will remain an absolute milestone, especially in India. For this I am deeply indebted to the late R Venkataraman.

Venkataraman visited the exhibition. In his inimitable fashion, he patted me on the back, and said: 'Sometimes crazy ideas culminate in exquisite exhibitions!'

R Venkataraman was always a guide and a philosopher. There are many reminiscences I have to share about him. Two of them relate to the establishment of institutions. It was his sagacity which facilitated the establishment of the Ved Vidya Pratisthan in Ujjain. He was anxious to have an institution which would record, document and study the entire tradition of Vedic recitation and intonation. Such an institution was then established.

More significant was his role in the establishment of the Indira Gandhi National Centre for the Arts. Indeed, I might say that he was the chief draftsman of the trust deed of this institution. He gave wise counsel towards its making.

The country and the nation will always remember him with gratitude.

A Music Aficionado

L Subramaniam

> *A simple man with deep love and understanding of music, RV balanced his human instincts effortlessly with the demands of presidential protocol.*

His Excellency R Venkataraman was one of the most humble, sensitive and cultured people I have ever come across. Every artiste is aware of his passion for music and dance, and the support he gave them. He was so attuned to culture – he always knew about artistes and their achievements, and had the graciousness to honour them during his tenure as president. He handpicked deserving artistes and bestowed national awards on them. He was also the vice-president of ICCR, and a lot of welcome changes happened during his tenure.

He was a connoisseur of music and dance and encouraged all artistes. It was also during his term as the president that artistes had the great privilege and honour of performing in the Rashtrapati Bhavan, where he converted the mini movie preview theatre into a concert hall for music performances. This attracted many political figures and administrative officers, who, under normal circumstances, would not have attended these performances.

I still remember my very first concert in Rashtrapati Bhavan and his personal interest to make sure the sound equipment, the atmosphere, were all suitable. He had also invited then Prime Minister Rajiv Gandhi and other distinguished guests to the concert.

Russia

During the Indian festival in Russia, I was asked to perform with Moscow Radio Television Orchestra. It was a special concert for the Indian and the Russian presidents, held at the Tchaikovsky Hall. Our president was scheduled to arrive on the same day and he had a reception to attend as well. It was the first time that an entire evening was dedicated to a living composer. I had the pleasure of performing my double violin concerto, and after the intermission, my 'Fantasy on Vedic Chants', which I was told the president was very fond of. We finished the first half of the concert and were waiting for the presidents to arrive for the second half. Due to his long travel from Delhi to Moscow and his tiring schedule, I was under the impression that R Venkataraman may not be able to arrive in time to attend the concert. On the contrary, he came in good time and we had the privilege of performing the composition, a tribute to my mother.

After the performance, we received a standing ovation, where our president was applauding too. The appreciation and support that he portrayed during that ovation made it one of the most important moments of my life. After the concert, when we were waiting for the presidents to leave, I was asked to come to meet Venkataraman. By the time I negotiated the crowd and reached them, the president was about to get into the car. In spite of security risks, as soon as he saw me, he just waited and we had a memorable conversation about the concert, which made all the security people tense, as he was out in the open outside Tchaikovsky Hall.

Subsequently, I had the privilege of having our president as a special guest on many occasions. I had the pleasure of being treated as a family member and a friend by him. Every time I went to visit him, whether it was in the Rashtrapati Bhavan in New Delhi or at the Kremlin in Moscow, he insisted I eat something or at least have a cup of coffee. He never made me feel like he was a president and I was a musician, which I can never forget. It was the same thing with First Lady Mrs Venkataraman. Subsequently, we became close friends and I met all his family members.

When I started the Lakshminarayana Global Music Festival in memory of my father and guru in Chennai on 11 January 1992, I wanted a message from our president since I felt he was a lucky charm for everything I started doing. Initially, due to protocol, I was informed officially that it would not be possible. But once the president was informed that it was a festival in honour of my father, I received a very warm message. Later, when the festival was conducted in Delhi, he very graciously accepted to be the chief guest and attend the performance. The Lakshminarayana Global Music Festival, which started as a very simple one-day affair in Chennai, has now grown to a global event, with legendary artists from all over the world. Since then, in every major step I took, I always consulted him, and had his blessings and best wishes. I was also greatly touched when he sent a condolence message when my first wife Viji passed away.

He was a grandfather figure to my children. Every time I had the opportunity to meet him, he used to enquire about my family and my children by name; he was very fond of children. Once, for New Year's Eve in Chennai, my family and I were invited to have dinner with Mr and Mrs Venkataraman, along with his daughter Lakshmi and her family. It was such a memorable evening, and we almost forgot he was the president. He was so simple and down to earth. He casually spoke to each of my children, enquiring about their education and offering sage advice. It was like my own father spending time with his grandchildren.

I am reminded of a humorous incident that occured once when I was in Rashtrapati Bhavan to see the president with my family. My elder son Narayana was very young at that time, hardly three years old; the president picked him up, seated him upon his lap affectionately and started talking to him. There was a bell next to the president that he used to call the attendant. In between the conversation, the president used the bell to order snacks for Viji, the children and me. Narayana observed it and rang the bell. The attendant came in and the president very politely told the attendant to leave. Narayana kept on ringing the bell, excited to see the uniformed attendant opening the door and coming in at his beck and call. I felt very uncomfortable and told my son very firmly that he should not behave like that in front of the president in the Rashtrapati Bhavan. Immediately, to my surprise, the president smiled and fully supported my son, letting him ring the bell, saying that after all he was a child and should be kept happy.

Even after he retired, I regularly visited him and his family and he spent many a memorable time with us. His daughter Lakshmi, her family and our family became very close when Lakshmi's daughter Tara started learning Western music and singing opera.

When I went to see him with my wife Kavita and the children, he spoke about one of his granddaughters Ranjani, who was focussing on Indian classical music and the other granddaughter, Tara, singing Western music. He persuaded her to come and sing for us and he was so happy that he brought his camera

Inspecting the Gandhigram Rural Industries

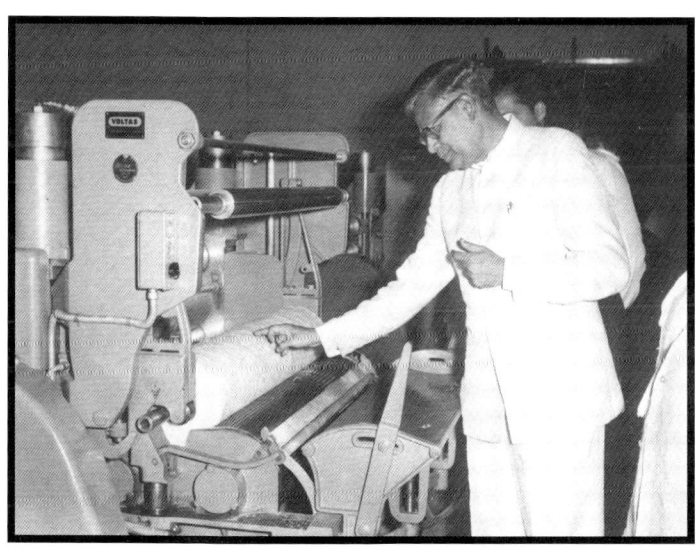

On a visit to the Voltas plant

A physically challenged girl tying a rakhi on RV's wrist

RV and Mrs Venkataraman surrounded by children

Inside Rashtrapati Bhavan with various dignitaries including Manmohan Singh (in turban), Shankar Dayal Sharma (on RV's left) and PV Narasimha Rao (on RV's right)

At the Republic Day celebrations in 1992

With Shankar Dayal Sharma (second from left), Chandra Shekhar (second from right) and Rajiv Gandhi (right) and others

Bestowing an award on JRD Tata

With APJ Abdul Kalam

Shaking hands with the Duke of Edinburgh at Buckingham Palace. HRH Queen Elizabeth II is standing next to the duke

At Moscow airport with Andrei Gromyko

With Former Prime Minister Rajiv Gandhi

(L-R) RV with Sonia Gandhi, Priyanka Gandhi Vadra and Rahul Gandhi

RV and Mrs Venkataraman with the Indian Davis Cup team

An avid photographer: RV at the Great Wall of China

With folk artistes

and started taking pictures. Then he began looking for an old cassette of MS Subbulakshmi, which he was fond of; he wanted to play it for Kavita. He eventually found the cassette, played it for her and then began discussing the music in great detail. He had a very deep knowledge of Indian music, but he was also very open-minded about other systems of music, which I could realise by the way he encouraged Tara.

He was an extremely spiritual person and I have had the pleasure of seeing him at the Mysore ashram of His Holiness Sri Ganapati Sachchidananda Swamiji on several occasions. He was a guiding light and assisted in the planning of many cultural activities. He was the chairman for the celebrations committee, where he was responsible in bringing many luminaries to the Mysore ashram, including His Holiness the Dalai Lama.

There were occasions where he was invited as chief guest and I have been also present but stayed at a distance as I didn't feel comfortable approaching him. But he used to spot me and come up to talk to me, unconcerned about protocol and formalities. He was such a simple, pure human being with a deep love for art and artistes.

Sometime I used to wonder, amazed at his simplicity, whether he even realised he was the president!

A Saint among Politicians

Padma Subrahmanyam

> *The other side of RV – a man of culture, who promoted all forms of art and was also interested in spirituality. Indeed, a well-rounded personality.*

R Venkataraman – a born leader – rose to the highest position that Indian politics offers. He was a favourite son of Mother India, who adorned him with the crown of the First Citizen of our country. Both he and our country deserved each other. It is not easy to find such a towering, multifaceted personality like him. I salute him, during his birth centenary, not merely for his having occupied that throne, not just for his role in the freedom struggle, not just for having played a vital part during the most difficult period of political turmoil, but from a humble angle of his having been a paternal personality to me and many others, with unparalleled human values. In short, he was a cultural catalyst.

RV *mama* (uncle) was a boyhood friend of my father, film director K Subrahmanyam, who was a freedom fighter and a cultural history maker. They grew up together, hand-in-hand and side-by-side, hailing from the same Tanjore district. My father was a few years older than him, and RV *mama* has seen all my siblings and me from our earliest days. Our families have one more thing in common – our unflinched devotion to the centenarian sage His Holiness Sri Sankaracharya of Kanchi. Apart from RV and my father being friends, his eldest daughter Padma and I were classmates. For her wedding, I danced the Meenakshi Kalyanam dance-drama at Abbotsbury. It was just one of the three weddings that I have performed for in my life.

RV *mama* was like a *karmaveera* from the Bhagavad Gita, ever cool, smiling and rock-steady under any circumstance. When he was nurturing the Tamil Nadu industry, which owes much to his pioneering efforts as the concerned minister, my brother Balakrishnan was making a documentary on the subject. His observation of how RV rejected a project is something that he reported to me, leaving a deep impression in my own evolution. Balakrishnan said that across the table he saw RV smiling all through, with very pleasing manners, and softly rejecting the proposal of the applicant. The rejection was firm, but so courteous that the man went with great satisfaction, even though empty-handed. What an extraordinary lesson this is for life! This was RV – the most lovable man with sincere human values.

RV's love for music and dance is well-known. He was the one who gave me all my mental power even during my late teens, and he proudly proclaimed me to be a 'constructive rebel'. He has seen me grow in the midst of opposition, and has solidly supported me in sticking to my convictions. He wanted my guru in research, TN Ramachandran, to write a book on Tanjore *karanas*, with photographs of the dance sculptures along with those of mine. But my guru did not live to complete that work. Years later when I published my book, *Karanas – Common Dance Codes of India and Indonesia,* in three volumes, RV *mama* gave me a scholarly and hearty foreword. I turned his dream into reality by publishing not only all the Tanjore Karanas, but those of Kumbakonam, Chidambaram, Prambanan (in Java) and those of Satara (which I designed), all these along with my pictures. When I wrote the book *Natyasastra and National Unity*, which I published in connection with the fiftieth anniversary of India's independence, he gave another great foreword, showing the oneness of Indian culture through common concepts in Sanskrit and Tamil.

RV was a visionary in the cultural world. When he was the minister for industries in Tamil Nadu, he thought of starting a college for traditional temple architecture and sculpture in Mahabalipuram. This institution has produced some of our best traditional sculptors, who are popular all over the world, building hundreds of Hindu/Jain/Buddhist temples. RV himself steered the building of the Uttara Swamimalai temple in New Delhi with the benign blessings of Sri Kanchi Mahaswami. For carving the main icon, His Holiness asked him to use the other half of the same stone in which the main deity of Tiruchendur temple was carved centuries ago. The search for this stone slab and the making of the idol is a miracle that RV himself narrated in an article. His work was hence not only rooted in the earth, but also vibrated in the metaphysical sphere with the unlimited blessings of Sri Acharya. Whatever he started had the Midas touch, thus flourishing with his blessings. For example, in my own life, his idea of a book with Tanjore sculptures and my dance photographs has turned into a reality with about six hundred illustrations in a separate volume, as part of my book, *Karanas – Common Codes of India and Indonesia*, which now finds a place among the works of many a library in the world.

When RV was the finance minister, he had to write his speech in the Parliament for budget presentation himself. Mama had had his cataract operation just around that time but in spite of this, he sat through the night and wrote the whole confidential script, much against the approval of the doctor. I cannot imagine anyone being more honest to one's work. When he was in Delhi, right from the time he was in the Planning Commission, I had the unique honour of staying as his guest. This continued even after he became the president. After the night stay, when we were having breakfast in the morning with both our families. I jocularly told him that the security in Rashtrapati Bhavan is so poor, that they cannot keep even the cats away. He readily retorted by saying, 'Yes I believe there are three hundred cats, along with the other (black)cats to guard.' He was always full of fun, but also full of profound thoughts.

My nephew Kannan's official name is Venkataraman. Wherever he went for his veena concerts, security men started following him. When he asked them the reason, they replied, 'Well, we have discovered that you are the grandson of the president of India and hence it is our duty to protect you.' Kannan could not convince them that there are many people with the same name. When we returned and narrated the joke to RV, he was not only amused, but also genuinely proud, and said, 'Subrahmanyam's grandson is my grandson also. I am proud to have a musician as my grandson.' We were all touched. Now RV *mama*'s granddaughter, Tara, is an extraordinary Western music singer and Ranjani is an accomplished Hindustani vocalist. His love for the youngsters made him cross over the generation gap.

After he relinquished the presidential office, RV *mama* took out more time for two of his passions. One was his stewardship of Kalakshetra in the cultural field and the other was his chairing the spiritually oriented service organisation, The All India Movement for Seva. The former was to see that the cultural empire founded by his dear friend Rukmini Devi did not dwindle after her death; the latter is a social service movement founded by His Holiness Swami Dayananda Saraswati, to provide education, medical care and hostel facility for tribals all over India. Until he fell down and hurt himself badly, RV was actively associated with both these bodies, for both were beyond the boundaries of political pressures, and provided great soul satisfaction in serving to protect heritage on one hand and instill development for the people who needed to be cared for on the other. I have had the privilege of being on the board of both these organisations when he chaired them.

When chairing one of his last meetings of the Kalakshetra Trust Board, we were discussing the choice of successor for Rajaram, the director of the great institution. RV *mama* shocked me when he suddenly turned to me in front of all the members and said, 'Why should we advertise for application? Why don't you take up this post? After all, you know that it was the last wish of Rukmini Devi. She had said it not only to me, but to others like Travancore Maharaja, the Russian artist Rorich and Sri Narayanaswamy (Chitra & Co). Even your father had a hint of it when she spoke to him.' I was perplexed. I could not negate it when it came from my father figure. But I could not accept either. I thanked him for the trust he had in me and politely requested that I needed to speak to him confidentially. I went to meet him with my brother Balakrishnan and explained the reasons for my compulsion to decline. I also strongly put across to him that Kalakshetra must be headed by someone who has grown there. The unanimous choice was Leela Samson.

RV *mama*'s interest in arts and culture was phenomenal. When the Chennai chapter of International Dance Alliance organised a joint show by several great dancers in Delhi, he not only presided over this unprecedented event, but also threw a special party in honour of us at the Rashtrapati Bhavan. His hospitality is evergreen in our memories. It was he who thought of honouring the traditional temple sculptors, Ganapati Sthapati and Muthaiah Sthapati, with Padma awards. It was because of his recommendation that the Nightingale of India, MS Subbulakshmi, was awarded the Bharat Ratna. Above all, it was he who chaired the committees to celebrate the Golden Jubilee of our dance school Nrithyodaya, as well as the committee to celebrate the birth centenary of my father, film director K Subrahmanyam, when a stamp was released in his memory.

When he was president of India, we had the singular honour of his hosting the projection of our telefilm, *Bharatiya Natyasastra*, at the Rashtrapati Bhavan. This film, based on my script, was directed by my brother Balakrishnan. Later, my third brother Krishnaswamy had the privilege of making a biographical film on him, with his full cooperation.

More than all these, it was under the leadership of RV that the birth centenary celebration of the Mahaswamy of Kanchi was planned and celebrated with his approval and blessings. Many of us thought of celebrating the birth centenary of RV – the saint among politicians (as described by Vasanth Sathe). His spirit is eternal. The 'Master' will rejoice and bless his family and extended family when we collectively pay our homage to him, who was truly a son of the globe, with his feet firmly planted in his motherland, nurtured by the collective cognisance of hundreds and thousands of generations.

RV's Contribution to the Arts

Shovana Narayan

The author talks about how R Venkataraman embodied the spirit of plurality, encouraging a confluence of three classical dance styles on one stage.

My first interaction with Former President Venkataraman took place when he was the union minister for finance in the early 1980s. Since I was the only serving officer who was a recognised classical dancer of the country and was being sponsored abroad by the Indian Council for Cultural Relations (ICCR), the issue of how to treat such official tours came to him for decision. Since then, I found a great friend in him. He not only attended my performances as much as he could, given his busy schedule, but also held lengthy discussions on the history of art and dance. Tradition and vision were intertwined in his personality, as he looked ahead and was up-to-date with the times. This aspect saw him, during his tenure as vice-president and ex-officio chairman of ICCR, moot the idea of bringing three dominant classical dance styles together on the same stage, in an era when experimentation was not very much the order. I was flattered when he asked me to do a kathak performance on this special evening, along with Yamini

Krishnamurthi (bharatanatyam) and Sonal Mansingh (odissi). For Delhi and India, it was a new idea. This programme that was presented in Delhi by the ICCR under the name Tridhara (The Three Streams) became a trendsetter for many more such programmes that followed later, and gradually became commonplace. Nowadays, epithets such as 'three in one ice-cream' that came our way at that point of time are never heard.

In one stroke, President Venkataraman, popularly known as RV, dealt with several issues. If Tridhara brought out the similarity in movements, theme and content, approaches to dance, and music and tenor, between the three classical dance forms, it also helped break down the latent feelings of cultural imperialism that runs like the invisible River Saraswati and unfortunately lays down deep foundations of divisiveness. Often, the debate relating to classicality centres on the issue of what constitutes *margi* and what constitutes *desi* as also *natyadharmi* and *lokadharmi*, and whether a style is true to the spirit and content of Bharatamuni's *Natyashastra*. In this endeavour, what is forgotten is the fact that almost all our classical dance forms have been reconstructed in the late nineteenth and twentieth centuries and have been consciously designed on the precepts enunciated in the *Natyashastra* and the *Abhinaya Darpan*. Starting with the late nineteenth century, art has been carefully crafted to fall within acceptable parameters. This period, under the patronage of Nawab Wajid Ali Shah of Oudh, saw items being arranged according to the *margi* system in kathak dance, and similarly by the Tanjore Quartet in the Sadir or Dasiattam dance form, later rechristened as bharatanatyam in the 1930s. In fact, at the time of India's independence, there were four recognised classical dance styles that gradually increased to eight by the year 2000.

Dwelling on the *Natyashastra* that enjoys pride of place for all artistes, it is pertinent to note that no dance or music form is especially mentioned in this mother of all treatises. The manner in which every movement of life is enumerated is akin to the dissection of human anatomy for a medical student. It was the quest for identity during the colonial period of Indian history and the class struggle in some parts of the country that fuelled the race for various performing art forms identifying themselves as the true inheritors of the *Natyashastra*. This question of assertion of identity was not an issue from a cultural point of view before the spate of invasions during the medieval period of Indian history, as there was largely one faith in the subcontinent. The issue of cultural and religious identity began only after the invaders established their rule, wherein rulers in certain areas followed a different religious faith from that followed by the local population. In the race for cultural supremacy with regional assertions by vested groups, the sagacity and secular spirit of RV was fully visible, as against the openly stated biases of many present-day leaders. Not only were his utterances extremely balanced and could not be faulted even by persons looking for faults, but as chairman of the ICCR, he ensured equitable representation of all dance forms on all occasions, especially inaugural functions, for those set the mood and made the statement for the nation.

The dance presentation 'The Dawn After' featuring kathak, Western classical ballet and Spanish flamenco, the first and only one of its kind till date, was cherished by RV. He would often discuss the similarity of movements and the difference in approach to a similar movement in the three dance styles. He would never tire of congratulating me on the production that he had witnessed, which had won raving reviews even from the 'traditionalists'. In this context, the discussions veered towards my costume comprising *churidar angarkha*, and he was happily surprised to learn about the existence of similar kinds of costumes during the Mauryan period (third century BC) and even in the Gupta period (fourth and fifth centuries AD) as evidenced from ancient India's wealth of sculptures dotting the various museums of our country. He stared at the comparative photographs for a long time, pointing out valuable similarities. It was he whose casual remark led me to embark on a voyage of discovery, studying sculptures especially between the third and sixth centuries AD, that showed the existence of a pair of vertical drums, the tabla and a 'sarod-like veena'.

Nurturing of cultural institutions reflecting Indian identity was extremely close to RV's heart. Rabindranath Tagore's vision and his establishment of Santiniketan, a place of all-inclusive learning, had served as a model for Rukmini Devi Arundale who, following Tagore's footsteps and ideals, laid the foundations of Kalakshetra in Chennai. It was RV's desire to see that the tree that had been nurtured by Rukminiji should lovingly be cared for, and that the progressive secular spirit prevailed, far removed from narrowmindedness. How often did he enlighten us on the synergy of the East and the West adopted by Rukminiji, whether in designing costumes or in the format and aesthetics of stage presentation, and on her as a pioneer who recognised the potency of 'internationalisation of art' and of 'institutionalising dance'. In order to ensure that the true inclusive plural secular spirit, the cornerstone of Rukminiji's vision, continued to prevail, RV included several people, including myself, from various parts of the country on the board of the institution.

During his tenure as the president of India, Rashtrapati Bhavan was not only a place that saw several political challenges, but was simultaneously a cultural hub exuding the fragrance of the rich cultural and philosophical traditions that have imbued India with pride. Before demitting the office of president, RV personally supervised the refurbishing and reactivation of the Rashtrapati Bhavan museum, donating most of the valuable gifts presented to him during his tenure as president to it.

Rare are such gestures seen from a person occupying such a high position.

But his humane streak was his most endearing quality. While he exhorted one and all to dream big and to strive for it, he was equally concerned about keeping intact one's integrity and ethics. He was particularly alive to the extraordinary needs of dancers as compared to other artists. All those who came into contact with him felt special, as though he or she was RV's particular friend. He became a friend, philosopher and guide to countless artistes. Without even mentioning or taking credit, he always tried to mitigate the problems of all those who came and wept on his shoulders. I, too, have shed tears before him on several occasions and have had the benefit of being rightfully guided by him. Another noticeable feature about him was his remarkable memory. No detail escaped him. He never tired in narrating how a certain visiting dignitary was so enamoured and engrossed with my dance that he even forgot to respond to RV's queries and observations.

President Venkataraman's remarkable ability to breathe the spirit of plurality and allow the fresh breeze of cultures of the world to nurture this plurality was reinforced when his two talented granddaughters became practitioners of Hindustani classical music and Western classical music respectively. He was a true example of the spirit of universal brotherhood, secularism and plurality, while not losing sight of tradition and humanity!

> *Reach high, for stars lie hidden in you. Dream deep, for every dream precedes the goal.*
> – Rabindranath Tagore

The Essence of a Truly Humanising Culture

Yamini Krishnamurthi

> *R Venkataraman was one of the few individuals who fully participated in the rich aesthetic experience of a dance performance and who could be uplifted to a spiritual plane during such performances.*

A festschrift in honour of Bharat Ratna R Venkataraman is the best tribute we can pay to an extraordinary individual, who has left his noble imprint on contemporary Indian history. The contributors to this volume have had the good fortune to work with him and therefore can provide an accurate and authentic account of RV and his multilayered personality. I feel it an ambiguous privilege to be asked to be one of the eminent contributors to this volume, as I was not a part of his personal and professional life. I knew him at a distance, but I had a good understanding of his spiritual side when he was present on the occasions of my performances. I have been a silent follower of RV, whose career graph climaxed with his becoming the eighth president of India. My tribute therefore does not rest singularly on RV, the statesman, RV, the minister and political leader, RV, the lawyer and administrator, RV, the freedom fighter and the social crusader, but on RV the man who, throughout his life, remained the most civilised and cultured human being.

I am a dancer, a passionate performer on stage to a limited audience. RV was a political leader, whose passionate activities were performed on the national stage for the benefit of the wider Indian masses. However divergent our interests and passions were, we were bound by the penetrative hermeneutic of music and dance that enabled us to reach a higher plane beyond the grasp of our limited reason and intellect.

The invention of classical arts, especially music and dance, is 'the supreme mystery in the science of man', to quote Levi-Strauss, the French anthropologist and ethnologist. It is difficult to analyse the ways in which these classical arts come to possess us as we go on stage to perform. The function of an artist is to communicate to the audience his or her rich experience of *satyam, shivam* and *sundaram* – all of them rolled into one unique aesthetic absorption, closely allied to the experience of the divine. The audience, on its part, enjoys the performance where form and content coalesce to provide an insight into the mysteries of the divine. The artist's performance – whether it is music or dance – is aesthetically pleasing and satisfying when the artist is successful in communicating this unique spiritual experience, that defies intellectual and cognitive understanding, to the audience.

I have been a dancer, with my whole life dedicated to this Indian classical art form. While as a dancer I have always felt happy at the accolades I received from the audience, there is a part in me that constantly sought to discern those few in the audience who would go beyond the aesthetically appealing form of dance to experience the invisible mysteries of the divine. Even if there happened to be one single individual among the audience who felt possessed by the art form and could be elevated to a spiritual plane during the period of performance, I would be elated. RV was one such person.

RV had truly been a patron of classical arts. He had this truly humanising culture that could apprehend in our classical art forms noble, subtle and profound thoughts, refined and lofty feelings. Underlying his varied personality as an astute administrator, a dynamic legislator, a believer in social justice and a statesman president, RV was a spiritual being representing the very best of humanity.

PERSONAL VIGNETTES

RV the Person

K Venkataraman

RV's public persona is well known and documented, but what was he like in private?

R Venkataraman was known as 'RV' to his friends and 'Anna' to all the junior members of his family. The latter appellation, meaning 'elder brother', is customarily used among certain families in Tamil Nadu.

In a long public life spanning more than seven decades, RV had cordial relationships all round. He wore many hats in his life, but never a mask. Ever smiling but never frivolous; patient but not weak; soft-spoken and courteous but firm, he nursed no animosity towards anyone. Though he was close to K Kamaraj, he had good relations with people like Satyamurti and Rajaji (C Rajagopalachari) as well. The latter, as chief minister of Madras state, once asked him to enquire into and report on the grievances of agricultural tenants in Thanjavur district. President VV Giri, when he was governor of Kerala, used to drop in unannounced, sometimes more than once on the same day, at 'Mohana', RV's residence when he was the industries minister in Madras, as they shared a long-standing friendship, both being labour leaders. In Parliament, RV had friendly relationships with members on both sides of the House. During his presidential election, he polled more votes than the Congress party controlled. He had good personal relationships with senior journalists but did not look for popularity through the press.

RV's personal life was no different from his public life. In his dealings, Anna was courteous, seldom angry, never speaking ill of others and providing constructive guidance to those who sought it. Many were invited to his home for lunch or tea; Rajiv Gandhi used to like the *vadas* and Madras coffee served by Mrs Janaki Venkataraman. Leading musicians and artistes were invited to perform in the Rashtrapati Bhavan theatre. In his retirement, at an advanced age, Anna still came to the portico to see his visitors off. Many were left wondering at his phenomenal memory for facts and faces even in old age.

Except for an interval during the 1970s, Anna was always busy, but interacted with the family in whatever time he had. In the 1940s, when he used to be away from home for several days at a stretch on trade union work, the children used to be surprised if he happened to stay at home for an extended period. He liked to have his family around at the dining table, but there was no political analysis or salacious gossip during meals. There was no recounting of the 'day in the office' either. Just simple family talk. He also liked to chat with the family for a short while, when he had his morning coffee.

Anna talked to his children and grandchildren in gentle, unobtrusive and affectionately teasing tones. He used to love playing chess or some other game with his grandchildren whenever he had time. He never gave them the impression that he was a highly placed man. When he was the finance minister, Sunil Gavaskar, the famous cricketer, came to meet him on some matter. When he told his grandson, then a ten-year-old, that Gavaskar had come, the boy could not believe that the great

Gavaskar had visited *his* grandfather! When, on his election as president, he was to move from the vice-president's house to Rashtrapati Bhavan, one of his granddaughters then staying with him wondered why he should move, because the existing house was good enough. During his funeral ceremony, the youngest granddaughter, then a fourteen-year-old, remarked that she did not know that her grandfather was so very important that the army and so many eminent people from the government came to pay homage.

Corruption and nepotism were alien to his nature; probity was ingrained. He left it to his children to secure their own school or college admissions. When invitations for the marriage of his first daughter were sent out, a business magnate came and offered to help in the celebrations. RV told him that no help was needed, but if the magnate was so particular, he could send two people from his region, well-versed in looking after guests in the dining hall, on the day of the wedding. RV did not believe in his daughters taking to politics – not that any of them were thus inclined. Imbibing his public spirit, however, all three are engaged in voluntary social work – Padma in the rehabilitation of leprosy-affected persons, Vijaya in improving the lot of construction workers, and Lakshmi in nurturing young entrepreneurs. Their mother, Janaki, was keen on helping spastic and physically-challenged children, and was a pioneer in introducing 'ahimsa silk', produced from silk extracted from silkworms without killing them. After retiring from the post of president, Anna also established a charitable trust (RV Foundation) with his own modest funds to help deserving persons for education or medical attention. One of the conditions of the trust is that no donations will be accepted, except from family members.

Anna organised his day well; taking care of his personal needs before breakfast at 9 a.m., having his major meal of the day at

1 p.m. and retiring to his room between 9.30 and 10 p.m. After retiring to his room, he used to check or update the family accounts in his copybook handwriting and on occasions, write in his diary. The diary that he kept as president came in useful when he was writing his book on his presidential years. He was not inclined to write about his other official years, saying that it would necessitate using the first person singular too often. It was his wont to write his own speeches too.

A vegetarian, he practised moderation in food. Janaki Venkataraman saw to it that he got the dishes he liked the most – simple food that he used to have even in his ancestral home. Though he became diabetic in his fifties, necessitating strictness in diet, the condition did not affect him much in terms of complications; he needed to resort to injecting a small dose of insulin only in his eighties. Sometimes he quoted in a subdued tone the stanza from the Bhagavad Gita, *'Yukta-ahara-viharasya, yukta cheshtasya karmasu. Yukta-swapna-avabodhasya yogo bhavati dukhaha'*, meaning, 'Yoga killeth out all pain for him who is regulated in eating and amusement, regulated in performing actions, regulated in sleeping and waking'. The emphasis on a regulated life was quite apposite to him, leave alone the eating. He used to say that he had learnt a trick from Sir CP Ramaswamy Iyer on how to avoid overeating in official dinners – take a piece of food from the plate, talk to the person by your side and put it down on the plate after talking; and repeat the procedure with other people around the table!

He walked regularly and did not do any strenuous physical exercise; perhaps his active public life kept him fit. There is a photograph in his albums, showing a slim RV keeping in step with the slowly moving jeep on which Jawaharlal Nehru is standing and waving to the crowds during the Avadi Congress. With advancing age, he managed his physical infirmities well; yet his overall good health surprised doctors who examined him in his last years. As finance minister, he had to surmount eye trouble and as president, ear trouble. He refused to go abroad for any treatment. As vice-president, he visited Ladakh without any discomfort, whereas his personal physician had to struggle due to the lack of oxygen at that altitude. In his post-presidential years, he had no personal attendant till the age of ninety-five, when he fractured his shoulder in a fall. He used to travel on the overnight train to Madurai to attend Gandhigram meetings without an attendant by his side. In the last year of his life, the doctors tried hard to have a pacemaker implanted in his heart, but he declined, saying that nature would take its course. He always took a walk around his garden, combining walking with instructions to his gardener. In the final year of his life, he mostly walked inside the house for twenty minutes at a time, three times a day, with his attendant in tow, and with the walking stick in hand but not placed on the ground.

RV was religious but not ritualistic. He did not get a horoscope made; he showed no interest in astrology. Though he and Janaki Venkataraman had great reverence for the Paramacharya of Kanchi, he had good relations with the heads of several other religious institutions as well. For some four decades, he was intimately involved in the development and running of the Malai Mandir in New Delhi. In his post-retirement years, he attended all the prayer meetings as often as possible. He even turned a student and attended the classes of Swami Dayananda Saraswati on the Vedas and Upanishads in Anaikatti near Coimbatore. He had no caste bias. His personal assistant for decades was from the so-called scheduled castes and his butler in Rashtrapati Bhavan belonged to the Islamic faith.

Anna liked to dress neatly, in crisp clothes. In public, he always wore trousers and a 'bush-shirt' or buttoned-up coat, usually *khadi*. At bedtime he wore a dhoti. When going to a temple, religious function, or a South Indian wedding, he wore a dhoti and kurta, sporting a *zari*-bordered *angavastram* on the right shoulder, if the occasion warranted it. Photography was a lifelong hobby, as was gardening. He had rows of banyan trees planted in Rashtrapati Bhavan. Later, President APJ Abdul Kalam presented him with a framed photograph of those trees grown up and spread out over the years. He had a library which he used particularly for writing his speeches; even in his post-presidential years, he mostly wrote his speeches with a yet steady hand. He rarely read fiction. He liked humour, but only in context. He had a large collection of music casettes, but found time to listen to them only after retirement. He never watched a movie at home and even when, on some political or official occasions, he went to a theatre and watched a movie, he was generally found dozing. He did not have much knowledge of film actors and personalities. When he was a minister in the then Madras state, a famous and beautiful actress came and greeted him at a party, but he could not recognise her, much to her righteous indignation!

Anna liked sports. He was an avid cricket fan, having played the game in his younger years, and used to watch it on television, often commenting spiritedly on what he thought were wrong field placements. However, he promptly got up, when it was bedtime or time for meals. In Rashtrapati Bhavan, apart from walking in the Mughal Gardens, he sometimes played badminton or golf. He also regularly spent half an hour in the billiards room after dinner. Barely a week before he was hospitalised for the last time, his attendant took a picture in the garden of RV using his walking stick as a golf club and a lime fruit as a golf ball – a sportsman till the end!

A Nation Finding its Feet
Our Experiences with R Venkataraman

Lloyd and Susanne Rudolph

> *A letter, written in 1957, captures the experience of two Americans watching RV campaign, and also provides a glimpse of a newly-formed democracy.*

R Venkataraman entered our life during the first year we did research in India and remained part of our Indian experience almost to the end of his life.

The letter below, written in March 1957, recounts how we accompanied him during his campaign for Parliament. It records our earliest experiences of Indian society, culture and politics. We have left it in its original language, which, we think, conveys the immediacy of our experience campaigning with RV, as we called him at the time. Campaigning with RV in the villages of Tanjore [now Thanjavur] district fifty-three years ago was a defining experience for our careers as scholars of Indian politics and government.

We arrived on the Indian subcontinent via the Khyber Pass in July 1956, after a six-week overland journey in a Land Rover through Europe and the Middle East. We were freshly minted Harvard PhDs with Ford Foundation Foreign Area Training

Fellowships. We told the foundation that we would study political development in India by spending six months in Rajasthan, a former princely state in the north, and Madras, formerly under British direct rule in the south. The result was our first book, *The Modernity of Tradition: Political Development in India.*

The following letter captures the immediate experience of campaigning with RV in 1957, but not its long-term effect on our thinking. Seymour Martin Lipset argued in an influential article in 1959, 'The Social Requisites of Democracy', that advanced levels of literariness, industrialisation and urbanisation were required for democracy to succeed.[1] Our experience of campaigning with R Venkataraman in Tanjore district among illiterate, poor voters made it abundantly clear that the universal franchise India had adopted at the time of Independence was working.

1956–57 was the first of the eleven research years we spent in India. RV continued to take an interest in us and our careers. On one of his visits to the US, as an Indian delegate to the UN in the early 1960s, he visited us in Cambridge, Massachusetts, where Susanne attempted to make *idlis* for his breakfast. The *idlis* were close to a disaster but RV cheerfully ate them. After holding important posts in government, RV became one of India's most distinguished and influential presidents. We wrote about his contribution as president in 'Redoing the constitutional design: from an interventionist to a regulatory state'.[2]

Perhaps our most cherished memories of R Venkataraman are our visits to Rashtrapati Bhavan. He reminisced about his

---

[1] See Lipset, SM, 'Some Social Requisites of Democracy: Economic Development and Political Legitimacy,' *American Political Science Review,* 53, March, 1959.
[2] Kohli, Atul (ed.), *The Success of India's Democracy,* Cambridge: Cambridge University Press, 2001.

campaign for MP in 1957 by showing us photo albums of that memorable trip, during which we had learned that India was going to be a successful democracy.

Railway Retiring Room

Tanjore
2 March 1957

Dear Families,

For the last few days we've been following an energetic Congress candidate, R Venkataraman, on his campaign for MP in remote villages of Tamil Nadu. Rover the Land Rover has teetered precariously on narrow mud tracks raised on eroding embankments overlooking the flooded paddy fields, churned through irrigation ditches, and splashed through muddy hollows – this country is wet! His constituency in Tanjore district, the rice bowl of South India, is said to be one of the most densely populated areas in all of India. The paddy is being harvested. The lean, muscular farm labourers bend their gleaming black bodies into the work of cutting the ears.

The lands surrounding Tanjore seem isolated and inaccessible. After following an obscure track across the lush fields that are dotted here and there with palm trees, the jeep skirts a tank. On the far side an ancient temple, black with time and lichen, raises its carved figures toward a pale blue morning sky. A single bird cries and rises as a village woman dips her brass pitcher into the water, raises it to her head, and moves off quietly toward the village. Beyond, the track passes rattan huts with thickly thatched roofs, surrounded by green banana trees. The track widens into the village street, little round naked boys run after the car on vigorously pounding legs, women look up from their task of sweeping the dusty road before their houses, an old man with a white cloth wrapped around his lean loins and his forehead painted with the three lines of white ash of the Shaivite, turns to look after the car.

The huts become more frequent, lanes lead off the main road, ahead rises an arch of dry leaves, beyond it signs of politics, small black and red flags fluttering from lines stretched high across the road as if to announce the opening of some rural American gas station. Huts with little covered front porches display the wares of local merchants; every second hut is brightly decked with election posters, and many display party flags.

Down the road ahead of us, energetically moving along, come two young men on bicycles, each with a large green, white, and saffron Congress party flag stuck into his handle bars. These are the bicycle volunteers, the workers who carry party messages from village to village, who arrange meetings for the candidate, who put up posters and distribute leaflets, and serve as the eyes and ears of whatever party they are backing. We pass a hut with the large black and red flag of the Dravidian Progressive Federation displayed in front, and a 1934 Ford touring car, also with [the same] flag, parked outside. We pass a cycle volunteer carrying the hammer and sickle of the CPI [Communist Party of India], and stop before a thatched hut bearing the Congress flag, heavy with posters.

Our Tamil network had started in Delhi. David Burgess, the well-connected American labour attaché, knows almost all the important labour people in India. He had introduced us to Mr Tripathi, MP, General Secretary of the Indian National Trade Union Congress, the Congress oriented national labour federation. Tripathi in turn had introduced us to R Venkataraman at the Parliament in Delhi. We had taken advantage of our brief acquaintance with Mr Venkataraman to ask him if we might observe his campaign, and he generously consented. We were a little worried about this project, since the American consulate and embassy have been telling all the Fulbright people to stay out of the countryside during the campaign, for fear that American observers might be misunderstood. Since we get no government money – we're on Ford Foundation Foreign Area Training Grants – no one attempted to give us advice. Madras, which has a US consulate, is almost as bad as Delhi in worrying about the awkward things Americans might do. Official caution – 'Don't do or say anything that might disturb the Indians' – is in the air.

All this notwithstanding, we couldn't resist the temptation to get out and see the campaign, and since RV was unimpressed with our worries, we set out after him in the company of his cousin Ramini.

R Venkataraman is a Brahmin, and most of the members of his immediate team appear to be Brahmins as well. Thus the young man who sits in the back of his jeep and sings campaign songs over the attached loudspeaker as we enter each village has shaved the front half of his head and wears a long tuft of hair pulled into a knot at the back in orthodox fashion. No one touches meat, or even eggs for that matter. There was general interest when we unpacked our hard-boiled eggs for lunch at one stop along the road. Did they taste different depending on whether they were soft or hard-boiled, someone wanted to know.

Apropos of Brahmins. We seem perpetually to be getting involved with former ruling classes on the run before the democratic onslaught. What the Rajputs, as former ruling caste, are to former princely Rajasthan, the Brahmins are to the South. Brahmins have for generations controlled the enormous temple properties of the South, and have developed a more visible Hinduism than we ever found in Rajasthan. They consolidated their position under the British, since their intellectual tradition gave them a jump on all others in the South as far as the new European-style education was concerned, and ultimately in the all-important civil service under the British.

Universal franchise has spelled, or is spelling, the end of their domination. Madras has a powerful anti-religious movement, whose main target is the Brahmins. At its best, this movement is bearer of a kind of Voltairian enlightenment. At its worst, it is mere communalism – the term used in this country for all movements that put caste or religious solidarity above all other considerations – combined with a kind of right radicalism. The Dravida Kazagham and Dravida Munnetra Kazagham, proponents of this point of view, have a full-fledged racial theory to back it up: according to them, the Aryan invaders who came from beyond Afghanistan and poured into the subcontinent some two to three thousand years ago, and who introduced the Vedic culture and Sanskrit script, 'occupied' the South as well. Their main representatives in the southland have been the Brahmins. Thus, according to DMK ideology, Brahmins are rank outsiders. [3]

Here in the state of Madras, Tamil is the local language – derived, like all Southern languages, from Dravidian rather than Sanskrit. The word Tamilian, used by the DK and DMK to designate the genuine local stock, has been redefined by them to exclude Brahmins. This effort to exclude Brahmins from the true Tamil society is re-enforced by the DMK and DK's vigorous anti-northernism, vaguely reminiscent of anti-Yankee feelings in the American south. According to the DMK the industrialising North is trying to do down the rural South – 'see how little industrial investment we got in the five-year plans.' The DMK also claims that the Hindi-speaking Sanskritic North is trying to culturally dominate the Dravidian South. 'They've put a resolution into the Constitution that Hindi shall become the

---

[3]For a subsequent, more elaborate version of the DMK story see Rudolph, Lloyd I, 'Dravidian Politics in Madras', *The Journal of Asian Studies,* 20 [3] May 1961, pp 283-97.

national language ...' The Dravidian South should assert its identity more. In fact, the Constitution should be amended to allow for the right of secession.

The DK and DMK viewpoint, in a gentler form, appears to have influenced Congress thinking in these parts. With exception of R Venkataraman, there are no Brahmins in the present Congress cabinet here, and the chief minister, a shrewd but unlettered man, comes from a socially mobile commercial caste.[4]

Anyhow, there we were, heading out into the constituency with RV. He is on very good terms with the chief minister, and doesn't share the estrangement many of his fellow Brahmins feels with respect to the new, lower-caste dominated Congress. A prematurely grey, handsome man with a kindly, gentle face, RV proved to have a sense of humour. He derives his political strength from the fact that he is president of 150 large and small labour unions in Madras. It is not extraordinary in Indian trade union life for one man to hold so many offices. Our friend Ashok Mehta of the Socialist Party does the same. Unions often choose some outstanding educated and professionally qualified and politically active individual as their president. Vice-presidents do the ordinary organisational work. The president, who plays a more ceremonial role, is called on when policy, regulatory and legal issues need attention.

The trade union men, many of them vice-presidents of important Madras unions, had come out in force to help R Venkataraman campaign. About thirty or forty had come the

---

[4]The chief minister, K Kamaraj Nadar, is of the Nadar caste. The Nadars' traditional occupation, according to the British Raj's census, was toddy tapping. Many of them have become successful business people. For the story of Nadar social mobility, see Rudolph, Susanne Hoeber and Lloyd I Rudolph, *The Modernity of Tradition,* Chicago: University of Chicago Press, 1967, and Hardgrave Robert, *The Nadars of Tamil Nad; The Political Culture of a Community in Change,* 1969, 2006.

250 miles from Madras, having taken leave for one month from their work in various companies to do so.

Two days ago, we accompanied RV as he campaigned in six villages. He held no large meetings as he had previously. Instead he held a series of informal meetings with village headmen. In two villages his conversation was mainly with the owner of the local coffee club (coffee shop to you), who was in each case also an important landowner. He had influence by [due to] the fact that everyone met in his establishment – or at least everyone with influence. In a third village he spoke with the headmen of three or four castes and repeated that process in a fourth. In another, he visited the panchayat head, and in one he spoke to a short-notice meeting of forty or so people. While he did his business, we went around with RV's former law partner, a portly Brahmin gentleman named Chakravarty, who turned out to be a splendid translator.

Lloyd explored the communications situation – how many radios and newspapers in the village, how often do people go to the movies – and Sue tried to find out how the women felt about voting. Villages of 5,000 or so souls seem to have around two or three battery sets, one belonging to the village panchayat (governing body of a village). The village gets at least one Tamil daily, and maybe thirty or so people subscribe themselves. Some villagers go the movies as much as three times a week, but once a month or less was more usual, Lloyd says. The ladies would all vote for a woman candidate. However, before doing so they would consult their husbands, Sue says.

We profited greatly from meeting and hearing the villagers of all stripes. They became something more than an abstraction to us. The villager is a thirty-year-old woman, with a lilac cotton sari wrapped into a skirt and with the end pulled up from the waist and over the shoulder to cover young bare breasts. [The villager is also] A young woman who says that women know better than men what other women want, especially for their children, and should therefore be elected. She says it in a determined, articulate way, emphasising her points with the clenched fist of one hand, while in the other arm she holds a child that leans, ill-looking, listlessly against her shoulder. The villager is a lean, small, grey-haired old woman, with enormous gold ornaments in drooping pierced earlobes, who looks vastly amused while some young women claim an independent judgment in voting matters, interrupts laughingly and says – 'We all vote the way our husbands tell us to.' The villager is a fortyish man with close-cropped hair and a day's growth of beard, wearing a white cloth wrapped ground length around his waist, who tells us that a certain landowner and two moneylenders are the best informed persons in the village. The villager is a landowner and shopkeeper, small and shy, who is said to be one of the most influential men in the village, but who defers, while answering our questions, to a fiery, bushy haired, intelligent youth with obvious DK inclinations. And finally, he is a sober-looking twenty-five-year-old, prematurely head of his family, who has gone to fourth class only but is substantially better informed about the Suez problem that many of his city neighbours.

Our campaign swing with R Venkataraman's has taught us that rural Indians may be non-literate but that they are informed and engaged. They have caught on fast to the political opportunities democracy offers.

My Grandfather: An Inspiration

Siddharth Ramachandran

R. Venkataraman's grandson reflects on how his grandfather's way of living and ethics influenced his and his cousins' characters and lives.

As a twelve-year-old, I was fascinated with the pomp and splendour of military processions and ceremonies. So I would grab any opportunity to see them in action. One such occasion was when my grandfather, then vice-president of India, was attending the 'passing-out' parade of the National Cadet Corps (NCC). This was a parade of an elite segment of the NCC, made up of school-going children from around the country, and thus a very prestigious affair, with the chiefs of all the three forces, along with the vice-president, in attendance. The navy admiral was chatting with me, and upon learning about my fascination with all things military, approached my grandfather, and suggested that I be inducted in the parade the following year. My grandfather replied, 'He will need to join his local school NCC first and rise up the ranks for that.' I must admit that, at that time, his response did not thrill me much – I would have loved to 'jump the gun' and be part of this elite cadre from the start. But his response was emblematic of the way he brought us up; indeed, it was representative of his deep commitment towards upholding the ethics of an elected officer or public servant.

This commitment did not just make him an honest and upright man, as he is often portrayed by the media, but also made him a policy-maker and an administrator who was immensely, and with amazing regularity, successful in impacting the ship of state, from the heady days of India's independence to this day. This is because Anna, as all of us called him, due to the Pattukkottai tradition of referring to senior males as elder brothers, strongly believed that power has a tendency to corrupt, and to wield power effectively and fruitfully, one needs to avoid, in some cases monastically, this tendency. There are two avenues for such corruption, he believed – through using power for monetary gains, and through using it to benefit friends and family. He abhorred the idea that, in an elected polity such as democratic India (whose Constitution he helped write), we would think of sons and daughters of powerful politicians as having the 'right' to share that power.

While we, his grandchildren, were explicitly prohibited from any actions that would even remotely gain an advantage from his office or status, we benefitted by getting the best civics lessons – better than anything we could get from our classrooms – in the functioning of the Indian political system, civil governance, labour movements, as well as about the United Nations Organisation (UN). After all, in one man, we had a resource who had years of experience in all of the above! We imbibed these lessons through his multiple late-night discussions on various topics, punctuated by actual events in which he had participated. Some interesting examples were of the way he convinced mighty landowners in the erstwhile Madras state to start investing their wealth in industries, by pairing the technical know-how of German industries with the wealth of the Indian landowners. Thus the agrarian Madras state was transformed into an industrial powerhouse. He also mentioned how, once, the recipe for instant *idlis* helped him, in his New York hotel apartment, to win over some critical friends in the diplomatic corps of the erstwhile Soviet Union.

But, as I mentioned earlier, perhaps the more important lessons we learnt related to the separation of power and officialdom from family. I feel immensely proud that all of us, his grandchildren, can state confidently that they owe their disparate careers today (development economics and finance, science and engineering, arts and music), not to a phone call he or someone else placed on our behalf, but to the education imparted by our grandparents and parents.

There are two other aspects of my grandfather that will forever be etched in my mind – his sense of discipline, and his interest in being a well-rounded individual. The former quality made him a voracious reader, with an undying thirst for knowledge and consequent ability to grasp the essence of fields outside his formal educational experience. This was probably his road to success as a policy maker and statesman over eight decades. His tremendous impact on the industrial development of Madras state was predicated by a deep knowledge, to the extent possible for a person not formally trained in the natural sciences, of the process by which heavy industry can impact the twin goals of technological development and employment. His ability to understand the best path forward for India's defence capabilities resulted in India choosing missile development and its spin-off, satellite launching, capabilities of direct relevance to agricultural development. Given his strict desire to keep work and family separate (and the fact that I was not born eight decades ago!), I was not directly privy to his work in these areas. Instead, I got to see how he approached problems – assembling experts for advice, doing a lot of reading and researching on his own, and only then reconvening the experts to make policy recommendations and decisions.

The latter quality (of striving to be a well-rounded individual) that I admired a lot, made him teach me chess and play with me almost every summer night I was on vacation in Delhi, and also play badminton well into his nineties! What impact did this have on him as a statesman? One particular anecdote that illustrates this well was his trip to the Khardung La pass, at 17,582 feet, in Ladakh. His motorcade got off at the pass and went on a small hike – he was the president of India at that time (in his late seventies) – accompanied by several members of the civilian administration and the military top brass. He was one among a few (other than all the army *jawans*, of course) that did not get mountain-sickness at all! This inspired the entire group, comprising people who were one to five decades younger than him, and helped them develop a deep sense of respect for the man, a common occurrence throughout his life. This quality also helped him develop a rapport with scientists, civil administrators as well as business people, and served him well as he helped steer the ship of state from the days of India's independence all the way to the last decade.

I truly miss my grandfather – I was fortunate to be able to spend a week with him just before he passed away (and yes, his mind and body was, amazingly, as alert and strong as ever) – for he was an inspiration like none other. The quality of his statesmanship, which emphasised the importance of the administrative outcome as much as the political one, impacted India for eight decades. For that reason, and for the fact that many of his generation, who had similar reasons for dedicating their lives to public service, have passed away, he will be cherished by India today and in the future.

Growing Up with Grandpa

Tara Venkatesan

R Venkataraman's granddaughter talks about how he gave her the strength to perform even in the most adverse situations.

'Anna, what's happening now?' I asked, tugging on my grandfather's buttoned Nehru-collar shirt for the fiftieth time. We were at a performance in Kalakshetra, the prestigious Bharatnatyam dance school, and also the only place in the world where anyone could get me to shut up. Sitting in the front row, watching the specks of light reflect off the shimmering jewellery and sets as the dancers re-enacted the Ramayana, 'Anna what's happening now?' was my repeat-after-every-two-seconds mantra. And ever-so-patiently, grandpa leaned down innumerable times to explain that Hanuman was still carrying a mountain. Nothing had changed in the last twenty seconds of my pestering, and nothing would change for at least another two minutes. That answer was good enough for me. The normally hyperactive two-year-old that I was sat in unusual silence, staring at the stage with rapt attention as the dancers twirled, leaped and … applause shattered the air. The performers all lined up on stage, taking their bows, and my grandfather stood up to garland them, so I stood up as well. It was the greatest thrill to follow him up on the stage. After he had congratulated everyone, the performers would bend down to pat my head or pick me up and giggle. Well, if I told you I was embarrassed or hesitant in the midst of all the attention, I would be lying! Basking in it, I would scramble at my grandfather's heels and look innocent and sweet until he walked offstage to get into the car, after which I would fall asleep immediately in his lap; it was way past my bedtime anyway.

As music aficionados, grandpa and I went to many concerts together: Indian classical music, Western classical music, and even fusion concerts. But music and dance were never just things we heard or saw at a concert. After school, I would trudge through the front door with my monstrous purple, flowery backpack, plonk it on the nearest sofa and hurry to join grandpa, who would be deeply engrossed in conversation with Uncle Pandit Ravi Shankarji (the sitarist), Mani Uncle (Dr L Subramaniam, the violinist), Aunty Shovana Narayan (the danseuse) and so on. I would listen, fascinated, as they would reminisce about old concerts, performances, or times together, and share memories. Now you might think that I'll say something like 'the experience was surreal' but truth be told, this was as normal as seeing my cousins at home!

Once, when I was about five years old, there was a world music concert held in honour of grandpa's ninetieth birthday. When he asked me whose performance I had liked the best, I turned around and gave the most unlikely answer – I wanted to sing like the soprano from the Netherlands. Opera? My mother Lakshmi looked slightly bewildered and incredulous. Who sang opera in India? Why would a five-year-old immersed in Indian classical art gravitate towards opera? More importantly, if opera was what I wanted to do, where were they going to go find an opera teacher in India? However, Anna simply said, 'Opera?

Go for it!' Coincidentally, the leading soprano in the country happened to live ten minutes away from our home.

I started performing when I was eight and Anna hardly ever missed a single show of mine. If he did, I would rush back home and give a blow-by-blow account of the night's events. The experience of performing was never complete until I heard him congratulate me with his favourite phrase, 'Wonderful, beautiful!' Then everything would be okay. I guess I always knew there would be a day when he would not be there to cheer me on; I knew there would come a time where I wouldn't see his lopsided grin or hear his clap of approval. *But that day will not come, can't come anytime soon,* I used to think to myself. The thought was reassuring. Life moved on.

16 January 2009

Six hundred people had already purchased passes to see a show featuring over forty children with me as the lead singer, to be presided over by the chief minister of Delhi and other dignitaries. But it was my ninety-nine-year-old grandfather whose presence I wanted most. Four days before the show, my mother had dashed out of the house, her brow furrowed, wringing her hands, uncharacteristically distracted. Anna had been admitted to the ICU and, as a former president of India, his condition bore national significance. The entire performance at the concert rested on my shoulders, but I was paralysed. Anna was taking a path that I had least expected him to take, one that I had absolutely no control over. For once, nothing that I said or did could have had any effect on his situation whatsoever. What difference did my insignificant performance make in comparison to his state? All I wanted to do was to curl into a ball and cry, but some part of me knew that grandpa would have insisted that 'the show must go on'.

After the concert, dignitaries and artists came up on stage to hand over the bouquets and make their final congratulatory speeches for the evening. But as each person came up to speak, they lapsed into their personal fond thoughts of grandpa being a true patron of the arts, how sad they were that he had missed the show and that at thirteen, I had made him proud. Ten days later, Anna passed away. I did not know what to feel. Sad because I had lost a companion and an inspiration? Angry at him for leaving me, for not saying, 'Wonderful, beautiful!' one last time? 'But the show must go on,' I reminded myself, 'The show must go on.' And it did. And that made all the difference in the world.

Tribute to Mama

Vyjayantimala Bali

> *R. Venkataraman was always deeply concerned about the well-being and progress of those around him. An artiste recounts fondly how 'Mama' guided her not only in her chosen career but also in the field of politics.*

On the occasion of the birth centenary 2010–2011 of respected R Venkataraman, I consider it my humble privilege to contribute an article as a tribute to a great leader, astute politician, statesman, and the eighth president of India. It is a well-known fact that during his term as president, Venkataraman faced the most challenging, critical and sensitive issues in contemporary Indian history with his administrative, intellectual and diplomatic skills. The power of decision-making in the interest of the country lay entirely with him. A weak president would have been a foil, but Venkataraman rose above that like a Titan, to find the right solutions. Such was his commendable strength of mind and spirit.

Venkataraman – Mama as I always used to address him – was a person of class, taste and humaneness, and what made him so remarkable was his vast knowledge in many areas and his understanding, be it politics, the Constitution of India, the inner workings of the Parliament (at his fingertips), home and international affairs, sports or the deep-rooted values and culture of our great country. A soft-spoken yet stern personality, he had a fantastic memory.

I feel happy that there were several occasions when I met him; I would turn to him in moments of joy as well as crisis in my life to seek his good advice. It is quite difficult for me to describe each and every meeting and incident. Still, I wish to recall maybe just a few of those unforgettable moments.

Only a few months after my dear husband Dr Bali's sudden demise – that had totally shattered me – I was told that there was a call from the vice-president's house and he wished to speak to me. Despite a heavy heart I took the phone. Mama came on the line and said he had called to ask me if I would accept an invitation to perform for the Indian Council of Cultural Relations (he was then the president of ICCR). For a moment, I was too dazed to say anything and my heart beat fast. How could he ask me to dance at this juncture, in spite of knowing my frame of mind? However, I did say that I was not sure of myself and my actions and I could not give an answer straightaway, but I would surely get back to him in a week's time. Mama said, 'I hope you'll say yes. It will be good for you.' Mama had always known about my passion and devotion to Bharatanatyam and now he was asking me to perform in New Delhi. I was in a dilemma. What should I do? What should I say? I kept asking myself repeatedly. Then I mustered up courage and talked to my family elders, friends, and musicians. I could hardly believe it when all of them said in one voice, 'You must accept. Remember what Doctorji always told you – keep on dancing. Bharatanatyam suits you best.' I prayed that whole night and his message came clearly in my mind. I knew I had to get back my energy, recharge myself and plunge into practice because I had been off dancing for quite some time. After four days I called up Mama and before he could say anything I said to him with tears rolling down my eyes, 'Mama, only you could make me come back to dance.' I performed at the Kamani auditorium in New Delhi in Mama's presence and blessings, and the evening was dedicated to Doctorji's memory.

When Mama became the president of India, he was the only president, unlike his predecessors, to patronise art and culture. He provided opportunites to all dancers and artistes to perform at Rashtrapati Bhavan. Such an honour by the head of the nation! This became a regular feature. I had the opportunity to perform more than once in the beautiful and compact Rashtrapati Bhavan auditorium. The audience consisted of highly interested and knowledgeable *rasikas* of art. Mama particularly liked my dancing the Bhairavi Svarajati 'Kanchi Kamakshi', a composition by Shyama Sastri known for its *sahitya* (words), raga (melody) and *tala* (rhythm). My performance was highly appreciated and Mama was happy.

Talking about my entry into politics – Rajiv Gandhi made me contest the parliamentary elections twice, in 1984 and 1989, from the South Madras constituency. I was very new to politics then and once my name was announced, the activities commenced at a frenetic pace. Everything seemed to be happening to me at the same time. A new type of lifestyle came about, which I had to adjust around. One huge responsibility that fell on me was that the earlier candidate of South Madras constituency was none other than dear Mama, who had won a huge victory from there. I could not imagine what I could do to replicate his victory, especially after a stalwart like him had set such a blazing trail. Revered Late Indira Gandhi's assuring hand symbol along with my sincere hard work paid off most successfully. After winning by a huge margin, my husband Dr Bali and I went to pay our respects to Mama and his wife Janaki Amma. They were touched and gave their blessings.

In 1991 when I was denied the Lok Sabha ticket for South Madras (for reasons unknown) although I was a sitting member of Parliament, Rajiv Gandhi promised me that he would induct me into the Rajya Sabha. Moreover, he himself spoke to Mama and a couple of others regarding this matter. Nearly three years went by and nothing happened. Even though I got to know that my name had come up for nomination, it failed to come through (again for reasons unknown). Finally, in 1993, I was nominated to the Rajya Sabha by the next president. The first thing I did was to meet Mama and Janaki Amma and take their blessings. However, Mama did say how nice it would have been had the swearing-in taken place when he was president. I was teary-eyed, because in my heart I too felt the same.

Once, when I called on Mama at Rashtrapati Bhavan, our conversation somehow drifted to sports. Mama suddenly asked me how my golf was going. I was quite taken aback and wondered how he knew about my passion for golf. Looking slightly amused, he told me he was well aware that I was a golfer, and so was he. I was surprised to know about his interest in golf; he even said that a special golf course had been put up for him to play regularly. 'Why don't you come early in the morning and play golf?' he asked. I was totally dumbfounded. Although I would have loved to take Mama's word seriously, I did not dare tell him that I was not in the habit of rising early. In the next few days, what a picture of his I saw in the papers – a veteran golfer, looking ever so smart and stylish in his golfing outfit and taking long strides with his golf stick! Such an amazing picture of Mama, so much so that I have preserved the paper clipping even today.

I would call on Mama and Janaki Amma now and then in Chennai to offer my *pranams*. The usual excellent coffee and snacks would be served, which I always relished with delight. After some time had passed, I heard and also read in the papers that Mama had suffered injuries due to a fall. I was very upset and went to see him in Chennai to enquire about his health. He greeted me with his usual smile. 'Come, come, you have not come to see me for a long time.' As I sat down and watched him, he did not show any pain or discomfort. He asked me about my dance, research work, travel and so on. As I left, I stopped at the doorway and looked back. He was looking at me and smiling. That is how I see him even today. Simple and dignified, profound in his conversations, an intellectual personality and above all, a noble human being. That is Mama for me. A man is remembered for his good deeds because they outlive him.

MESSAGES

I am glad to know that the R Venkataraman Birth Centenary Editorial Board joins Rupa Publications in bringing out a compilation of articles in the memory of Late R Venkataraman, the eighth president of India.

R Venkataraman made significant contributions in the social, cultural, economical and political affairs of the country. He was a great patriot, an adept administrator and a veteran parliamentarian. He served with distinction in various capacities in public life and ultimately rose to occupy the highest office of the nation. Known for his dignity and fair play, he skilfully guided the country through a testing period of coalition politics.

His multifaceted personality as a writer, politician, and above all, a good human being won him a prominent place in the hearts of the people of India. I have special regard and respect for him. He did not allow party considerations to come in the way of our personal relations.

I extend my best wishes to the R Venkataraman Birth Centenary Editorial Board and Rupa Publications for their endeavour and also wish for the successful publication of the compilation of articles.

Atal Bihari Vajpayee

I first met R Venkataraman when he visited Kashmir in the mid-1960s while I was still Sadr-i-Riyasat. After I moved to Delhi in 1967, our meetings became more frequent, and continued to grow as time progressed. Venkataraman became vice-president and then president and we used to meet on many occasions. It was always a great pleasure to interact with him on matters of mutual interest, such as the Shaiva tradition of South India.

R Venkataraman was a remarkable personality. A clear thinker and a fine administrator, he brought to every assignment a mature and progressive outlook. During his tenure as president he had to face some difficult situations, which he did with great tact and dignity.

My meetings with him continued even after he had retired from public life. He remained clear-headed and articulate till the very end. Through the pages of this volume I pay my homage to his memory and to all the contributions that he made to the nation during his long and fruitful life

Karan Singh

R Venkataraman was a practical idealist. He devoted his entire life to the cause of India in various capacities. He was a freedom fighter who was imprisoned by the British government during the Quit India Movement in 1942. After his release, he became associated with trade union activities and, with his legal acumen, contributed handsomely to the field of labour law. His understanding of the problems and points of view of workers would undoubtedly have stood him in good stead during the decade he was a minister in Tamil Nadu (then Madras state). It is during this decade that the foundations were laid for all-round development of the state, particularly in the field of industry, and Venkataramanji made a seminal contribution to this achievement, which has enabled Tamil Nadu to attain its present position among the leading states of the union.

Venkataramanji belonged to that generation of leaders which built this nation after Independence. He was a member of the Constituent Assembly and was elected to the first Lok Sabha. He was a member of the Planning Commission. After some years he became finance minister and defence minister in the union government, both key portfolios. He went on to become the vice-president and finally the president of India. He occupied these high positions with distinction and aplomb.

It is not as though there were no ups and downs in his political life. But he faced them with equanimity and always remained true to himself. In every sense of the term, he was a man of unquestionable integrity.

I had the privilege of knowing him as a member of Parliament, as union minister, vice president and president, and what struck me were his human qualities and his intellect. He carried power lightly. After his retirement, and particularly in his later years, when he seldom went out, I spent many hours with him. He remained deeply interested in national and international affairs. He was not happy about the weaknesses developing in our polity and feared that institutions were being enfeebled. He spoke freely about personalities and policies, but there was no malice or ill-will in his criticism. His approach was always positive and constructive. His interest in international affairs had been sharpened by his experiences as a delegate to the UN General Assembly and his association with the UN Administrative Tribunal for twenty-four years.

Venkataraman was a god-fearing man, with a deep understanding of, and belief in, the cultural heritage of India. At the same time, he was a modern man, forward-looking and fully aware of global trends. He was a decent, dignified and fair-minded human being. I am glad to have this opportunity to pay my heartfelt tribute to a true gentleman.

KC Pant

I have had good opportunities to serve with R Venkataraman in different capacities and have developed great respect for him. First, I knew him well when he was the defence minister of India, while I was chief of army staff and chairman, chief of staff. Subsequently, when I was the governor of the important north-eastern state, I had the pleasure of taking him around while he was vice-president of India. Later, as governor of Jammu and Kashmir, I interacted with him when he was president of the country.

In all these, I found that it was a pleasure working with him. He had the complete confidence of Indira Gandhi, then prime minister of India. He was deeply interested in the security of the nation and in the progress of the armed forces, particularly their professional efficiency and welfare. On the political side, he was extremely keen about the unity and integrity of India, and took deep interest particularly in dealing with the backward tribal states and solving their intricate problems. On Jammu and Kashmir, the most vital state with its complex problems, he always rendered extremely sound advice. Fully appreciative of our efforts and achievements in dealing with a proxy war, he was also very sympathetic and considerate to the people of the state.

In all the assignments that he held, he mixed freely with the people and made every effort to obtain a broad idea of their views on various issues. During discussions, he elicited considerable knowledge of the state of affairs and could contribute significantly towards reaching decisions. I consider his contribution towards the build-up of the nation significant indeed. God bless his noble soul.

General KV Krishna Rao

Late R Venkataraman was a unique personality – a man of few words with a benign smile. He brought a special touch to every office he occupied. Hailing from Tamil Nadu, he adapted to national politics in Delhi without a problem. A man of learning, he had his own way of bringing his deep knowledge of men and matters to bear on every decision he took. As union minister for finance and defence, he made a mark as an administrator and policy maker.

I came to know him really well when he became vice-president and chairman of the Rajya Sabha. He had wanted me to be the deputy chairman to assist him in running the House. But Rajivji appointed me minister of state for parliamentary affairs instead, in which capacity I worked with him. He managed the House with quiet diplomacy, gave the backbenchers and newcomers an opportunity to be heard, and encouraged healthy debate.

It was but natural that he move to the Rashrapati Bhavan in 1987. There, as successor to Sardar Giani Zail Singh, he served as a friend, philosopher and guide to the government and successive prime ministers at a turbulent time. He brought dignity and prestige to the position of president, bridging the gap between the government and the opposition and helping the young prime minister, Late Rajiv Gandhi, steer the nation through difficult situations.

He will be long remembered for his eloquent speeches, administrative ability and wise counsel. He was a towering leader, a proud Indian, and a clean politician who made a great contribution to the nation's life and public morality.

Margaret Alva

I am glad to know that the birth centenary of Late R Venkataraman, former president of India, is being observed and a commemorative volume is being brought out on the occasion.

I extend my warm greetings and felicitations to the organisers and convey my best wishes for the successful publication of the book.

Pranab Mukherjee

It is with deep respect and gratitude that I remember Late President Ramaswamy Venkataraman and the connection with him that I enjoyed over the years.

After four decades of strong and growing relations between our countries, Venkataraman was the first president of India ever to pay a state visit to Germany. He undertook this step shortly after acceding to his high office. Thus, we first met in the auspicious year of 1989, right before the fall of the Berlin Wall. Of course, attention in Germany was then focussed on the impending breakthrough towards democracy in Eastern Europe. During our first conversation, we discussed the policies of Mikhail Gorbachev and their wider consequences. With equal emphasis, however, Former President Venkataraman underlined the importance of strengthening relations between Europe and other parts of the world. In very concrete terms, he laid out the ascent of India as an economic and technological power – a development that was then well under way, but still met with the scepticism of many outside observers. In hindsight, it is clear to all that the end of the era of opposing military and ideological blocs opened the way for an ever further and deeper interconnection in the world at large and most definitely between India and Germany.

Just one and a half years later – a very short time in the rhythm of such events – the presidential couple was our host during a state visit to India. My wife and I vividly remember the warm welcome they gave us at the magnificent Rashtrapati Bhavan, where we stayed for a couple of days. We especially enjoyed a walk we took in the morning hours with the former president and Mrs Venkataraman in the vast and wonderfully fragrant gardens.

In official conversations, we discussed issues ranging from the international situation – the Gulf War had just ended – to economic cooperation. On Former President Venkataraman's initiative, we set up a German–Indian Consultative Group as a framework for private and frank discussions of members of Parliament, but also people from various walks of life. Involving civil society in international relations was then still quite a novel thing. Having bid farewell to our hosts, my wife and I went on to visit Agra, Madras and Bombay – indulging in an experience of Indian culture and history and receiving a strong first-hand impression of the dynamic economic development under way.

I was pleased that our cooperation continued, even after President Venkataraman and I both had left our offices. We met as old friends at the Global Convention on Peace and Non-Violence, which the former president convened at New Delhi in 2004. I deeply felt the privilege of joining him in an effort inspired by the teachings of the Mahatma – the best tradition that India has given to the world. I will remember President Venkataraman as the perfect embodiment both of the wisdom of an ancient culture and the proud aspirations of a rising young nation.

Richard von Weizsäcker

Ramaswamy Venkataraman, who held the portfolio of labour in the then Madras state in 1957 and handled the subjects of labour and industry as a member of Planning Commission of India in 1967 and onwards, was a true friend of those belonging to the lower tier of society. Venkataraman also took up the organisation of the labour section of the Madras Congress Committee in 1944. His commitment towards the labour class inspired him to initiate publication of *Labour Law Journal* in 1949, to disseminate important decisions pertaining to labour. He was also closely associated with trade union activity as the founder of several unions, including those of plantation workers, estate staff, dock workers, railway workers and working journalists. Even in his home district of Thanjavur he associated himself with agricultural workers to improve their working conditions. His commitment towards the working class was infinite. He attended the 1952 session of the International Labour Organisation as a workers' delegate. He was also leader of the Indian delegation to the 42nd session of the International Labour Conference at Geneva in 1958. Even after holding the highest constitutional office in the country, RV remained sympathetic and compassionate towards the labour class.

He was born in a village in Thanjavur district in 1910. RV established himself as an eminent advocate and started practice in the High Court, Madras, in 1935, and in the Supreme Court in 1951. While practising law, Venkataraman was drawn into the movement for India's freedom from British colonial subjugation. He became an ardent follower of Gandhiji and participated in the Quit India Movement of 1942. He was also imprisoned for two years. His public life, which started in 1942, was illustrious as well as exemplary. Probably he was the only politician from the southern state of Madras/Tamil Nadu who never lost any election. This reflects his proximity to people, including the common man. Venkataraman was also a reputed parliamentarian with apt knowledge of rules and procedures. He was an orator, statesman and administrator who will always be remembered for his clear vision and commitment. Venkataraman served as a minister in the Madras government, member of the Planning Commission, union finance minister, union defence minister, vice-president of India and president of India. He conducted the proceedings of the Rajya Sabha in an impartial manner and gave no opportunity that would lead to uproar in the House. His integrity was beyond doubt.

Apart from holding various posts in the government and being active in politics, he was deeply involved in promotion of art and culture. Venkataraman continued his involvement in this field even after relinquishing the highest office of the president of India. He was the chairman of the governing body of Kalakshetra Foundation, Chennai, and Gandhi Gram Trust. He also served as president of Bharatiya Vidya Bhavan and patron of HelpAge India and Global Cancer Concern. Venkataraman also took keen interest in development of IGNCA, New Delhi.

As a true son of the motherland, Venkataraman performed all his duties with distinction, unblemished by private interests, and continued his commitment towards the labour class throughout his life. We all have much to learn from his style of functioning, which was all the time accurate and served the larger public interest. I am sure that his career as a politician, public servant and a friend of the working class will continue to inspire the younger generation for times to come.

Sheila Dikshit

I was in my twenties, when, in Chennai, I heard R Venkataraman talk to the public before the first general elections. The impression that I got about him from that talk was confirmed when I came in close contact with him as a teacher of Vedanta. That impression, 'Here is a brilliant, clean leader' was indelible.

When I initiated a movement for *seva*, I discussed with him the vision and mode of achieving it. It did not take time for him to grasp the vision and present a feasible plan of how to go about it. On my request, he agreed to be the chairperson of this all-India *seva* venture.

He loved to stay with me at the *gurukulam* in Anaikatti. I used to discuss national and international issues with him, and I was always delighted to see his clarity. I saw him as a positive thinker, even though he had to go through the pain of seeing mediocrity and corruption in our national political leadership in responsible positions. Concerned about regionalism, he said that there should be an electoral change. Unless the contesting parties have a standing in the nation, in terms of a certain minimum per cent of the national electorate, they should not be eligible to contest the parliamentary election. That is clarity.

A Gandhian, RV, as we used to call him fondly, was always a contributor. The thought of grabbing and hoarding was alien to him. From the days of the freedom struggle, he lived a life given to the cause of the nation, always upholding dharma. He was highly committed, with an insight, to the spiritual oneness as unfolded by the Gita. And this helped him relate to all forms of religious prayers without any tinge of patronising attitude.

Bharat was lucky to have him as its president. In him was the fulfilment of its bigness and profundity.

Swami Dayananda Saraswati

The esteem, admiration and love the pontiff of Avadhoota Datta Peetham, Mysore, Sri Sri Ganapathi Sachchidananda Swamiji has for R Venkataraman, the eighth president of India, is reflected in these lines below:

We place on record our deep appreciation for this fascinating person who went on a momentous journey from Rajamadam village to Rashtrapati Bhavan as the president of India. Venkataraman was a scholar, an academician of the highest order and a lover of Vedic scriptures. He had the cherished privilege of being the honorary chairman of the Sri Ganapathi Sachchidananda Ashrama and Datta Peetham Celebrations Committee for more than a decade. Under his able guidance, Datta Peetham built a classical music auditorium, the very popular Nada Mantapam, Sri Datta Venkateswara shrine, a charming temple in Mysore, and a charity clinic. He actively supported Sri Ganapathi Sachchidananda Veda Patashala, which has completed twenty-five years of its useful existence at the time of writing.

Venkataraman was of the view that Sadguru's grace is crucial in man's spiritual journey. It evoked great interest when he would discuss these matters with us.

Venkataraman was a witness to all the celebrated festivals and detailed programmes that took place such as Maha Shivratri, Navaratri celebrations, the gaiety and grandeur of Sri Dattatreya Jayanti and Shankara Jayanti, which used to be clebrated with great éclat and fervour in the *peetham*. He was an anchor during that festive occasion, relieving the confusion and creating bonhomie with all the devotees of Datta Peetham. He ensured that the current of life should flow with vigour and vitality based on dharma. With the blessings of God, Venkataraman became part and parcel of the Datta family. He always appreciated the grand tolerant nature of Sri Swamiji, who believed in harmonising society and maintaining a cordial relationship with all faiths. He used to say 'Swamiji is born for the welfare and guidance of mankind and he is for all ages'.

'Do not waste the gift of human life,' Venkataraman once said. He would relate many events and recollections from his administrative life to enthrall Swamiji for hours. The rich experience and acumen he got from his active public life, along with a distinguished academic career as lawyer, added flavour to these moments. The activities he undertook, his zeal for life, and active participation in international events made him a unique figure in the public life of Indian statesmen.

I am happy to give this message on the occasion of R Venkataraman's birth centenary. He led his life by example and may it be the torch for future generations to come.

Jaya Guru Datta.

Sri Sri Ganapathi Sachchidananda Swamiji

Contributors

AP Venkateswaran

AP Venkateswaran joined the Indian Foreign Service in 1952, and has served at India's diplomatic missions in Czechoslovakia, USA, Ethiopia, USSR and the FRG in various capacities. He also served as the Indian high commissioner to Fiji and South Pacific territories, and as ambassador of India to the Syrian Arab Republic, ambassador and permanent representative of India to the UN and ambassador to China. Later, he was appointed India's foreign secretary. He was also chairman of the Board of Governors of the Indian Institute of Management, Ahmedabad. He is now settled in Bangalore, where he has founded the *Asia Centre*, and also occasionally contributes articles to journals and newspapers.

Amjad Ali Khan

Sarod maestro Ustad Amjad Ali Khan has performed at various national and international venues, including the WOMAD Festival, the Edinburgh Music Festival, and UNESCO. He has represented India in the first World Arts Summit in Venice in 1991. In Boston, Massachusetts, 20 April 1984 has been declared as Amjad Ali Khan Day. He has been awarded the Gandhi UNESCO Medal, and has received the 'Commander of the Order of Arts and Letters' from the French Government, as well as the Fukuoka Cultural Grand Prize in Japan in 2004. He has also received the UNESCO award, the Padma Vibhushan, UNICEF's National Ambassadorship, and has been nominated for a Grammy award in the best traditional world music album category (2010).

Atal Bihari Vajpayee

Atal Bihari Vajpayee is a former prime minister of India, and former president of the Bharatiya Janata Party (BJP). He was a founder-member of the Bharatiya Jana Sangh, a forerunner of the BJP. He was the leader of opposition, Lok Sabha, in 1996–97. He was twice elected prime minister of India, in 1996 and in 1998. He is also a published poet.

DN Patodia

DN Patodia is a businessman and industrialist. He has done his MA from Calcutta University. He is a former member of the Lok Sabha (1967–71). He was the parliamentary secretary of the Swatantra Party, and president of FICCI (1985–86).

Swami Dayananda Saraswati

Swami Dayananda Saraswati is an acclaimed spiritual teacher. In 1962 he was initiated into *sanyasa*, a committed life of learning and teaching. He teaches short and long-term courses in the teaching institutions he has founded in India and USA. Swamiji has also founded the Hindu Dharma Acarya Sabha consisting of heads of different seats of learning in Hindu tradition, besides working towards harmony among world religions. He is also the founder and an active executive of the All India Movement for Seva, working in the field of education and healthcare in India's rural areas.

Era Sezhiyan

Era Sezhiyan was a member of Parliament (Lok Sabha 1962–77 and Rajya Sabha 1978–84) and chairman of Public Accounts Committee (1971–73). He was the founder-member of the Janata party in 1977 and the Janata Dal in 1988. He retired in 2000 from active party politics. However he participates in seminars of public importance and writes for *The Hindu*, *Frontline* and *Mainstream* as well as *Dinamani* and *Sangoli* in Tamil. He is senior fellow of Institute of Social Sciences, New Delhi. He can be contacted at: *erasezhiyan@gmail.com*.

Fali Sam Nariman

Fali Sam Nariman (born 10 January 1929) is a distinguished Indian Constitutional jurist, and senior advocate to the Supreme Court of India since 1971. He has been the president of the Bar Association of India since 1991, and is now its president emeritus. He is one of India's most distinguished constitutional lawyers and an internationally recognised authority on international arbitration. He was the additional solicitor general of India from May 1972 and resigned his office on 26 June 1975, the day after the proclamation of the Internal Emergency.

He has been awarded the Padma Bhushan (1991), Padma Vibhushan (2007) and the Gruber Prize for Justice (2002) and was a nominated member of the Rajya Sabha (1999–2005). His autobiography is titled *Before Memory Fades*.

G Ramachandran

G Ramachandran topped the Indian Administrative Services examination in 1949. He has held a number of posts in the central and state governments. He was the private secretary to C Rajagopalachari, as well as the collector of Coimbatore, the joint secretary and subsequently secretary, finance and planning in Madras. He moved to Delhi in 1969, where he served as joint secretary, and later additional secretary to then Prime Minister Indira Gandhi. He was also member-secretary of the Sixth Finance Commission, the expenditure and financial secretary, and the executive director for India, Bangladesh and Bhutan in Asian Development Bank. After retirement, he served as a part-time director of the Reserve Bank of India (1995–2000)

Lord Geoffrey Howe of Aberavon

Geoffrey Howe served as a cabinet minister for all but the last three weeks of Margaret Thatcher's government: as chancellor of the exchequer (1979–83), as foreign and commonwealth secretary (1983–89) and finally as deputy prime minister (1989–90). He entered the House of Lords in July 1992. Appointed Queen's Counsel in 1965, he served in Edward Heath's government as Solicitor General (1970–72) and Minister for Trade & Consumer Affairs (1972–74). He was the chairman of the International Monetary Fund Interim Committee (1982–83). International Advisory Boards on which he has served include those of J.P. Morgan, Stanford University, the Carlyle Partnership and Fuji (Mitzuho) Bank. He was the chairman of the Framlington Russian Investment Fund and on the advisory council of the Supreme Rada of Ukraine. He is now president of the Great Britain–China Centre.

Gopalkrishna Gandhi

Gopalkrishna Gandhi has been a member of the Indian Administrative Service. He was secretary to R Venkataraman when he was the vice president of India (1985–1987), and became his joint secretary when he was president of India (1987–1992). He served as India's high commissioner in South Africa and Lesotho (1996–1997) and in Sri Lanka (2000–2002). He was ambassador of India in Norway and Iceland (2002–2004). He served as secretary to President KR Narayanan from 1997 to 2000. He was governor of West Bengal from 2004 to 2009.

Inder Malhotra

Inder Malhotra has been a syndicated columnist since taking premature retirement as editor of *The Times of India*, New Delhi (1978–86). Previously, he worked for *The Statesman* for fifteen years, first as the political correspondent and chief of bureau, then as deputy editor. He also wrote for *The Guardian* (1965–95). He is both a Nehru Fellow (1986–87) and a Woodrow Wilson Fellow (1992–93). He has lectured widely, in India and abroad. His publications include *Indira Gandhi: A Personal & Political Biography* (1989), *Dynasties Of India And Beyond* (2003), and a fresh biography of Indira Gandhi (2006). He is now working on a book on *Indian Security: Past, Present and Future*.

K Natwar Singh

K Natwar Singh was a member of the Indian Foreign Service for thirty-one years. He was part of Prime Minister Indira Gandhi's staff (1966–71). He was also India's ambassador to Pakistan (1980–82), the secretary-general of the 7th NAM

Summit, minister of state (1984–89), member of the Lok Sabha (1984–1989 and 1998–1999) and member of the Rajya Sabha (2002–2008). He was India's external affairs minister from 2005 to 2006. A recipient of the Padma Bhushan award (1984), he has authored several books, including *My China Dairy* and most recently, *Yours Sincerely*.

K Parasaran

K Parasaran is a renowned senior advocate. He was appointed the central government senior standing counsel in the Madras High Court in 1971. In 1976, he was appointed advocate-general of Tamil Nadu. He was appointed the solicitor general of India in February 1980 and held that post till 1983. On 9 August 1983 he was appointed the attorney general for India. He was also the president, Indian Society of Criminology (1984–1985); president, Bar Association of India (1984–1987). He was awarded the Padma Bhushan in 2003.

K Subrahmanyam

K Subrahmanyam (19 January 1929–2 February 2011) was a prominent international strategic affairs analyst, journalist and former civil servant. He was the founding director of the New Delhi-based Institute for Defence Studies and Analyses, the chairman of India's Joint Intelligence Committee, fourth member, Board of Revenue, Government of Tamil Nadu, home secretary, Government of Tamil Nadu, additional secretary, Cabinet Secretariat, New Delhi, and union secretary for Defence Production in the Ministry of Defence. He was appointed convenor of India's first National Security Council Advisory Board in 1998.

Dr K Venkataraman

Dr Krishnaswamy Venkataraman has a PhD in Economics. He has served in the Indian Administrative Service and the United Nations Industrial Development Organization. He is the founder chairman of Public Expenditure Round Table, a Chennai NGO, and has authored several books. He married Padma, R Venkataraman's eldest daughter, in 1962. They have two daughters, Meera and Shobana.

KC Pant

Krishna Chandra Pant is a former cabinet minister in the Government of India. He has been elected to the Lok Sabha four times. He was elected to the Rajya Sabha in 1978 and was leader of the House (1979–1980). As a union minister, he held the portfolios of defence, finance, steel and heavy engineering, home affairs, electronics, atomic energy, and science and technology. He was the first chairman of the advisory board on energy. He was also deputy chairman of the Planning Commission of India (2000–2004).

KS Narayanan

KS Narayanan is the chairman emeritus of Chemplast Sanmar Limited. He was for many years the promoter and managing director of The India Cements Ltd, the largest manufacturer of cement in South India. He was also promoter director of Chemplast Sanmar Limited, Sanmar Shipping Limited, WS Industries Ltd., and many others. He was the founder-president of Indo-American Chamber of Commerce – Southern Region (1969–70) and past president of the Hindustan Chamber of Commerce (1975–76). He was also the sheriff of Madras (1974).

He was the honorary consul of Denmark for South India (1975–88). He has been involved in the management of several educational and charitable organisations. His sons N Sankar and N Kumar are well-known in industrial and sports circles.

General KV Krishna Rao

General KV Krishna Rao is a former chief of army staff of the Indian Army. He was commissioned into the Indian Army in 1942. During the 1971 war against Pakistan, his division captured the Sylhet area and liberated northeast Bangladesh. General Rao retired as chief of army staff and chairman, chiefs of staff, in 1983 and was appointed governor of Nagaland, Manipur and Tripura in June 1984. He was the governor of Jammu & Kashmir from 11 July 1989 to 19 January 1990 and from 13 March 1993 to 2 May 1998.

KV Ramanathan

KV Ramanathan is a retired officer of the Tamil Nadu cadre of the Indian Administrative Service, and has held a number of senior posts under both the state and central governments. After seven years as secretary to the Government of India, he was, when member-secretary of the Planning Commission, deputed to the Asian Development Bank in Manila as executive director for India, Bangladesh and Bhutan. From December 1988 to May 1991, he was the resident editor of the *Indian Express*, Madras. A lover of classical Carnatic music, he was the editor of *Sruti* magazine (2003–2007). He now lives in retirement in Chennai.

Dr Kapila Vatsyayan

Dr Kapila Vatsyayan is a scholar, author, linguist, dancer, ethnographer, cultural policy maker, and above all, an art historian. She was formerly secretary, Department of Arts, Ministry of Education, Government of India, and is currently a nominated member of the Rajya Sabha and a life trustee of the India International Centre. She has been the academic director of the Indira Gandhi National Centre for the Arts and member, UNESCO Executive Board. She has taught at the Universities of Delhi, Banaras, Philadelphia, and California (Santa Cruz). She is a recipient of the Jawaharlal Nehru Fellowship. She has been honoured with D. Litt. (honoris causa) from several universities in India and abroad. She has been associated with the establishment and development of many libraries, museums and archival repositories. She was responsible for negotiating cultural agreements with foreign countries and for formulating, executing and administering bilateral programmes of exchanges.

She is a recipient of many awards, and is the author of nearly twenty books and over 200 research papers.

Dr Karan Singh

Dr Karan Singh is the titular maharaja of Jammu and Kashmir. He served as governor of the State of Jammu and Kashmir (1965–1967), union minister for tourism and civil aviation (1967–1973), minister of health and family planning (1973–1977) and minister of education and culture (1979–1980). He is chancellor of Banaras Hindu University, and was earlier chancellor of Jammu and Kashmir University, and Jawaharlal Nehru University. Presently, he is an MP in the Rajya Sabha, chairman of the All India Congress Committee Foreign Affairs

Department, president of the Indian Council for Cultural Relations, India's ambassador to UNESCO and chairman of the Auroville Foundation.

Dr L Subramaniam

Dr L Subramaniam is India's foremost violinist, the only musician who has performed/recorded Carnatic classical music, Western classical music and also composed for and conducted major orchestras. He has collaborated with a wide range of renowned musicians, from different genres of music. He is the founder-director of the Lakshminarayana Global Music Festival, the biggest global music festival in India. He has received several awards and honours, including the Padma Bhushan and the Sangeet Natak Akademi Award.

Lloyd I Rudolph and Susanne H Rudolph

Lloyd I Rudolph and Susanne Hoeber Rudolph are professors of Political Science Emeriti of the University of Chicago. Recently, they have written a three-volume book on India, *Explaining India Democracy: A Fifty-Year Perspective*. They have been teaching and writing about India since 1956 when they drove overland in a Land Rover from London. Currently, they divide their time between Jaipur, California and Vermont.

M Hamid Ansari

Mohammad Hamid Ansari is the vice president of India and ex-officio chairman of the Rajya Sabha. He joined the Indian Foreign Service (IFS) in 1961 and was India's ambassador to several countries including Saudi Arabia, United Arab Emirates, Afghanistan, Iran, and the Indian high commissioner to Australia. He was also India's permanent representative to the United

Nations, vice chancellor of the Aligarh Muslim University and chairman, Fifth Statutory National Commission for Minorities. He received the Padma Shri in 1984.

MK Narayanan

MK Narayanan is a former member of the Indian Police Service and has served in various capacities, mainly in the areas of intelligence, security and strategic matters, from 1955 to 1992. Subsequently, he was a member of several committees constituted by the Government of India, dealing with intelligence, security, counter-terrorism and counter-intelligence. He was the senior advisor and national security advisor to the prime minister of India (2004–2010) and has been the governor of West Bengal since January 2010. He is widely recognised as one of the foremost experts on security and strategic matters. He is a recipient of several awards, including the Padma Shri.

MK Venkatachalam

MK Venkatachalam was a member of the Indian Revenue Service (1944). He served in the field as income tax officer, Mumbai, (1945–55) and as assistant commissioner in Tamil Nadu and Kerala (1955–57). He also served in different capacities in the departments of economic affairs, banking and revenue in the Ministry of Finance. After retirement in 1980, he became a financial adviser in then newly established Housing Development Finance Corporation (HDFC) Ltd. As per the advice of Late R Venkataraman, he has served the Sree Swaminatha Swami Seva Samaj from 1999 onwards, first as vice-president till 2006, and later as president.

MM Pallam Raju

MM Pallam Raju is the minister of state for defence, Government of India. He is also a member of the 15th Lok Sabha. He is a member of the Indian National Congress, and represents the Kakinada constituency of Andhra Pradesh. He has served as a director on the boards of Indian Airlines and Air India (1994–1997). Between August 2004 and January 2006, he was the chairman of the Parliamentary Standing Committee on Information Technology. He has represented India in the United Nations General Assembly in New York in October 2004 and at the SAFMA Conference in Pakistan in May 2005.

MS Parthasarathy

MS Parthasarathy is the former president, Federation of Association of Small Scale Industries of India, and the founder-president of National Confederation of Small Industries of India, Chennai. He was a member of the Planning Commission, Government of India. He is the chairman of the group, Tech Plaastic Industrie.

Margaret Alva

Margaret Alva served four terms in the Rajya Sabha, from 1974–1998 before being elected to the Lok Sabha in 1999. She served as minister in the Rajiv Gandhi and Narasimha Rao governments, and as general secretary of the All India Congress Committee from 2004–2009. She was appointed governor of Uttarakhand in August 2009.

Meira Kumar

Meira Kumar is a five-time member of Parliament. She was elected the first woman speaker of the Lok Sabha on 3 June 2009. She is a lawyer and a former diplomat. Prior to being a member of the 15th Lok Sabha, she was elected to the 8th, 11th, 12th and 14th Lok Sabha, where she remained cabinet minister in the Ministry of Social Justice and Empowerment (2004–2009). She is a keen sportswoman and holds medals for rifle shooting. She is also a published poet.

Dr Najma Heptulla

Dr Najma Heptulla is the vice-president of the Bharatiya Janata Party. She was a Rajya Sabha member from Rajasthan (July 2004–July 2010). Since 1980, she has been a member of the Rajya Sabha from Maharashtra for four terms – 1980, 1986, 1992 and 1998. She was also the deputy chairperson of the Rajya Sabha (1985–1986 and 1988–2004). Among her other notable achievements are being the head of the Indian Council of Cultural Affairs, heading the women parliamentarians' group of the Inter-Parliamentary Union in 1993 and being nominated by the United Nations Development Programme as its human development ambassador.

P Murari

P Murari served in the Indian Administrative Service from 1957 till 1992. He has held many distinguished positions, including additional secretary, Ministry of Industry, secretary, Ministry of Food Processing Industries and secretary, Ministry of Information and Broadcasting in the Government of India. He has undertaken many special projects for the Government of India and has chaired numerous high level commissions and committees. He has also represented India in the Asian Productivity Council. He retired as secretary to the president of India in August 1992 and is currently adviser to the president of FICCI. He has a number of important publications to his credit.

PC Alexander

PC Alexander (20 March 1921–10 August 2011) was the governor of Tamil Nadu from 1988 to 1990 and the governor of Maharashtra from 1993 to 2002. He also had additional charge of Goa from 1996 to 1998. He was a member of the Rajya Sabha, representing Maharashtra as an independent candidate (29 July 2002–2 April 2008). He was considered as a candidate for the post of the president of India in 2002. He had extended stints with the United Nations and India's Ministry of Commerce and was the principal secretary for both Former Prime Ministers Indira Gandhi and Rajiv Gandhi. He also served as the Indian high commissioner to the Court of St. James's. He had written four books.

PR Ramasubrahmaneya Rajha

PR Ramasubrahmaneya Rajha is the chairman of the Ramco Group of Companies, as well as the managing trustee of Raja Charity Trust and PAC Ramasamy Raja Education Charity Trust. He is also president, Rajapalayam Chamber of Commerce & Industry, chairman, Bharatiya Vidya Bhavan's Gandhi Vidyashram, Kodaikanal, charter president, Rajapalaiyam Rotary Club and a member of the Special Task Force for Industrial Development, Government of Tamil Nadu. He has founded a number of educational institutions, promoted several charity programmes and undertaken the renovation of several temples in South India.

Dr Padma Subrahmanyam

Dr Padma Subrahmanyam is an Indian Bharatanatyam dancer, research scholar, choreographer, music composer, musician, teacher and author. She has performed in India as well as abroad. Several films and documentaries have been made in her honour. She is a recipient of several prestigious awards, including the Sangeet Natak Akademi Award (1983), the Nehru Award from the Soviet Union (1983) the Fukoka Asian Cultural Prize from Japan, Kalidas Samman, Bharata Sastra Rakshamani and the Padma Bhushan (2003).

Pranab Mukherjee

Pranab Mukherjee is the minister of finance, government of India. He started his political career as a Rajya Sabha member from the Congress party in 1969, and went on to hold several ministerial posts, such as deputy minister, industrial development (February 1973 to January 1974), minister of state for finance (October1974 to December1975), cabinet minister of commerce (January 1993 to February 1995), minister of external affairs (February 1995 to May 1996 and October 2006 to May 2009), minister of defence (May 2004 to 24 October 2006). He is also leader of the House, Lok Sabha, June 2004 till date

Admiral (Retd) RH Tahiliani

Admiral (Retd) RH Tahiliani was born on 12 May 1930 in Karachi. He joined the erstwhile Royal Indian Navy in March 1948, and retired as Chief of Naval Staff on 30 November 1987. He was the governor of Sikkim from 1990–1994. Presently, he is engaged in social work with the Servants of People Society.

Dr RK Pachauri

Dr Rajendra Kumar Pachauri is a prominent researcher on environmental subjects, recognised internationally for his efforts to build up and disseminate greater knowledge about manmade climate change and to lay the foundations for measures needed to counteract such change. He is the chair of the Nobel Peace Prize-winning Intergovernmental Panel on Climate Change (IPCC). He is also director general of TERI (The Energy and Resources Institute), a major independent research organisation providing knowledge on energy, environment, forestry, biotechnology, and the conservation of natural resources. Since July 2009, he has also served as director of the Yale Climate and Energy Institute at Yale University.

Dr Richard von Weizsäcker

Dr Richard von Weizsäcker was president of the Federal Republic of Germany (1984–1994), governing mayor of West Berlin (1981–1984), vice-president of the German Parliament (1969–1981). He was also the president of the German Lutheran Church Council Laureate of the Heinrich Heine (1991) and Leo Baeck Awards (1994) and the chairman of the Bergedorf Round Table of the Körber Foundation. He has written a number of books on various subjects.

Sheila Dikshit

Sheila Dikshit is the chief minister of Delhi. She is a member of the Indian National Congress. She is the second woman chief minister of Delhi and represents the New Delhi Constituency in Delhi's legislative assembly. She has also served as a union minister (1986–1989), first as the minister of state for Parliamentary

Affairs and later as a minister of state in the prime minister's office. She represented India in the UN Commission on Status of Women for five years (1984–89).

Dr Shovana Narayan

Shovana Narayan is India's most celebrated kathak guru and danseuse. In her career spanning several decades, she has performed in several prestigious national and international festivals. She has collaborated with well-known Indian and Western dancers and musicians, and has performed before several heads of states and governments all over the world.

She is the recipient of numerous awards, including the Padma Shri Award (1992), the Sangeet Natak Akademi award (1999–2000), the Parishad Samman, Rajiv Gandhi Puraskar, Indira Priyadarshini Samman and many more. She has authored several books and numerous articles on the subject of dance and is also a visiting lecturer to several universities in India and abroad.

Siddharth Ramachandran

Siddharth Ramachandran (born 22 July 1970) is the grandson of R Venkataraman. His formative years were spent in Kanpur, Uttar Pradesh. Siddharth is a scientist by profession, who got his Bachelor's degree from IIT-Kanpur, and a PhD in the United States of America. He worked for a decade in the world-famous Bell Laboratories in the US, and is now a professor at Boston University, US. He has received many professional accolades in his field of expertise, including the title of Fellow of the Optical Society of America.

Sri Ganapati Sachchidananda Swamiji

His Holiness Parama Pujya Sri Ganapati Sachchidananda Swamiji is the pontiff of Avadhoota Datta Peetham at Sri Ganapati Sachchidananda Ashrama in Mysore. He has been propagating Vedic culture, Nama Sanirtan tradition and Kriya Yoga. Swamiji is a guru in the Dattatreya Avadhoota lineage. Swamiji has composed over 3,000 *bhajans* and is well-known for his music therapy. He is also involved in a number of charitable programmes.

TS Sankaran

TS Sankaran retired from the Indian Administrative Service in 1984 after having served in several important official positions, both in his home state of Tamil Nadu and in the central government. A large part of his official life was spent in fields like labour, land reforms and community development/*panchayati raj*. After retirement he continues to evince an active interest in matters pertaining to labour, labour policy and labour administration, with special emphasis on the unorganized sector. He had also been chairman of the Central Advisory Contract Labour Board. Currently, he is the president of the National Labour Law Association.

Tara Venkatesan

The youngest granddaughter of R Venkataraman, sixteen-year-old Tara is an eleventh grade student at the American Embassy School in Delhi, as well as a rising Western classical musician. She has sung internationally for various dignitaries including the president of Austria, president of the European Council, mayor of Salzburg, prime minister of India and the Dalai Lama. She has also performed at the closing ceremony of the Commonwealth Games 2010, the Singapore Live 2010 with the Vienna Chamber Orchestra, and is a recording artist for Walt Disney. She has been featured on CNN, Austrian, Indian and Asian TV channels, as well as in major newspapers. Tara also created Music 4 Kids By Kids, a programme for underprivileged children, at the age of twelve. She has been bestowed the iCongo award in India and the NESA award in Asia and the Middle East.

Dr VS Arunachalam

Dr VS Arunachalam is the founder chairman, Center for Study of Science, Technology and Policy (CSTEP), distinguished service professor in the departments of engineering and public policy, material science and engineering at the Robotics Institute of Carnegie Mellon University, Pittsburgh, Pennsylvania, and an honorary professor in the School of Engineering, University of Warwick, UK. He was the past president and fellow of the Indian National Academy of Engineering, Indian Institute of Metals and a fellow of the Indian National Science Academy and Indian Academy of Sciences. He is also the first Indian to be elected as a fellow of the Royal Academy of Engineering, UK. He is a recipient of numerous awards including the Padma Vibhushan, Padma Bhushan and the SS Bhatnagar Prize for Engineering Sciences. Recently, the Indian National Academy of Engineering conferred upon him the Lifetime Contribution Award in Engineering.

Dr Vyjayantimala Bali

Dr Vyjayantimala Bali is a well-known actress, Bharatanatyam dancer as well as a parliamentarian. She has performed before many eminent statesmen and dignitaries like Former President

S Radhakrishnan, Former Prime Ministers Jawaharlal Nehru and Indira Gandhi, Her Majesty Queen Elizabeth II, President Eisenhower and at many international forums. She has conceived, directed and presented several dance-dramas and through her research work, led to the revival of several dance forms. She has won awards and accolades for her roles in films such as *Madhumati, Naya Daur, Sangam* and *Devdas*. She contested from the South Madras constituency and served two consecutive terms in the Lok Sabha in 1984 and 1989. She was nominated to the Rajya Sabha in 1993. She has been bestowed the Padma Shri award (1968), the Sangeet Natak Akademi award (1982), and the Living Legend in Entertainment Award by FICCI.

Dr Yamini Krishnamurthi

Dr Yamini Krishnamurthi is an eminent bharatanatyam and kuchipudi danseuse. She played a significant role in popularising the kuchipudi style of dance. She has received many awards, including the Padma Shri and the Padma Bhushan. She has also published her autobiography, *A Passion For Dance*. She now imparts dance lessons at her institute, Yamini School of Dance, Hauz Khas, New Delhi.

Appendix
Ramaswamy Venkataraman: A Profile[1]

Lok Sabha Secretariat

A true nationalist, a firm believer in secularism, democracy and Gandhian principle of non-violence, a reputed legal luminary, an eminent trade union leader, a renowned economist, a distinguished Parliamentarian and above all, a humanitarian to the core, Shri Ramaswamy Venkataraman the eighth President of the Republic of India – has attained the pinnacle of glory as the head of the largest democracy in the world, neither by luck nor by chance, but by sheer force of his personality, dedication, devotion and commitment. He uniquely combines in him some outstanding traits – unassuming simplicity, transparent sincerity and honesty of purpose, which endears him to one and all.

---

[1] Reproduced with permission from the Lok Sabha publication *Ramaswamy Venkataraman – President in Parliament.*

Early Life

Shri Ramaswamy Venkataraman, popularly called 'RV' by his friends and admirers, was born on 4 December, 1910 in Rajamadam Village in the world famous ancient temple city of Thanjavur district in Tamil Nadu. Shri Venkataraman's father, late Shri K Ramaswami Iyer, was a lawyer of repute in the district, known for its rich cultural heritage. Young Venkataraman thus grew up in a traditional but alive atmosphere. This had made a deep imprint on him and helped him develop into a pious, virtuous and dedicated individual. The love of his country made him join the Indian National Congress and take part in the many struggles it had launched for the liberation of the country from foreign yoke.

Shri Venkataraman had his initial education in Thanjavur itself. He did his Bachelor of Laws from the Law College in Madras and obtained a Master's Degree in Economics from the Madras University. A true patriot as he is, after completing his formal education, he decided not to get into Government service and thus be a slave of the British. Instead he chose to practise law and enrolled himself first in the High Court of Madras in 1935 and later in the Supreme Court. Even when he was at Madras, his dedication to the cause of social service remained undiminished and he continued to evince keen interest in ameliorating the lot of agricultural workers in his home district of Thanjavur.

In 1938, he was married to Janaki Devi, whose parents were then settled in Myanmar (Burma). As a true traditional and devoted wife, Janaki Venkataraman has always remained by the side of her husband and has performed her household duties with religious zeal. Soon, theirs became a happy and contented family blessed as they were with three daughters.

Role in the Freedom Movement

Like many of the leaders, who were then in the vanguard of the freedom struggle, Shri Venkataraman too came under the profound influence of Gandhiji, early in his life. The Mahatma and his distinct philosophy had a deep impact on Shri Venkataraman and his thoughts, words and actions provided him a beacon light. So fascinated was he by this colossus of a man and so irresistible was the call given by the Mahatma that he gave up his lucrative legal practice and plunged into the freedom struggle. He took active part in the 'Quit India Movement' of 1942 for which he was detained for two years by the British Government under the Defence of India Rules (DIR). After his release from prison in 1944, and moved by the poverty of the masses, the misery of the landless labour, and the plight of the industrial labour, he became a Trade Union Leader and took up their cause.

His keen interest in the legal matters continued nevertheless. It was in recognition of his legal acumen that he was deputed in 1946 by the Government of India to Malaya and Singapore for defending members of Subhash Chandra Bose's India Independence League who were charged by the British with collaborating with the Japanese. The Panel consisted of eminent lawyers like K. Bhashiyam of Madras, K.F. Nariman of Bombay and P.N. Sapru of Allahabad.

Shri Venkataraman has an extraordinary legal acumen. Once a group of youngsters were sentenced to death for killing a British Officer in a frenzy. Shri C. Rajagopalachari had tried to secure pardon for the condemned boys in view of their tender age, but failed. The date of hanging had been fixed, and all hopes had been given up. However, Shri Venkataraman discovered a legal way to get the hanging stayed. With the help of a Counsel in England, he got a petition filed in the Privy Council which resulted in the stay of the hanging. Rajaji, impressed as he was with Venkataraman's achievement paid him a rare compliment: 'a very intelligent lawyer'.

From 1947 to 1950, he was the Secretary of the Madras Provincial Bar Federation. His long experience of handling labour matters and his establishment of the *Labour Law Journal* (LLJ) – a prestigious publication – in 1949 turned him into an expert in the field of industrial law. The *Labour Law Journal* ultimately came to be known as the most valuable reference manual for trade unions and lawyers engaged in labour cases. In recognition of his deep knowledge in legal matters, the Government of India sent him as the leader of the Indian delegation to the Metal Trade Committee of the International Labour Organisation in Geneva, in 1952. Subsequently in 1958, he was appointed the leader of the Indian Delegation to the 42nd session of the International Labour Conference in Geneva. He was also a member of the prestigious United Nations Administrative Tribunal from 1955 to 1979, and remained its President for more than ten years from 1968 to 1979. In a rare gesture of recognition of invaluable services to the UN Administrative Tribunal, he was designated its honorary President for life.

Entry into Active Politics

It is from the grassroot level that Shri Venkataraman has risen to the dizzy heights of his career culminating in his occupation of the exalted office of the President of world's largest democracy. In his younger days, he came under the influence of Shri Satyamurthiji, a doyen in the field of Parliamentary politics. Another great politician and pragmatic socialist, who was mainly responsible for bringing Venkataraman into active politics was Late Kumaraswamy Kamaraj. It was the late Kamaraj who had put Venkataraman incharge of the Labour Wing of the Tamil

Nadu Congress Committee (TNCC). In a short spell of time, Venkataraman developed an effective rapport with the workers owing allegiance to the Congress and working in urban industries, plantations and estates, ports and docks and railways.

Shri Venkataraman believes in sincere work. In 1957, Shri Venkataraman was re-elected to the Second Lok Sabha and he was offered a place in the Union Council of Ministers. However, when the Chief Minister of Madras asked him to join his cabinet, Shri Venkataraman readily agreed to the wishes of Shri Kamaraj.

Knowing the abilities of Shri Venkataraman, K. Kamaraj entrusted him with various important portfolios like Industries, Labour, Cooperation, Power, Transport and Commercial Taxes from 1957 to 1967. During this period, he also served as the Leader of the House in the Madras Legislative Council. When he took charge as the Industry Minister, Tamil Nadu was largely an agricultural state with negligible industrial growth. But with his dexterity and skilful handling of affairs he soon brought the state high on the industrial map of India. He is, in fact, considered the 'father of industrialisation' in Tamil Nadu. He introduced many innovations, such as, setting up of industrial cooperatives for small tea growers, promotion of cooperative textile mills and encouraged, for the first time in the State, the establishment of large scale industries like paper, aluminium and cement. He also introduced the first long-distance buses in the State. When he left the Industry Ministry in 1967, Tamil Nadu had become the third most industrialised State of the countiy.

Being an active Congress worker since pre-independence days, RV occupied various party posts. Besides being the Secretary of the Tamil Nadu Congress Committee from 1952–54, he was also one of the Secretaries of the Reception Committee of the Avadi session of the Congress. He also served on the Working

Committee of the TNCC from 1952–67 and established his reputation as an able party ideologue, an efficient leader, a trusted friend and a man dedicated to work.

As a Parliamentarian

RV's parliamentary career began in 1950 when he was first elected to the Provisional Parliament (1950–52) and during these two years he actively participated in various discussions and established himself as an eloquent parliamentarian. The then Speaker, Shri G.V. Mavalankar, was so impressed with his performance that he nominated him as a delegate to the Commonwealth Parliamentary Conference in New Zealand in 1950. Later, he was elected to the First Lok Sabha (1952–57) and again to the Second Lok Sabha (1957–1962). He, however, resigned in 1957 to join K. Kamaraj's Cabinet in Tamil Nadu (then Madras). He became, once again, a Member of the Sixth Lok Sabha (1977–80) and the Seventh Lok Sabha (1980–84) whereafter, he was called upon to occupy the nation's second highest office – the Vice-Presidentship.

An able Parliamentarian and a forceful speaker, Ramaswamy Venkataraman evinced keen interest in a wide range of subjects. He always used to come fully prepared for parliamentary debates and discussions. His parliamentary skill and eloquence, coupled with a constructive approach to the problems facing the country earned him a prominent place in his Party. Even the members of Opposition admired him for his deep understanding and appreciation of the issues and problems that came up before the House. During his initial years in Parliament, his contribution, even as an ordinary member of Lok Sabha, was indeed remarkable. In the First Lok Sabha, he was one of the founders of a 'ginger group' which mobilised effective backing in the Party to Government's progressive socio-economic programmes and policies. His scholarly contribution during the debate on the Constitution amendment relating to 'Right to property' will always be remembered. He convinced Late Panditji that the change in article 31 should apply to all types of property to ensure equity as between the rural and urban sectors. Pandit Nehru agreed to amend the bill to this effect even after its introduction in Parliament. It was Venkataraman's effective eloquence that impressed Panditji and brought him closer to the nation's topmost leaders.

On general issues facing the country, Venkataraman was quite forthcoming. His parliamentary skills and acumen were well-recognised and appreciated in the initial years itself when he was given the honour to second the Motion of Thanks to the President Shri Rajendra Prasad for his first address to the Joint Sitting of Parliament. Speaking on the motion on 19 May, 1952 he *inter alia* said:

> ...Unemployment is a scourge. It is indeed a veiy unhappy situation that an able-bodied man, a man who is ready, able and willing to work, should be denied work and unless we are able to combat the mass retrenchment and unemployment that are consequent upon fall in prices and the fall in production, the veiy thing which we welcome as a measure that is intended to benefit the lower classes will prove to be a measure of great harm to those classes...

Realising fully the efficacy of the Press in our Parliamentary polity, he has always stood in favour of freedom of thought and expression. In his view, the role of the press was very vital in transforming the ideals of the Constitution into a reality. Speaking on this issue in the same debate[2], he said:

---

[2] *L.S.Deb.*, 19 May, 1952.

I am very glad that Government intend to appoint a Press Commission which will go into the question of the organisation of the Press monopolies, if any, existing in it, the conditions of working journalists who sustain the entire organisation and all aspects of the Press, so that freedom of thought and expression which we have embodied in the Constitution will become a reality. Freedom of thought and expression cannot obtain, unless the Press is a strong one, and independent one and is not controlled by merchants, traders and speculators who may use the Press for their own purposes...

There is yet another instance of his Parliamentary skill which stood highlighted when he spoke on the question of rationalisation in the textile mills. When the late T.T. Krishnamachari and Gulzari Lai Nanda were locked in a bitter fight over the induction of automatic looms, Venkataraman brought forward a formula of "rationalisation without tears" by which automation would be introduced provided the surplus labour could be otherwise absorbed. It was an impressive parliamentary debate and his compromise formula was readily accepted by Panditji.

His approach to the subjects under discussions in the House, the laborious and painstaking homework which he used to undertake before coming to participate in the discussion, his deep penetrating thoughts, his confidence and straightforwardness contributed in shaping him as one of the most distinguished Parliamentarians.

Owing to his rich and outstanding Parliamentary performance in Lok Sabha, he was elected to various prestigious Parliamentary Standing Committees *viz.*, Committee of Privileges, Committee on Estimates and Committee on Public Accounts.

He has also been a pioneer in suggesting the introduction of the Committee system to make elected governments more responsive to the needs and demands of the people. In his view, the Committees, like Public Accounts and the Estimates, where members deal with matters without any party affiliations and whose proceedings are not published, could help find 'genuine solutions' to some of the glaring problems confronting the nation.

Apart from his ability and eminence as a Parliamentarian, Venkataraman possesses an abundant fund of wit and humour with which he could silence his opponents in Parliament. Once, when the late Jyotirmoy Bosu, a stormy petrel, kept frequently interrupting him, Venkataraman quipped: 'Mr. Chairman, Mr. Jyotirmoy Bosu is a veiy experienced member of Parliament.... In fact, he is so much in the habit of differing that even when I say he is good, he will differ.' On yet another occasion he said: 'Jyotirmoy is like Winston Churchill. He would like to be the bridegroom in a marriage party and the dead body at a funeral' which perhaps silenced Bosu for the rest of the day.

During this period, besides effectively performing his role as an able and active Parliamentarian, he also held various positions in the Party organisation. He was the Secretary of the Congress Party in Parliament (1954-55); member of All India Congress Committee (AICC) (1952-67); All India Congress Working Committee (AICWC) (1980-84) and the Congress Parliamentary Board (CPB) (1981-84).

In recognition of his parliamentary experience, expertise and oratorical skill, he was sent as a delegate to the United Nations General Assembly as part of the Indian delegation in the years 1953, 1955, 1956, 1958, 1959, 1960 and 1961, where too he made a distinct mark of his own.

As a Renowned Economist

A renowned economist, Venkataraman brought to Parliament his expertise in the areas of finance and planning. He served as a Member, Planning Commission from 1967 to 1971. The subjects entrusted to him were industry, labour, power, transport, communications and railways. Regarding the importance of planning with special inference to industrial development, he once observed:

> During the last eighteen years of planning, the economy has been taken out of the traditional rut and a sense of dynamism infused in it. The rate of investment and national income have been substantially stepped up. Structural changes conducive to growth and development have been brought about.

He was a member of the Economic Affairs Committee of the Union Cabinet and also served as Governor of the International Bank of Reconstruction and Development (IBRD) and the Asian Development Bank (ADB).

Venkataraman's views on economic matters are well-known and are discernible from his Address to the Indian Chamber of Commerce in Calcutta, where he said:

> It is incumbent upon business leaders and managers to do some soul-searching and self-introspection in their work styles—styles of living and styles of problem solving. In our situation, the State must play an active part in the management of the nation's economy, it can do so best through the totality of planning. Planning does not necessarily mean controls, planning means having a vision of the future, having a well thought out approach for development of key sectors, a well articulated policy towards acquiring and developing technologies.

He called upon economists to formulate time bound targets for the elimination of poverty and completion of work on the design and content of anti-poverty programmes. This is quite evident from the speech he made while inaugurating the 68th All India Economic Conference in Ahmedabad on 25 December, 1975. He said:

> Even though economic progress was substantial since independence, we have not overcome the basic problem of mass poverty. Planning has been instrumental in putting the countiy's economy on the path of sustained progress despite severe odds. The problem between efficient use of resources, self-reliance and poverty eradication was not simple.

While speaking on the 'Role of Planning in Industrial Development', on 10 September, 1969, Venkataraman said:

> Soon after independence, we adopted planning as a means to accelerate economic development. To the newly independent countries, political freedom was only first and initial step in the arduous path towards the ultimate objective of improving the economic social status of their large mass of people, steeped in ignorance and poverty and of uniting and welding them into progressive and prosperous nations. Economic development thus became the prime concern of the Governments in the post-independence era in the most underdeveloped countries.

According to him, the profitability of an enterprise does not depend on the sector to which it belongs but on good management and sound policies. He believes that with the expansion of resources and infrastructure in the country, it is no longer necessary to retain the shackles of controls which have built-in undue rigidities and delays.

Industrialisation, he opines, is *sine-qua-non* for rapid economic development of a nation It occupies a central and pivotal position in every programme of planned economic development. Industrialisation and economic development have become so integrated with each other that the economic progress of a nation is often assessed in terms of the measure of its success in transforming its agricultural economy into a modern industrial one. Increased production and productivity are the hall-marks of national wealth and prosperity. Industrialisation thus provides the key to rising income, employment, wealth and prosperity.

A firm believer in international economic co-operation among the developing countries, he lays great(er) emphasis on the South-South dialogue, because if developing countries realise their potential increase the economic interaction with each other, they would be better able to minimise the economic dictates and high handedness sometimes resorted to by developed nations.

As an economist in politics, Venkataraman looks back with pride at the striking progress the country has made in the last four decades despite the population explosion. He describes the population explosion as:

> the single biggest factor against the success of our economic programmes, all the more, the population growth rate is even higher than the economic growth.

As a Union Minister

In January 1980, Shri Venkataraman, in view of his vast experience in the Tamil Nadu Cabinet, was accorded the honour of serving the country as Minister of Finance. By dint of his administrative skills and the far-reaching economic reforms that he introduced, he proved himself as one of India's ablest Finance Ministers and guided the nation in the difficult years along the path of planned economy.

The economic policy that he adopted was sound and two-pronged. On the one hand, he believed in increasing the goods and services to absorb the excess liquidity and on the other, followed a fairly tight money policy, both in regard to credit for non-productive purposes and also to check non-planned expenditure. He was the first Finance Minister who introduced the scheme of Bearer Bonds which netted over Rs 1,000 crores.

A straightforward and pragmatic economist, RV believes that cash assistance and subsidies are inevitable for the development of exports. This is evident from his following observations made in the House on 18 August, 1981 while speaking on the Export-Import Bank of India Bill:

> We cannot do away with cash assistance and subsidies for our export because our balance of payment position is so difficult that unless by a concerted effort at improving the exports, we reach a sort of balance in our payment position, the country's progress will be retarded. Therefore, taking into account the overall needs of the country, it is very necessary to promote exports and that promotion will have to be done by giving a certain amount of subsidies and certain amount of assistance.

Venkataraman has always argued for the nation's self-reliance in all spheres. As Defence Minister, he emphasised the importance of scientific research in Defence. During his tenure as Defence Minister, he did everything possible to strengthen national defence, without funds being wasted. Not only did he introduce several projects for manufacture of rockets, missiles, battle-tanks and light combat aircraft, but also worked with extreme dedication and constant vigilance, towards achieving indigenous production.

He has had full faith in the patriotic sense of the Defence forces. Reinforcing his faith in our Defence forces while speaking in the Lok Sabha on Espionage Activities Bill on 20 December, 1983 he said:

> As against one per cent of possible blacksheeps in our Defence forces, 99 per cent are patriotic and have the sense of duty and they will not let down this country. The recent events have shown clearly that if ever such an opportunity occurs, then the person who is involved, will bring it to the notice of the higher authorities and then see that this is burst.

Not only as Minister of Finance and Defence, but in whatever capacity any responsibility was shouldered by him throughout this period, he carried it out with a distinction leaving an indelible imprint of his own.

As Vice-President

RV was unanimously elected as the Vice-President of the Indian Republic on 22 August 1984. It was a measure of his eminence that he was a consensus candidate for this august office. After taking oath as India's Vice-President, he pledged to work for communal harmony and national integration.

On 19 January 1985, when he arrived to preside over the sitting of Rajya Sabha as its *ex-officio* Chairman, he was accorded a warm welcome by all sections of the House. Late Shri Rajiv Gandhi, the then Prime Minister, led the Members in expressing the hope that RV would live upto the 'distinguished tradition' set by his illustrious predecessors like Dr. S. Radhakrishnan and with his dignity and sense of humour would continue to maintain the high standards already set. Responding to their sentiments, Shri Venkataraman said that he was aware of the tradition set by persons of the eminence of Dr. S. Radhakrishnan and Dr. Zakir Hussain and would endeavour to follow their footsteps.

As the Chairman of Rajya Sabha, RV enjoyed the distinction of being equally respected both by the ruling party and the opposition. There were several occasions when situations in the House became tense and tumultuous but by his exemplary patience and extraordinary forbearance, he invariably succeeded in defusing the tension and the surcharged atmosphere. By his liberal approach, amiable disposition, largeness of heart and an abiding sense of impartiality, he won the appreciation of all Members notwithstanding the parties they belonged to. The manner in which he conducted the House at the time of debates on certain controversial issues such as the 'President-Prime Minister correspondence', the Fairfax issue etc. evoked friendliness from all quarters. By providing adequate opportunities to opposition Members to express their views fully and with his personal attributes of reasonableness and maturity, he proved to be an excellent moderator between the warring groups of Parliamentarians and established for himself a reputation of fair play and political even-handedness. As the presiding deity of the House, he delivered a number of rulings which will go down as landmarks in our parliamentary history both for their content and literary fervour.

Shri Venkataraman was always conscious of affording equal opportunity to each and every member of the House to express his or her views fully and without interruption. He defended, with utmost concern, the rights and privileges of the members both inside and outside the House. On 8 March 1984, when some members raised the question of interference with the legitimate duties of the honourable members, he intervened and observed:

> You remember that sometime back there was a question raised about tapping of telephones and at that time I gave a ruling. I know that you **are** going to mention

this. So, I again reiterate what I said then. I must, however, say that any *mala fide* action or interference with the legitimate duties of the Hon'ble Members of this House, if proved, will not have the protection of this ruling. I repeat with respect to the observations of the Hon'ble Speaker.

Again on 6 May 1987, when a Member of the House was shouted down and interrupted in going ahead with his observations which were not to the liking of others, the Chairman intervened to say:

> What is happening is the negation of democracy. Every member is entitled to express his opinion. You may agree, you may disagree, you cannot shout him down. Then there will be no Parliament.

As the President

Shri R. Venkataraman achieved the pinnacle of glory when he was elected, on 25 July 1987, as the Eighth Head of the Indian Republic. It was indeed a well deserved honour. It was also a colossal responsibility to defend, protect and preserve the Constitution of India. Addressing the members of Parliament soon after his elevation to the highest office of the land, Shri Venkataraman acknowledged, with transparent sincerity and utmost humility, the heavy duty cast on him and observed:

> I am deeply conscious of the honour bestowed on me by the people of India. As I enter this office today, in all humility, I wish to assure the nation that I shall endeavour to deserve the trust and confidence reposed in me.... It will be my constant endeavour to play my due role in clearing mistrust, in strengthening the

foundations of mutual understanding and confidence and in building bridges of respect between people and institutions. I appeal to all fellow citizens of this ancient land to march with firm unwavering steps towards the goal of a peaceful and prosperous India.

A firm and decisive man, Shri Venkataraman was called upon to occupy the high office at a time when the country needed besides a constitutional and ceremonial Head of State, also a statesman *par excellence*. His election as President was hailed by people from a cross sections of our polity and world leaders. The newspapers, in their editorials, eulogised the choice of Shri Venkataraman and qualities of his head and heart Welcoming his election *The Hindustan Times* wrote on 17 July 1987:

> Venkataraman assumes office at a critical juncture in the history of the nation. His experience, sagacity and farsightedness will stand him in good stead in fulfilling his responsibilities as Head of State.

The *Patriot,* in its editorial, described Shri Venkataraman as 'a symbol of spirit and sanity. His distinguished public life', the paper commented, 'has been marked as much by a high standard of performance in several capacities in which he has served the country, as by an unswerving commitment to parliamentary democracy and its essential norms.'

In the history of the Indian Republic, no Head of the State has perhaps been faced with so many crisis situations, as Shri Venkataraman was called upon to handle during his tenure. With his vast reservoir of experience, coupled with his knowledge of politics and administration, he displayed his judgment, maturity and sagacity in handling sensitive situations arising out of a 'Hung Parliament'. Though he had limited workable options in hand particularly when the Janata Dal Government had fallen and when there was no single party with absolute majority in the Tenth Lok Sabha, Venkataraman proved beyond doubt that the President must have the capacity and wisdom to read between the lines of the Constitution. Displaying rare acumen and statecraft, he took bold initiatives in solving the problems he faced, disregarding the inherent risk of criticism in seeming to step outside the ostensibly restricted framework of his obligations and authorities.

His decision on unprecedented constitutional questions was widely acclaimed because of his disciplined adherence to the path charted out by the Constitution. On one of the occasions, when the Indian polity was in distress, he remarked:

> The office of the President is like an emergency light. It comes on automatically when there is a crisis and goes off automatically when the crisis passes.

In his long and multifaceted career, Venkataraman has been successful in whatever position or responsibility he has been entrusted with. Be it the Industries portfolio in Tamil Nadu, the Defence and Finance portfolios at the Centre, Chairmanship of the Rajya Sabha, the Vice-Presidentship and the Presidentship of the country – Venkataraman has functioned with efficiency and equanimity. It has been his firm belief that ethical norms must be observed by all those who are in public life and it is perhaps because of this conviction that his image has remained splendorous all through his political career.

As a Great Humanist

Venkataraman's greatness lies in his unassuming simplicity and intense love for his fellow countrymen. In his own words, 'I am the humble servant of the people'. He is also a patient listener, a good conversationalist and has a sense of humour that very few people possess. No one has ever seen him losing his composure even in the worst of situations. As a great secularist he firmly believes in India's composite culture and its unity in diversity. Religion for him is not merely dogmatic but a practical one aimed at serving the humanity. In his own words:

> Service of our weaker brethren is the service of God. It might do us all a great deal of good to confine religion to our shrines or our homes or, best of all, to our hearts. The temples, mosques, churches and other places of worship so released could shelter millions of houseless people—Hindus, Muslims, Christians and others alike. Even God might be pleased as He would be relieved as a part of His responsibility to mankind. True religion is humanity. And humanity is the God-head.

This amply demonstrates the great levels of his thought.

He possesses a rare equanimity, like the *Sthithapragnya*, the *Bhagavad Gita* speaks of. Viccissitudes, personal or political, have left no work on his visage. Even the most complex problem does not baffle him. He gets into the pith and substance instantly. He reminds one of the mythological bird, *hans,* which is credited with sieving from a bowl of milk only its milk content, leaving behind the water. Inebrity of power or ego-centrism is alien to his nature. Having expressed his clear opinion, he always abides by the general will.

A great man at heart, Shri Venkataraman has always been concerned with the terrorist onslaughts that continue in the strife-torn states of India. Hundreds of innocent men, women and children are killed brutally and this pains the heart of every true Indian. He, like an upright citizen, believes that communalism, beyond any shadow of doubt is a canker eating into the vitals of the nation. Elaborating his views while speaking at the Defence College in New Delhi, Venkataraman touched upon terrorism that stalks the countr today. He said:

> Day after day, come reports of death; persons shot down only because they belong to a particular community. If terrorists think that they can compel a state to surrender to terrorism they are either living in a paradise of their own or are ignorant of history. State power is more potent than sporadic violence.

Shri Venkataraman, a great votary of peace and cooperation, is very optimistic about the future of the world but threats of a nuclear holocaust dampens even his spirits. Speaking on the 'Hiroshima Day' in New Delhi on 6 August, 1985, he said:

> In my view, we should have to educate ourselves as much as others that the possession of nuclear arms does not ensure invulnerability of a nation. It is a colossal delusion to imagine that nuclear arms add to economic or moral strength that it affords security to a nation. It is my conviction that nuclear disarmament is imperative and should precede general disarmament. I feel that there can no longer be a limited use of nuclear weapons. Once it is unleashed, the entire world will be engulfed, irrespective of the user's intent

Recipient of National and International Honours

Venkataraman has been honoured with several distinctive Awards for his dedicated service in various fields by various institutions. Amongst his innumerable achievements, some stand out because of their splendour. He was awarded the Doctor of Laws *(Honoris Causa)* by the University of Madras, University of Nagarjuna, University of Burdwan and University of Philippines.

He is Honorary Fellow, Madras Medical College and Doctor of Social Sciences, University of Roorkee. The University of Philippines, honoured him with Doctor of Laws *(honoris causa)* at a special convocation.

He has been awarded *'Tamra Patra'* for his participation in the freedom struggle when he risked his life for the freedom of his nation. He has also received the Soviet prize for a travelogue of his mentor, Late Shri K. Kamaraj's visit to the socialist countries. Shri Venkataraman has also served the United Nations Organisation (UNO) in different capacities for many years. He was thus awarded the Souvenir by the Secretary-General U.N. for distinguished service as President of the UN Administrative Tribunal. Because of his religious thoughts and pious acts he was given the title of *'Sat Seva Ratna'* by his holiness Shankaracharya of Kancheepuram for services rendered in constructing the temple for Lord Subrumaniam.

All through- his life he has accomplished many commendable tasks and has received due recognition for them.

His saga thus aptly epitomises the qualities of a *Nishkama Karm-yogi*. The Bhagavad Gita says:

यद्यदाचरति श्रेष्ठस्तत्तदेवेतरो जन:।
स यत्प्रमाणं कुरूते लोकस्तदनुवर्तते।।

(Whatever the Best doeth, that the lower kind of man puts into practice; the standard he creates, the people follow).